PURPOSE
AND
MEANING
IN THE WORKPLACE

PURPOSE AND MEANING

IN THE WORKPLACE

edited by

Bryan J. Dik, Zinta S. Byrne, and Michael F. Steger

AMERICAN PSYCHOLOGICAL ASSOCIATION • WASHINGTON, DC

Published by
American Psychological Association
750 First Street, NE
Washington, DC 20002
www.apa.org

To order
APA Order Department
P.O. Box 92984
Washington, DC 20090-2984
Tel: (800) 374-2721; Direct: (202) 336-5510
Fax: (202) 336-5502; TDD/TTY: (202) 336-6123
Online: www.apa.org/pubs/books
E-mail: order@apa.org

In the U.K., Europe, Africa, and the Middle East, copies may be ordered from
American Psychological Association
3 Henrietta Street
Covent Garden, London
WC2E 8LU England

Typeset in Meridien by Circle Graphics, Inc., Columbia, MD

Printer: Edwards Brothers, Inc., Lillington, NC
Cover Designer: Mercury Publishing Services, Inc., Rockville, MD

The opinions and statements published are the responsibility of the authors, and such opinions and statements do not necessarily represent the policies of the American Psychological Association.

Library of Congress Cataloging-in-Publication Data

Purpose and meaning in the workplace / edited by Bryan J. Dik, Zinta S. Byrne, and Michael F. Steger. — First edition.
    pages cm
 Includes bibliographical references and index.
 ISBN 978-1-4338-1314-6 — ISBN 1-4338-1314-9 1. Career development—Psychological aspects. 2. Job satisfaction. 3. Work—Psychological aspects. 4. Employees—Psychology. I. Dik, Bryan J. II. Byrne, Zinta S. III. Steger, Michael F. IV. American Psychological Association.

 HF5381.P876 2013
 658.3001'9—dc23
                                    2012043235

British Library Cataloguing-in-Publication Data
A CIP record is available from the British Library.

Printed in the United States of America
First Edition

http://dx.doi.org/10.1037/14183-000

To my grandfathers, Ralph Dik, Howard P. Longstreet,
and Ross W. Winters,
faithful examples of how to work and live
with purpose and meaning.
—Bryan J. Dik

To my father, J. P. M. Stofberg, who showed me what it meant
to derive purpose and meaning from work.
—Zinta S. Byrne

To Ava, Rowan, and LeAnn, who enable me to do better work
and remind me of what is meaningful.
—Michael F. Steger

Contents

III

Leading a Meaningful Organization   171

Contributors

Blake E. Ashforth, PhD, W. P. Carey School of Business, Arizona State University, Tempe

Justin M. Berg, PhD candidate, The Wharton School, University of Pennsylvania, Philadelphia

Zinta S. Byrne, PhD, Colorado State University, Fort Collins

Amanda L. Christensen, PhD candidate, W. P. Carey School of Business, Arizona State University, Tempe

Bryan J. Dik, PhD, Colorado State University, Fort Collins

Jane E. Dutton, PhD, Ross School of Business, University of Michigan, Ann Arbor

Elana Feldman, PhD candidate, Boston University School of Management, Boston, MA

Steven Fellows, PhD candidate, Boston University School of Management, Boston, MA

Lauren Garrison, MS, Colorado State University, Denver

Douglas T. Hall, PhD, Boston University School of Management, Boston, MA

Jo-Ida C. Hansen, PhD, University of Minnesota, Twin Cities

Paul J. Hartung, PhD, Northeast Ohio Medical University, Rootstown

William A. Kahn, PhD, Boston University School of Management, Boston, MA

Najung Kim, PhD candidate, Carroll School of Management, Boston College, Chestnut Hill, MA

Glen E. Kreiner, PhD, Smeal College of Business, Pennsylvania State University, State College

Robert W. Lent, PhD, University of Maryland, College Park

Douglas A. Lepisto, PhD candidate, Carroll School of Management, Boston College, Chestnut Hill, MA

Michael K. Muchiri, PhD, School of Management and Information Systems, CQUniversity, Rockhampton, Queensland, Australia

David G. Myers, PhD, Hope College, Holland, MI

Camille Pradies, PhD candidate, Carroll School of Management, Boston College, Chestnut Hill, MA

Michael G. Pratt, PhD, Carroll School of Management, Boston College, Chestnut Hill, MA

Stefanie Putter, MS, C Cubed, Denver, CO

Michael F. Steger, PhD, Colorado State University, Fort Collins; North-West University, Vanderbijlpark, South Africa

Dianne R. Stober, PhD, C Cubed, Fort Collins, CO

Brian J. Taber, PhD, Oakland University, Rochester, MI

Fred O. Walumbwa, PhD, W. P. Carey School of Business, Arizona State University, Tempe

Amy Wrzesniewski, PhD, Yale School of Management, Yale University, New Haven, CT

David G. Myers

Foreword

> There are still two sorts of jobs. Of one sort, a [person] can truly say, "I am doing work which is worth doing. It would still be worth doing if nobody paid for it. But as I have no private means, and need to be fed and housed and clothed, I must be paid while I do it." The other kind of job is that in which people do work whose sole purpose is that of the earning of money; work which need not be, ought not to be, or would not be, done by anyone in the whole world unless it were paid.
>
> —C. S. Lewis, *The World's Last Night*

I write from Holland, Michigan, which in 2010 was named "America's second happiest city" by the Gallup Organization (based on data from its daily Gallup-Healthways Well-Being Index; http://well-beingindex.com/). Having come to know several of the CEOs of Holland's major corporations during my 43 years at Hope College, I conclude that their efforts to create purpose and meaning in the workplace have borne some fruit. As religiously motivated humane capitalists, they have operated their businesses not only to create products and profits but also to provide quality of life for their workers (their "members," as the 7,500-employee Haworth, Inc., respectfully calls its staff).

These companies were, and some still are, locally owned ventures whose owners and workers rubbed shoulders at the grocery store, in worship, and at school soccer games. "Why do I do what I do?" mused Haworth founder G. W. Haworth to me (87 years old, born in a sod house on a Nebraska homestead). "I look out my office window and see all those cars in the parking lot. All those people are depending on me to provide for their car payments, their mortgages, their livelihood." As we together toured his main office furniture manufacturing plant, where workers were designing and industriously producing work environments that aimed to suit workers' needs, the seemingly universal facial response to seeing their legendary founder was a broad smile and a warm greeting.

Among the most remarkable people I have known here was industrialist John Donnelly, whose company, the Donnelly Corporation (now Magna Donnelly), manufactured most mirrors found in U.S.-made cars. Part of his effort to do good, beyond making safety-enhancing car mirrors, was to create meaningful, involving work experiences. To involve his employees with a sense of entrepreneurial teamwork, Donnelly organized them into Scanlon plan–guided, self-managed work groups. When times were good, as they generally were, employees shared in the profits; when times were bad, top executives took pay cuts. In this company, the parking lot had no executive parking spaces. After seeing the aging Donnelly slip on the parking lot ice one day, his employees plotted a gift: a parking lot sign near his office designating John Donnelly's parking place. Although grateful, he promptly removed the sign and hung it in his office. For Donnelly, an idea about the self-esteem and involvement of every employee was more important than a parking place or another million car mirrors.

Shortly before his death at the age of 74, Donnelly wrote me, "What will I have achieved in life if all I have done is to make car mirrors—there has to be more to it than that." A devout Catholic, Donnelly was inspired by his faith to focus on what he could do for the greater good rather than what he could gain for himself alone.

Another huge local employer, Herman Miller, Inc. (America's second largest office furniture manufacturer), has repeatedly been both a "most admired company" and one of the "100 best companies to work for" in *Fortune* executive surveys (Herman Miller, Inc., 2010).[1] While under the leadership of its founder D. J. DePree and sons Hugh DePree and Max DePree (author of *Leadership Is an Art*, on employee-empowering management), Herman Miller functioned as if people mattered. It organized its workers into small teams. Long before most Americans knew about the Japanese corporation-as-family model, Herman Miller employees were participating in decisions about their work, sharing in the company's profits, and becoming company stockholders after only a year of service. Instead of a human resources director, the company had a "Vice President for People," whose concerns included nurturing employee morale, fostering employee suggestions, and facilitating communications.

Underlying this participative approach to management is a corporate philosophy that workers are happier and more productive when

---

[1]Herman Miller, Inc. (2010, March 5). *Herman Miller again tops industry in FORTUNE's "most admired" companies survey* [Press release]. Retrieved from http://www.hermanmiller.com/about-us/press/press-releases/all/herman-miller-again-tops-industry-in-fortunes-most-admired-companies-survey.html

they are respected, cared about, and involved. Max DePree (1989) wrote, "Words such as love, warmth, personal chemistry are certainly pertinent" (p. 60).[2] To judge from informal comments heard over the back fence and about town, Herman Miller's participative management made for a workforce with much higher than average morale, and even today some of that ethos survives (although the CEO's salary is no longer constrained, as it was under the DePrees, to 20 times the average full-time worker's compensation).

For Herman Miller's humane capitalists, high-level employee morale was good for business. Compared with depressed employees, those with higher levels of well-being often have lower medical costs, higher work efficiency, and less absenteeism (Ford, Cerasoli, Higgins, & Deccesare, 2011[3]; Shockley, Ispas, Rossi, & Levine, 2012[4]). Thus, just as investing in prenatal care and preventive well-baby care can reduce net medical costs, so can investing in employee well-being help the bottom line. By 2011, every dollar invested in Herman Miller in 1990 was worth nearly $9.

Such success has also marked the Fleetwood Group, a 165-employee manufacturer of educational furniture and wireless electronic clickers. When the founder gave 45% of the company to his employees, who later bought out other family stockholders, it paved the way for the Fleetwood Group to become one of America's first employee stock ownership plans (ESOP) companies. Today, every employee owns part of the company and, as a group, they own 100% of Fleetwood. The more years they work, the more they own, yet no one owns more than 5%. Like every CEO, Doug Ruch works for his stockholders, who just happen to also be his employees.

As a company that endorses "servant leadership" and "respect and care for each team member–owner" (Fleetwood Group, n.d.)[5], Fleetwood prioritizes people above profits. Thus, when orders lagged during the recent recession, the employee–owners communicated to leadership that job security meant more to them than profits. Ergo, the company paid otherwise idle workers to do community service: answering phones, building Habitat for Humanity houses, and the like. In tough times and in good, the company tithes the business proceeds, with contributions averaging more than $6,000 per employee.

---

[2]DePree, M. (1989). *Leadership is an art.* New York, NY: Doubleday.

[3]Ford, M. T., Cerasoli, C. P., Higgins, J. A., & Deccesare, A. L. (2011). Relationships between psychological, physical, and behavioural health and work performance: A review and meta-analysis. *Work & Stress, 25,* 185–204.

[4]Shockley, K. M., Ispas, D., Rossi, M. E., & Levine, E. L. (2012). A meta-analytic investigation of the relationship between state affect, discrete emotions, and organizational performance. *Human Performance, 25,* 377–411.

[5]Fleetwood Group. (n.d.). *About us: Christ centered . . . employee owned.* Retrieved from http://www.fleetwoodgroup.com/about-us.htm

Fleetwood employees "act like they own the place," noted Ruch. Employee ownership attracts and retains talented people, "drives dedication," and gives Fleetwood "a sustainable competitive advantage." With stock growth averaging 17% a year, Fleetwood was named the 2006 National ESOP of the Year. Ruch seeks to sustain the "ownership culture" and to inspire his employee–colleagues to share his own keen sense of calling. As a faith-motivated person, he quoted Frederick Buechner (1993): "The place God calls you to is the place where your deep gladness and the world's deep hunger meet" (p. 95).[6]

Another multi-thousand Holland employer, the Prince Corporation, began with its invention of the automotive lighted visor and expanded to produce a host of interior dashboard car parts. Its family owners, who are well known for their support of conservative political and religious causes, also managed to create an employee-supportive corporate culture, complete with a spectacular (and free) employee health–fitness club that employees raved about. One employee, after the company's sale in the aftermath of its founder's sudden death, reflected on its former culture: "I've been asked hundreds of times why I worked where I did with my education and my only answer has always been, 'You'd just have to work there to understand.'" The founding family's locally invested wealth was also partly returned to our community through their gifts of the city's senior citizen complex, its arts center, and a renewed downtown, complete with an environmentally friendly snow-melt system that uses waste hot water to warm streets and sidewalks. When the company was sold, employees took out a full-page newspaper ad saying simply, "Thank you, Elsa," after the founder's widow gave them $100 million from the cash proceeds.

Some of these companies have also enabled people to balance family life with meaningful work through family friendly flextime and job-sharing opportunities. That also is true of Worth Publishers, with whom I have worked closely as one of its authors for nearly 3 decades. The women who lead the company (as president and publisher) have supported their staff by adjusting their work schedules and locations to suit their avocational needs. My texts and their teaching supplements are created thanks to editorial, artistic, and marketing leadership talent who work from home offices from Alaska to Florida. My longtime book development editor, who formerly worked in the company's New York office, now works 30 hours a week from a home office in Anchorage, with no lost time in daily travel and few work-related clothing, meal, and transportation expenses. At home, she is free to work at 6 A.M. while her children sleep and to adjust her daytime hours around family commitments.

---

[6]Buechner, F. (1993). *Wishful thinking: A theological ABC.* New York, NY: HarperOne.

Across varied occupations, some people view their work as a *job*, an unfulfilling but necessary way to make money. Others view their work as a *career*, an opportunity to advance from one position to a better position. The rest—those of us who may view our work as a *calling*, a fulfilling and socially useful activity, or who view our work as engaging and fulfilling—report the highest satisfaction with their work and with their lives. For example, all of us who work together at Worth Publishers to create teaching products feel blessed with meaningful work—work through which we can aim to do good while doing well.

Purpose and Meaning in the Workplace offers counselors, human resources managers, and organizational leaders insights for creating the meaningful sort of work to which I refer in this foreword. This volume's all-star team of contributors provides ideas for matching employee strengths to job tasks, creating work environments that optimize employee engagement, crafting jobs that express and affirm workers' gifts, and coaching staff on career planning. By so doing, the volume offers possibilities for making every community a happier place.

Kudos to Bryan J. Dik, Zinta S. Byrne, Michael F. Steger, and their contributing authors for their state-of-the-art reflections on how organizational policies, workplace leaders, career counselors, and employees themselves can create work in which people can engage as a meaningful career and possibly even a purposeful calling—work that feels intrinsically worth doing, even if nobody is paid for it.

PURPOSE
AND
MEANING
IN THE WORKPLACE

Bryan J. Dik, Zinta S. Byrne, and Michael F. Steger

Introduction
Toward an Integrative Science and Practice of Meaningful Work

What does your work mean? This question is as critical as it is common. Most full-time employees spend more of their waking hours working than doing anything else (e.g., Bureau of Labor Statistics, 2012; Organization for Economic Co-operation and Development, 2012). For that reason alone, the question demands attention. The question becomes pressing when one considers that work is, for most people, a necessity and, often (although not always), central to their identity. This is evident when people are asked what they do and they respond with the preface "I *am* a ___," when children are asked what they want to *be* when they grow up, or when someone faces retirement after years of building a successful career. Of course, work has always meant different things to different people. For some, a job is a necessary evil, a requirement for paying the bills, or simply a way to help pass the time. For others, work is a barometer for testing their self-worth; it provides a status ladder to climb and tangible rewards useful for evaluating professional progress. Yet, as the accumulating theory and

http://dx.doi.org/10.1037/14183-001
Purpose and Meaning in the Workplace, B. J. Dik, Z. S. Byrne, and M. F. Steger (Editors)

research detailed in this volume show, many people also want their work to matter in an existential sense. They want their work to enable their personal growth, to help them optimize their inner potential, to make sense of life, and to give them a path to pursue their purpose. These aspirations are at the heart of this volume. From a diversity of perspectives, expert scholars show us the importance of—and the answers to—the questions "What makes work meaningful?" and "What can individuals and organizations do to make work *more* meaningful?"

Concepts and Definitions

At its most fundamental level, *meaningful work* is work that is subjectively judged to matter, be significant, possess the capacity to serve some greater good, and feed the creation of meaning in one's broader life (Steger, Dik, & Duffy, 2012). Meaningful work also has been referred to as *meaning in work* (Pratt & Ashforth, 2003). Because the interchange of terms and their inconsistent use create confusion in the literature, some clarification is needed before we proceed. Steger et al.'s (2012) definition of *meaningful work* refers to the overall degree or amount of meaning people perceive or find in their work. This meaningfulness is thought to arise from work that people find worthwhile, as well as from work that gives people a sense of purpose. *Purpose* refers to "people's identification of, and intention to pursue, particular highly valued, overarching life goals" (Steger & Dik, 2010, p. 133). Although this definition of *purpose* refers to aims and aspirations for life writ large, scholars have long recognized that people feel work is more meaningful if there is some point or purpose to their work duties (e.g., Hackman & Oldham, 1976, 1980). One of the ambitions of meaningful work research is to examine whether engaging in this kind of work extends the benefits of meaning from the workplace into the rest of one's life. Purpose is one of the ways in which work activity can deliver benefits outside of work, particularly if someone feels that the purpose of her or his work is to serve some greater good or provide benefits to other people (e.g., Grant, 2007). Thus, if people judge their work to be meaningful or find substantial meaning in work, we then surmise that they feel their work matters and that it supports their purpose in life or helps them contribute to the world around them in a way they believe is important.

Meaning in work has been contrasted with *meaning of work* (Pratt & Ashforth, 2003). Although it is common to see these phrases used interchangeably (Rosso, Dekas, & Wrzesniewski, 2010), we distinguish them as follows: *Meaning in work* refers to the amount of meaning people experience, whereas *meaning of work* refers to the specific content of work that provides people with meaning. Put another way, meaning in work is the answer to the question "How meaningful is your work?" and meaning of work is the answer to the question "What makes it so?" People can have widely disparate answers to these questions. For many who find their work meaningful, the source of meaning is the people, whether coworkers, clients, or community (e.g., Wrzesniewski, Dutton, & Debebe, 2003). But at their core, questions about meaningful work are about optimal work experiences, beneficial synergies between work and the rest of life, and finding work that resonates with the entirety of one's personality, values, and passions.

Growing Interest, but Fragmented

In his landmark project, *Working,* Terkel (1972) observed that work was often about more than acquiring sustenance and enduring stupefaction: It was about a search for meaning in everyday life. His sense of the scope of work's impact on workers has been reflected in scholarly efforts to understand how work can transcend crude labor. In work psychology and management research, much of the initial examination of meaningful work was in reaction to criticism of worker apathy and efforts to improve the management of organizations (e.g., Mayo, 1933; Whitehead, 1935), both issues that emerged during the human relations movement of the 1920s. For example, some considered research in job satisfaction the study of the personal meaning of work (e.g., Schaffer, 1953). Other early efforts investigated constructs such as work centrality (Dubin, 1956), job involvement (Lodahl & Kejner, 1965), intrinsic work motivation (Herzberg, Mausner, & Snyderman, 1959), and work values (Super, 1962). Drawing a distinction between motivation and meaningful work, Hackman and Oldham (1976, 1980) proposed the job characteristics theory, which states that key characteristics of the job trigger a psychological state of felt meaningfulness that, in turn, triggers motivation, resulting in job satisfaction and productivity. In kind, Guion and Landy (1972), along with others (e.g., Quintanilla, 1991), suggested that people assess the meaning or significance of work by making sense of the work situation and the potential consequences for their work activities. Sustaining the belief that meaningful work cultivates motivation, Kahn (1990) purported that employees' sense of meaningfulness fosters their engagement (i.e., a motivational state wherein one invests oneself cognitively, physically, and emotionally into one's work role), a construct that has since garnered considerable attention from researchers and practitioners. Arguably, each of the dominant theoretical paradigms within vocational psychology (i.e., person–environment fit, developmental, social–cognitive career theory, constructivist) also incorporated, as they developed, considerations of personal meaningfulness and purpose, if often only implicitly (Chen, 2001; Dik, Duffy, & Eldridge, 2009).

Building on these steady streams of inquiry, research on meaningful work and closely related topics has increased exponentially in recent years. For example, the number of research publications on work as a *calling*, defined as a transcendent summons to purposeful work that serves the greater good (e.g., Dik & Duffy, 2009), has more than quadrupled in the past half decade. Workplace spirituality has been described as one of the fastest growing areas of new scholarly inquiry (Giacalone, Jurkiewicz, & Fry, 2005). Research on prosocial work motivation (e.g., Grant, 2009) has also generated headlines and sparked new conversations about the potential of work to benefit people. In addition, the influential positive psychology movement has further extended its reach into workplace research, resulting in the publication of resources such as the *Oxford Handbook of Positive Psychology and Work* (Linley, Harrington, & Page, 2010) and the *Oxford Handbook of Positive Organizational Scholarship* (Cameron & Spreitzer, 2012).

As is often the case with rapidly expanding domains of research, scholarly attention drawing from diverse disciplines has resulted in something of an identity problem for purpose and meaning in work. Rosso et al. (2010) described meaningful work scholarship as highly fragmented, following a course marked by "relatively distinct domains of study . . . and many missed opportunities for these domains to build on each other . . . [leaving] this research difficult to interpret as a whole" (p. 93). That they reached this conclusion after a review that focused narrowly on the organizational studies literature (appropriate given their publication outlet, *Research in Organizational Behavior*) without also incorporating research from related disciplines further highlights the fragmented nature of scholarship related to purpose and meaning at work.

To summarize, although the research in this area has proliferated, it is anything but unified. Furthermore, recent years have seen a parallel influx of popular books, Internet resources, seminars, webinars, and practitioners helping to create purposeful, mission-driven workplaces. Therein lies the impetus for this volume, the first to bring together the best thinking and research from across relevant disciplines to offer a panoramic view of purpose and meaning in the workplace in a way that both encourages unified ongoing scholarship and conversation and helps bridge the gap between science and practice.

This conversation is occurring at a challenging yet crucial time. Change in today's world of work is abrupt and nonlinear and unpredictable. The marketplace is global, and increased diversity has put social norms in flux. Media coverage of this new normal is ubiquitous and probably sensationalized; it is worth noting that claims of rapid change and instability have been common since at least the 1930s (Cascio, 2010). Nevertheless, it is difficult to avoid getting anxious when one of the few things one can predict is uncertainty. A 2010 Bureau of Labor Statistics report revealed that individuals born between 1957 and 1964 held an average of 11 jobs between the ages of 18 and 44 years; that is a different job every 2.4 years! Overall job satisfaction trends have been heading downward since 2009 (Society for Human Resource Management, 2011), suggesting that this new norm may not be so great. In such an environment, how does one find purpose and meaning in work?

It seems that many employees may be struggling with this question. A survey of approximately 100,000 workers across North America, Europe, and the Asia Pacific region found that 51% of the respondents said yes to the question "Would you take a lesser role or lower wage if you felt that your work contributed to something more important or meaningful to you or your organization?" (Kelly Services, 2009). Yet, in the 2012 edition of this report, slightly fewer than half of the 170,000 workers surveyed said that their current employment provided them with a sense of meaning (Kelly Services, 2012). Thus, it seems that more and more employees may feel that there has to be more to work than pay or promotions, whether or not they believe that their employer helps them find purpose and meaning. With evidence of a widespread desire to give back (Hewlett, Sherbin, & Sumberg, 2009), the time is right for both organizations and individuals to invest in more purpose-driven, meaningful workplaces, ones marked by missions to develop people and communities as much as they enhance profitability. The fusion of work and dignity, as well as identity and positive change, and the cultivation of talent for pursuit of beyond-the-self goals: These are hallmarks of purpose and meaning in the workplace.

Purpose of This Volume

The overarching mission of *Purpose and Meaning in the Workplace* is to provide a resource that supports paradigm integration and assimilation of cross-disciplinary theory and research related to purpose and meaning in the workplace in a way that highlights clearly defined, empirically derived practical applications. We invited leading theorists, researchers, and applied professionals within counseling and vocational psychology, industrial and organizational psychology, organizational behavior, and management to respond to the following central questions: What are we learning about meaningful work, and in what specific ways can the science make a difference for people working in the trenches? What strategies can managers, human resource professionals, consultants, counselors, and employees implement to help make workplaces more meaningful? What effects might such strategies have on employee health, happiness, sense of purpose, and productivity?

Authors' contributions appraise the current state of theory and research on meaningful work; outline the far-reaching implications of meaningful work for personal and organizational well-being; and suggest directions for future theory, research, practice, and application. Furthermore, each chapter emphasizes practical application by providing a quick-glance "Focus on the Workplace" table that offers a concise summary of approximately five to 10 specific recommendations for fostering purpose and meaning at work. For each recommendation, authors note its level of support across three domains: (a) tested in practice, (b) derived from theory, and (c) supported by research evidence.

The result is a fascinating, accessible, and highly practical collection of 10 chapters that provide a multifaceted overview of social science research on purpose and meaning in the workplace while offering clear recommendations for how this research translates into practice. Part I, "Cultivating a Meaningful Career," focuses on how individual employees might navigate their career choice and development process in a way that fosters purpose and meaning. In the section's opening chapter (Chapter 1), Paul J. Hartung and Brian J. Taber provide an overview of the emerging career construction theory, describing in detail how its principles translate, through the Career Construction Interview, into a captivating approach for helping individuals identify narrative themes that express the purpose and meaning they may experience or wish to experience in their work and lives. Jo-Ida C. Hansen follows in Chapter 2 by summarizing the current state of the research on person–environment fit, long a dominant paradigm in applied psychology. She points to a number of highly practical strategies for leveraging fit to increase a sense of meaningfulness at work. In Chapter 3, Douglas T. Hall, Elana Feldman, and Najung Kim describe how the protean career orientation translates into meaningful work, as protean employees strive to create and maintain meaningfulness by changing their work in a self-directed and values-driven approach.

Part II, "Meaning Making on the Job," moves beyond individual development over the course of a career to tackle the question of how meaningfulness and purpose might be pursued day to day and within in an organizational context. Justin M. Berg, Jane E. Dutton, and Amy Wrzesniewski lead off this section with a rich exploration of how employees actively shape their tasks, relationships, and cognitive frameworks on the job to increase meaningfulness through a process called *job crafting* (Chapter 4). William A. Kahn and Steven Fellows follow in Chapter 5 with an overview of employee engagement, a motivational state that some feel is a behavioral and an attitudinal manifestation of meaning and purpose expressed at work, and the contextual factors from which workers are ennobled and engagement arises. Blake E. Ashforth and Glen E. Kreiner (Chapter 6) summarize what is known about how employees doing *dirty work*—undesirable, stigmatized, socially tainted occupations—often construct positive meaning and purpose in their jobs. In Chapter 7, Robert W. Lent explores the utility of social–cognitive career theory for understanding how multiple hedonic and eudemonic variables dynamically influence work satisfaction through processes that also suggest strategies for making work meaningful. All four chapters in this section offer actionable and practical suggestions for creating and maintaining the conditions needed to foster a sense of purpose and meaning on the job.

Finally, the focus of Part III, "Leading a Meaningful Organization," is on practices that organizational leaders might implement to promote a purposeful and meaningful workplace. In Chapter 8, Michael G. Pratt, Camille Pradies, and Douglas A. Lepisto describe how organizations influence purpose and meaning at work by tying specific organizational practices to a new five-orientation approach for understanding how people conceptualize work as worthwhile and significant. Fred O. Walumbwa, Amanda L. Christensen, and Michael K. Muchiri devote Chapter 9 to a compelling exploration of theory, research, and practical implications regarding transformational leadership, an approach they suggest "perhaps provides the most intuitive link to meaningful work" (p. 198) among leadership theories. Dianne R. Stober, Stefanie Putter, and Lauren Garrison close this section and the book by outlining specific strategies in Chapter 10 that executive and organizational coaches might use to help leaders more effectively promote purpose and meaning within their organizations.

Our Vision for Purpose and Meaning in the Workplace

Reading these outstanding chapters and interacting with their authors gave us the opportunity to further reflect on the reasons why we originally thought a book like this was needed. As we previously noted, there is a strong thirst for purpose and meaning in the workplace. Although research suggests that employees who experience work as meaningful may enhance an organization's financial bottom line (e.g., less absenteeism and lower intentions to leave an organization; Steger et al., 2012), we feel that meaningful work is an important target in its own right, and our authors suggest the same in their chapters. Purpose and meaning at work can be a rightful expectation held by employees of themselves and their organizations and is one that is achievable. Of course, arguing that all work should be meaningful necessitates some clear strategies for making that possible. What makes purpose and meaning flourish in the workplace?

Elsewhere, we have offered that employers and leaders can take concrete steps to make meaningful work more likely (e.g., Byrne, Palmer, Smith, & Weidert, 2011; Dik, Steger, Fitch-Martin, & Onder, in press; Steger et al., 2012). Some of these steps echo recommendations that have been made and repeated for decades, yet are still all too often overlooked; others reflect more recent developments, such as those highlighted in this volume. What are these steps? At minimum, employees and followers should feel respected as individuals and valued for their unique contributions (Moorman & Byrne, 2005). Prioritizing respect and value for employees points to the necessity of including, to a legitimate degree, employees' perspectives in decisions about working conditions and new directions for the organization (Byrne, Kiersch, Weidert, & Smith, 2011). It also means that workers should be afforded, where appropriate, autonomy in executing their duties. Meaningful work is likely fostered when employees are given a clear understanding of how their organization functions and when they are given all of the information and resources they need to do their jobs (Byrne, Palmer, et al., 2011; Hackman & Oldham, 1976, 1980). Meaningful work also is likely fostered when individuals understand how their personal attributes—interests, abilities, values, and personality—have uniquely equipped them to do their work well (Dik et al., 2009). In a similar vein, leaders should help employees see how their work aligns with and supports the organization's mission (discussed in a number of this book's chapters), and every effort should be made to craft organizational missions that support an organization's ability to make a positive difference in its supporting communities and the broader world, thereby engendering a genuine focus on the greater good. These suggestions may also make it easier for employees to become engaged at work, providing another route to meaning and purpose (Byrne, Palmer, et al., 2011).

Beyond these suggestions, the experts who have contributed to this volume offer forward-thinking strategies drawn from multiple fields of scholarship and throughout the world of work, from individual career pursuits through organizational systems up to executives setting the course. The chapters speak strongly for themselves, but we indulge ourselves here by briefly considering some of the themes we felt emerged in this volume. Although each author or team of authors approached the issue of purpose and meaning in the workplace from a slightly different perspective, there was convergence around four high-level themes. First, several contributors noted how meaning and purpose are socially constructed. Particularly in the workplace, individual workers interact to create collective identity and culture, which, in turn, is uniquely interpreted by individual workers. Second, purposeful and meaningful work is attainable only when people successfully align their values with their aspirations. When this alignment is accomplished in the workplace, workers' efforts are continually invested in meaningful pursuits. Third, meaningful and purposeful work requires individual action to make work tasks feed a broader purpose. This means that workers should ideally be active crafters of their work experiences, fully engaged and committed to applying themselves to their work. Fourth, individual employees can only do so much. Poorly designed and dehumanizing workplaces likely thwart the experience and expression of purpose and meaning. However, leaders who thoughtfully design their work culture to support meaningful work can harvest the benefits of a dedicated, impassioned, and invested workforce.

We invite you to form your own conclusions, derive your own themes, and draw your own inspirations for future research and practical application from each chapter. Furthermore, we hope that this book will guide you in learning more about the unique perspectives of different fields toward purpose and meaning in the workplace, and also how these different fields can come together to further promote our understanding of purpose and meaning in the workplace. This is the first edited volume to provide a multidisciplinary approach to purpose and meaning in the workplace, which means that the research necessary to deliver the promise of meaningful work is just beginning. Our hope is that this book becomes one of many important milestones in the growth of cross-disciplinary research and practice in meaningful work, and we eagerly look forward to the next wave of research on meaningful work that is already building on the horizon. Although each chapter in this book contains evidence-based ideas for practice, it seems apparent that practitioners of all stripes have a wealth of ideas for fostering purpose and meaning that have yet to be tested, and academicians have theories and empirical evidence that are awaiting application. Together, science and practice can join in a dynamic conversation to accelerate and advance our understanding and application of purpose and meaning in the workplace.

References

Bureau of Labor Statistics. (2010). Number of jobs held, labor market activity, and earnings growth among the youngest Baby Boomers: Results from a longitudinal survey [Press release]. Retrieved from http://www.bls.gov/news.release/archives/nlsoy_09102010.pdf

Bureau of Labor Statistics. (2012). *American time use survey—2011 results* (USDL-12-1246). Retrieved from http://www.bls.gov/news.release/atus.toc.htm

Byrne, Z. S., Kiersch, C. E., Weidert, J. M., & Smith, C. L. (2011). The justice-based face organizations. In M. A. Sarlak (Ed.), *The new faces of organizations in the 21st century* (Vol. 4, pp. 95–163). Toronto, Canada: North American Institute of Science and Information Technology.

Byrne, Z. S., Palmer, C. E., Smith, C. L., & Weidert, J. M. (2011). The engaged employee face of organizations. In M. A. Sarlak (Ed.), *The new faces of organizations in the 21st century* (Vol. 1, pp. 93–135). Toronto, Canada: North American Institute of Science and Information Technology.

Cameron, K. S., & Spreitzer, G. M. (Eds.). (2012). *The Oxford handbook of positive organizational scholarship*. Oxford, England: Oxford University Press.

Cascio, W. F. (2010). The changing world of work. In P. A. Linley, S. Harrington, & N. Page (Eds.), *The Oxford handbook of positive psychology and work* (pp. 13–23). Oxford, England: Oxford University Press.

Chen, C. P. (2001). On exploring meanings: Combining humanistic and career psychology theories in counselling. *Counselling Psychology Quarterly, 14*, 317–330. doi:10.1080/09515070110091308

Dik, B. J., & Duffy, R. D. (2009). Calling and vocation at work: Definitions and prospects for research and practice. *The Counseling Psychologist, 37*, 424–450. doi:10.1177/0011000008316430

Dik, B. J., Duffy, R. D., & Eldridge, B. M. (2009). Calling and vocation in career counseling: Recommendations for promoting meaningful work. *Professional Psychology: Research and Practice, 40*, 625–632. doi:10.1037/a0015547

Dik, B. J., Steger, M. F., Fitch-Martin, A., & Onder, C. (in press). Cultivating meaningfulness at work. In C. Routledge & J. Hicks (Eds.), *The experience of meaning in life: Classical perspectives, emerging themes, and controversies*. New York, NY: Springer-Verlag.

Dubin, R. (1956). Industrial worker's worlds: A study of the central life interests of industrial workers. *Social Problems, 3*, 131–142. doi:10.2307/799133

Giacalone, R. A., Jurkiewicz, C. L., & Fry, L. W. (2005). From advocacy to science: The next steps in workplace spirituality research. In R. F. Paloutzian & C. L. Park (Eds.), *Handbook of the psychology of religion and spirituality* (pp. 515–528). New York, NY: Guilford Press.

Grant, A. M. (2007). Relational job design and the motivation to make a prosocial difference. *Academy of Management Review, 32*, 393–417. doi:10.5465/AMR.2007.24351328

Grant, A. M. (2009). Putting self-interest out of business? Contributions and unanswered questions from use-inspired research on prosocial motivation. *Industrial and Organizational Psychology, 2*, 94–98. doi:10.1111/j.1754-9434.2008.01113.x

Guion, R. M., & Landy, F. J. (1972). The meaning of work and the motivation to work. *Organizational Behavior and Human Performance, 7*, 308–339. doi:10.1016/0030-5073(72)90020-7

Hackman, J., & Oldham, G. R. (1976). Motivation through the design of work: Test of a theory. *Organizational Behavior and Human Performance, 16,* 250–279. doi:10.1016/0030-5073(76)90016-7

Hackman, J., & Oldham, G. R. (1980). *Work redesign.* Reading, MA: Addison-Wesley.

Herzberg, F., Mausner, B., & Snyderman, B. B. (1959). *The motivation to work.* New York, NY: Wiley.

Hewlett, S. A., Sherbin, L., & Sumberg, K. (2009, July–August). How Gen Y & Boomers will reshape your agenda. *Harvard Business Review, 87,* 71–76.

Kahn, W. A. (1990). Psychological conditions of personal engagement and disengagement at work. *Academy of Management Journal, 33,* 692–724. doi:10.2307/256287

Kelly Services. (2009). *Generational crossovers in the workforce—Opinions revealed.* Retrieved from http://www.smartmanager.com.au/res/content/au/smartmanager/en/docs/kelly_services_generational_crossovers_in_the_workplace_09.pdf

Kelly Services. (2012). *Acquisition and retention in the war for talent: Kelly Global Workforce Index.* Retrieved from http://www.kellyocg.com/Knowledge/Kelly_Global_Workforce_Index/Acquisition_and_Retention_in_the_War_for_Talent/

Linley, P. A., Harrington, S., & Page, N. (Eds.). (2010). *The Oxford handbook of positive psychology and work.* Oxford, England: Oxford University Press.

Lodahl, T. M., & Kejner, M. (1965). The definition and measurement of job involvement. *Journal of Applied Psychology, 49,* 24–33. doi:10.1037/h0021692

Mayo, E. (1933). *The human problems of an industrial civilization.* New York, NY: Macmillan.

Moorman, R., & Byrne, Z. S. (2005). What is the role of justice in promoting organizational citizenship behavior? In J. Greenberg & J. A. Colquitt (Eds.), *Handbook of organizational justice: Fundamental questions about fairness in the workplace* (pp. 355–382). Mahwah, NJ: Erlbaum.

Organization for Economic Co-operation and Development. (2012). *Average usual weekly hours worked on the main job.* Retrieved from http://stats.oecd.org/Index.aspx?DatasetCode=ANHRS#

Pratt, M. G., & Ashforth, B. E. (2003). Fostering meaningfulness in working and at work. In K. S. Cameron, J. E. Dutton, & R. E. Quinn (Eds.), *Positive organizational scholarship: Foundations for a new discipline* (pp. 309–327). San Francisco, CA: Berrett-Koehler.

Quintanilla, S. (1991). Introduction: The meaning of work. *European Work & Organizational Psychologist, 1,* 81–90. doi:10.1080/09602009108408514

Rosso, B. D., Dekas, K. H., & Wrzesniewski, A. (2010). On the meaning of work: A theoretical integration and review. *Research in Organizational Behavior, 30,* 91–127. doi:10.1016/j.riob.2010.09.001

Schaffer, R. H. (1953). Job satisfaction as related to need satisfaction in work. *Psychological Monographs: General and Applied, 67*(14, Whole No. 364). doi:10.1037/h0093658

Society for Human Resource Management. (2011). *2011 employee job satisfaction and engagement: Gratification and commitment at work in a sluggish economy.* Retrieved from http://www.shrm.org/research/survey findings/articles/pages/employeejobsatisfactionandengagement.aspx

Steger, M. F., & Dik, B. J. (2010). Work as meaning: Individual and organizational benefits of engaging in meaningful work. In P. A. Linley, S. Harrington, & N. Page (Eds.), *The Oxford handbook of positive psychology and work* (pp. 131–142). Oxford, England: Oxford University Press.

Steger, M. F., Dik, B. J., & Duffy, R. D. (2012). Measuring meaningful work: The Work and Meaning Inventory (WAMI). *Journal of Career Assessment, 20,* 322–337. doi:10.1177/1069072711436160

Super, D. E. (1962). The structure of work values in relation to status, achievement, interest, and adjustment. *Journal of Applied Psychology, 46,* 231–239. doi:10.1037/h0040109

Terkel, S. (1972). *Working.* New York, NY: Avon Books.

Whitehead, T. N. (1935). Social relationships in the factory: A study of an industrial group. *Human Factors, 9,* 381–382.

Wrzesniewski, A., Dutton, J. E., & Debebe, G. (2003). Interpersonal sensemaking and the meaning of work. *Research in Organizational Behavior, 25,* 93–135. doi:10.1016/S0191-3085(03)25003-6

CULTIVATING A
MEANINGFUL CAREER

Paul J. Hartung and Brian J. Taber

Career Construction
Heeding the Call of the Heart

1

Efforts and courage are not enough without purpose
and direction.
                                        —*John F. Kennedy*

Making a living is not the same thing as making a life.
                                        —*Maya Angelou*

W ork holds promise for making a life when it purposefully
heeds and enacts the call of the heart. A universal human
activity and location for performing a social role, work has
long been extolled as a cardinal virtue. In writings of preemi-
nent scholars such as Adler (1931) and Erikson (1963), successful engagement in work represents a hallmark of human
psychosocial adjustment. Along with love, play, and community, work at its best offers a core context for constructing
self and contributing to society in ways heartfelt, personally
meaningful, and socially relevant.

Unfortunately, work's promise as a wellspring for living
a life of personal and social consequence often goes unfulfilled, yielding disdain, dissatisfaction, discouragement, and
disengagement. In modern and postmodern times, work for
many people has meant at most a means of survival, render-
ing little in the way of opportunity for enacting and fulfilling a life purpose (Blustein, 2006). So it appears that work's
promise fails most when workers find work disappointingly
absent in their lives or when work only offers a living in

http://dx.doi.org/10.1037/14183-002
Purpose and Meaning in the Workplace, B. J. Dik, Z. S. Byrne, and M. F. Steger
(Editors)

the form of a paycheck. Likewise, work can disappoint when it lets a person meet the cultural mandate to make a living by performing as a worker in a social role yet does not offer, because of various internal and external forces, a means of making a life in the form of a purpose that responds to the yearnings of the heart. Because the work role occupies and offers promise for much of human life, this volume's aim to consider ways to foster purpose and meaning reflects keenly on humans' search to personally fulfill the promise of work.

Career construction—a theory of vocational behavior and a system of career counseling—assists workers suffering from work's unfulfilled promise to articulate, author, and enact their life-career stories in ways that heed the call of the heart (Savickas, 2005, 2011a). Career construction proceeds from the fundamental premise that work devoid of meaning fails to echo the hurt of a heart that hungers for healing. Viewing work too as a social contribution, career construction asserts that personally meaningful work must also matter to society. In this way, career construction aligns with the neoclassical perspective on "career as calling" (cf. Bunderson & Thompson, 2009; Hall & Chandler, 2005). However, whereas a neoclassical approach assumes an external source of the call, such as divine inspiration or destiny, career construction also aligns with a modern view of calling (Bunderson & Thompson, 2009) in that it interprets calling as arising from a strong inner sense of purpose and direction (Savickas, 2011a), as well as from duty to contribute to the welfare of others. Put simply, career construction views calling as emerging from within workers themselves rather than from sources emanating from without. Consequently, counseling workers for career construction concentrates on imbuing work and career with private meaning derived from experienced problems, preoccupations, and pains—what career construction describes as a hole in the heart—and turning that meaning into work that matters to self and society (Savickas, 2011a).

By melding its constructivist career counseling base with differential and developmental career psychology, career construction incorporates long-standing vocational guidance and career education models and methods (Savickas, 2011a). *Vocational guidance,* epitomized by Holland's (1997) vocational personality and work environments model, assists workers with choosing educational programs and occupations. *Career education,* epitomized by Super's (1990) vocational development model, helps people learn how to ready themselves to make such choices. As a counseling scheme, career construction uses narrative methods to discover the unexamined and hidden reasons workers make themselves into who they are, move along particular life-career pathways, and enact themselves as they do in the workplace (Savickas, 2009b).

In this chapter, we review and apply the principles of career construction theory and practice to indicate how they naturally reflect and advance the notion of career as calling and thereby promote meaning and purpose in workers and workplaces. To do so, we first situate career construction within the context of work in contemporary life, noting particularly how the fields of career development and vocational psychology must now once again adapt—this time, to effectively meet the needs of people trying to make a life in a 21st-century world of extraordinary instability and workplaces shifting beyond the walls of organizations. Within this context, we then consider how perspectives on work have evolved in keeping with and in response to changing times and how these changing perspectives mirror workers' relationships to work as jobs, careers, and callings (Bellah, Madsen, Sullivan, Swidler, & Tipton, 1985). A review of career construction's core principles leads to applying the theory to counseling practice for life-career design. We conclude the chapter by considering evidence to support career construction and future directions for research and practice. These directions aim to increase the validity and viability of career construction for assisting workers in narrating and shaping their identities so as to create meaning within themselves that can sustain them in their work and workplaces.

Work and Career Services in Contemporary Life

Changing times and a fluctuating world of work prompt increased emphasis on meaning. Workers cast into a sea of job loss, workplace stress, and work inopportunity brought by severe economic downturn, *dejobbing* (the shift of work from jobs to activities and assignments), corporate failure, and organizational restructuring search to comprehend their places in an uncertain world. Meanwhile, work continually gets redefined to meet contemporary conditions. Conceptions of career as vertical movement through a sequence of positions within an organizational workplace now give way to notions of career unbounded by such limits. Organizational structures in constant flux and offering little security require workers to be adaptable, self-reflective, self-regulating, and self-managing. These qualities represent hallmarks of effectively navigating a new era of boundaryless (Arthur & Rousseau, 1996) and protean (Hall, 1976) careers in which workers must direct themselves rather than be directed by organizations that are no longer stable (Briscoe, Hall, & DeMuth, 2006).

Today, most workers cannot rely on a steady work world such as once existed in the 20th century. With job security effectively a bygone assurance, contemporary times demand self-reliance and self-directedness whereby workers must create security and stability within themselves (Savickas et al., 2009; Sullivan, 2011) and through their relationships to the social world (Richardson et al., 2009). Critical to this process of becoming self-directed is the ability to narrate a personal identity with coherence and enact it with intentionality. Workers today more than ever must be able to articulate clearly their own answers to the identity questions (Baumeister, 1999) of who they are, who they are becoming, and what is important to them in the work role.

Against this backdrop of revolutionary change in the 21st-century digital and global age, practitioners in the fields of vocational psychology and career development must now innovate and update their theories and practices. If they do so successfully, they will more effectively meet the needs of today's workers who feel undone by work's failed promise and by organizations that no longer exchange company loyalty for job security (Savickas, 2011a; Savickas & Baker, 2005; Sullivan, 2011). Longstanding career models and methods of (a) vocational guidance (i.e., matching people to jobs; e.g., Holland, 1997; Lofquist & Dawis, 1991; Parsons, 1909) and (b) career education (i.e., readying people for educational and vocational decision making; Super, 1990) must now be augmented by (c) career counseling systems and services (i.e., assisting people with life-career design; e.g., Amundson, 2003; Cochran, 1997; Savickas, 2011a; Savickas et al. 2009). Career construction (Savickas, 2005, 2011a) offers counselors, organizational consultants, human resource professionals, life coaches, and researchers both a conceptual model for comprehending vocational behavior and a practical method for assisting today's workers in constructing meaning within themselves and navigating a fluctuating, complex, and uncertain world and workplace.

Evolving Perspectives on Work: Job, Career, Calling

As the world has evolved, so too have perspectives on work, such as those seen in the concepts of boundaryless and protean careers. Evolving perspectives on work reflect both changing times (Savickas & Baker, 2005) and variations in how people relate to their work (Bellah et al., 1985). Revised understandings of individual careers have arisen largely in response to changes in the nature of work and the workplace itself (Savickas & Baker, 2005). Early 20th-century industrialization and urbanization moved work's location from farms to factories. This ushered in the rise of vocational guidance services that assisted youth and a growing immigrant population in securing jobs (Parsons, 1909). Eventually, this development and the need to classify personnel for military service during World Wars I and II fueled the development of guidance and placement services and a shift from work to occupation whereby people related to their work as a job providing sustenance and material gain. By the mid-20th century, with the rise of large corporations and organizations, a new perspective emerged in the form of work as a life-span hierarchical progression through a developmental sequence of positions within an organization (Super, 1957). Attendant with this change came a relationship to work as a career with opportunity for workplace achievement, advancement up an organizational ladder, and increased social status.

Contemporary conditions find perspectives on work shifting again— this time, to reflect the meaning and purpose work serves in people's lives. An unprecedented sea change has reshaped the world as an interconnected, globalized, knowledge-based system. Movement from the industrial age to the digital age, rampant instability, and the restructuring of work have combined to shift the predominant focus from workers in organizations to workers unbounded by organizational structures. Feeling uncertain and insignificant in an ambiguous and unstable world, workers today search for meaning and must do so by creating stability within themselves. In response, career development has evolved a constructivist–social–constructionist perspective on career as a vehicle for life design through which people use work to craft personally meaningful and socially productive lives (Savickas et al., 2009). Rather than fitting self to jobs or readying self to develop a career, workers now must focus increasingly on constructing self in work rather than advancing self in an organization. They may most effectively do so by narrating their identities coherently, adapting to changing circumstances in self and situation, and imbuing their lives with intentionality (Savickas et al., 2009). This change in perspective parallels a relationship between person and work as calling accompanying a profound sense of purpose and mission.

In accordance with changing times, then, longstanding perspectives on work evolve to keep pace and advance their relevance for 21st-century workers. Perspectives on work as an objective match between person and job and as a subjective cycle of self in career over the lifespan are now augmented by a perspective on work as a projective calling realized through self-reflective life design (Savickas, 2011b; Savickas et al., 2009). Career construction honors and integrates the job and career perspectives on work into a holistic framework that advances vital possibilities for work as calling. In this way, work becomes a vehicle for a self-making project wherein people construct themselves and author their lives with purpose rather than merely relate to work as an actor in a job or as an agent in a career (Savickas, 2009a, 2011a). Career construction combines perspectives on work as object (job), subject (career), and project (calling) in its core principles for comprehending vocational behavior and in its practices for counseling workers to heed the call of their hearts and use work to become themselves more completely. Career construction's core principles comprehend career as a complex of personal traits, social tasks, and life themes.

Career Construction: Core Principles for Life Design

As a theory, career construction unifies three principal perspectives on vocational behavior and its development: *individual differences* (Holland, 1997), *individual development* (Super, 1990), and *individual design* (Savickas, 2011a; Savickas et al., 2009). From an individual differences perspective, workers are perceived as actors who fit into suitable work environments. An individual development perspective describes workers as agents who manage the role of work in their lives. And an individual design perspective characterizes workers as authors who write their own life-career stories. Combined in career construction theory, these three perspectives offer a comprehensive and synergistic view on vocational behavior and development.

DIFFERENCES

Career construction uses the individual differences perspective to comprehend career choice content as a function of matching worker traits to occupational environments. Career choice content reflects what specific job or occupation an individual selects and enacts. When individuals align their traits (e.g., interests, abilities, and personality) with analogous job characteristics and requirements, they succeed as actors who fit themselves into a workplace. Workers who know what vocational types they resemble according to the Realistic, Investigative, Artistic, Social, Enterprising, and Conventional (RIASEC) model (Holland, 1997), for example, can better connect to workplaces that may support those workers.

DEVELOPMENT

Career construction uses the individual development perspective to comprehend career growth and change in the context of a worker's whole life. Career context concerns how an individual manages life roles, navigates transitions, and meets social expectations about work across the life course. When individuals deal effectively with developmental tasks, they succeed as agents in managing their careers and fitting work into their lives. Workers who adapt to life-span (Super, 1990) developmental concerns ready themselves to more effectively manage the role of work and the workplace in their lives.

DESIGN

Career construction augments conceptions of vocational behavior and development as matching self to jobs and managing careers over the life span. It does so by setting as its foundation the individual design perspective to construe the purpose and meaning workers may give to work. Career construal involves self-defining stories individuals tell that reveal why they move in a particular life-career direction. When individuals coherently narrate their life themes and enact them with purposeful engagement in vocational choice and adjustment, they succeed as authors of work in their lives.

In sum, career construction comprehends workers in three possible ways: (a) as actors who resemble social scripts that fit corresponding work environments, (b) as agents who develop readiness for fitting work into life, and (c) as authors who reflexively form themselves through work. The first two perspectives translate into practices of, respectively, vocational guidance for person–job matching and education for career management. The third perspective translates into counseling practice for life-career meaning. Career construction uses guidance methods when clients most need to choose an occupation. It uses education methods when clients most need to improve their readiness to choose and learn how to adapt. Career construction uses counseling methods when clients most need to clarify their identity, purpose, and direction in life. It is when work's purpose dims or dies because of changes in self or situation that career construction counseling most helps workers reshape their life careers in ways that heed the call of their hearts.

Career Construction Counseling

As a counseling scheme, career construction assists workers in attaining a clear sense of self, identity, and mission by narrating their life stories. In so doing, it increases capacity to purposefully and meaningfully match self to jobs and manage a career. The *Career Construction Interview* (CCI; American Psychological Association [APA], 2009; Savickas, 1989, 1998, 2009b, 2011a) serves as the central method for career construction. Although best used whole, users may select components of the CCI for focused self-reflection according to need and circumstance. The

CCI contains six questions that elicit stories about early childhood role models, magazines, movies, books, sayings, school subjects, leisure, and early autobiographical memories. Before responding to these questions, clients are asked to tell the story of how they believe counseling can be useful to them as they construct their careers. The response to this preliminary question indicates the client's agenda for counseling, self-perceived current problem, goals for solving it, and the solution he or she is already thinking about. Relating the answer to this initial question to the responses made to all of the other six questions keeps clients mindful of their stated problem and the extent to which they believe they have addressed it. As the client relates self-defining responses to the CCI questions, the counselor listens closely, asks follow-up questions, and makes reflective statements to clarify meaning. Each CCI question elicits small stories about choices and movement through life. Counselor and client then work together to shape the themes and patterns culled from these microstories into a macronarrative about the client's core problem or preoccupation, motives, goals, adaptive strategies, and self-view.

ROLE MODELS

Human beings enter the world without instructions on how life should be lived. Accordingly, as children, they look to others to provide ways of solving life's problems. When counselors ask clients about their role models or the heroes and heroines they admired as children, stories emerge that reveal the template they have used for constructing a self and determining how life should be lived successfully. Consciously selected role models share a dilemma similar to the client's own and show a way to solve the problem. When clients imitate their own childhood role models, they develop coping strategies relevant to solving their problem and form values and interests for specific activities. Understanding why a client selected particular role models provides a window into that client's view of an ideal self, life goals, and solutions to a central life problem. Of course, as clients describe their role models, they, in fact, describe themselves (Savickas, 1989, 1998, 2009b, 2011a).

Clients typically identify with more than one role model as they construct a self. Consequently, they incorporate personally salient aspects from different role models with respect to interests, attitudes, capabilities, values, and personality that they then synthesize into a meaningful whole that is unique to them (Gibson, 2004). Accordingly, the CCI asks for three childhood role models that can come from anywhere—cartoons, super heroes or heroines, a renowned person, or someone from the neighborhood. Role models can be real or fictitious, famous or known only to the client, and may originate from a variety of sources, and they all share one common attribute: The client purposefully selected them to provide a blueprint for constructing a self.

Once identified, the counselor moves to discern what the client admired about these heroes or heroines and how the client is like and different from them. Client–hero/heroine similarities indicate characteristics the client has incorporated into self. Dissimilarities yield characteristics the client may wish to incorporate or has not found personally useful. Follow-up questions ascertain characteristics the client admired about these individuals. Here, the focus remains on the client's perceptions of what is admired about these role models rather than factual accuracy. In discussing role models, patterns emerge that signal resources the client possesses to adapt to the challenges of living.

The influence of childhood role models persists in adulthood. For example, a young man identified Superman as one of his heroes. When asked what he admired about Superman, he identified "being able to save people facing a crisis" as a central characteristic. Later, he commented that while growing up, he wished someone had been there for him during his own moments of crisis. As an adult, he worked as a psychiatric social worker in a hospital emergency department, conducting emergency assessments of people experiencing crises in their lives. His work in this setting allowed him to be there for others and in so doing heal the hole in his own heart from others not being there for him. In this way, then, his work held deep personal meaning for him and mattered to others.

FAVORITE MAGAZINES AND TELEVISION SHOWS

Magazines provide vicarious environments, or *settings,* in which workers immerse themselves (Savickas, 1989, 1998, 2009b, 2011a). In these purposefully selected settings, workers nurture interests that fit their personalities. Magazines incorporate content designed to attract an audience with specific interests. Consequently, they can be conceptualized according to RIASEC types (Holland, 1997). For example, the *National Enquirer* tabloid and *In Touch Weekly* magazine expose readers to human interest stories and may hint about a client's preference for a relational or social environment. In contrast, magazines such as *Hunting* and *Popular Mechanics* indicate a preference for a physical or realistic type of environment. Knowing what magazines a client reads consistently for pleasure and what she or he likes about them offers insights into where the client would most like to enact the self that she or he has constructed.

Some clients may not read any particular magazines consistently. Instead, they may identify a number of television shows that they watch on a regular basis. Identifying and describing favorite television shows provides another way to discern a client's preferred setting for enacting self. As with magazines, counselors ask questions to learn what the client likes about a particular show. For example, a young woman liked *CSI: Miami* because it showed how crime scene evidence is collected and used to solve crimes. Her interest in using data to solve problems hinted at her preference for investigative environments. These types of settings would likely provide the place for her to be who she is and enact the work role meaningfully.

FAVORITE BOOKS AND MOVIES

Stories in the form of books and movies attract an individual's attention when they have a plot that resembles the person's own principal problem, preoccupation, and pain (Savickas, 1989, 1998, 2009b, 2011a). An individual feels drawn to the story because it offers a life script for dealing successfully with a core problem and a central character who constitutes an ideal self. Like a role model, the central character shows the person how to manage a seemingly impossible plight. We hear of and perhaps have our own stories about people reading a book or seeing a movie that changed their lives. Favorite stories thus empower a person who may, for the first time, understand with great clarity a core personal life problem. The experience can be transformative because one comes to see oneself as capable of overcoming difficulties. Exploring clients' favorite stories entails their telling the story of a book or movie in their own words, including most-admired characters and their characteristics. In recounting the story, clients relate how they may move toward a more preferred self-narrative that fosters purposeful movement in work and the workplace.

For example, a client identified *1984* as his favorite book and Winston Smith as his favorite character in the story. As a child, the client received a diagnosis of a mood disorder. Consequently, his parents became, in his words, "overly protective" and closely monitored his activities. Winston Smith, although he lived under the ever-watchful eye of Big Brother, found ways to escape to a life he coveted. Like Winston Smith, the client, too, found ways to circumvent the intrusive nature of his parents' monitoring. As an adult, he found that through his artwork he was free to express himself fully without others looking over his shoulder and telling him what to do.

LEISURE

When unconstrained by the demands of work and other life roles, people typically engage in leisure. Responses to inquiries about leisure activities and hobbies reveal how clients develop skills and attitudes that overcome feelings of weakness and inferiority that often surface in the workplace. As clients tell about their leisure activities, counselors may listen for what they are rehearsing: achievement, creativity, nurturance, or obedience. In their leisure activities, clients may be listeners, learners, competitors, team members, problem solvers, or observers. They engage these skills to foster their success in the workplace. For example, a woman executive enjoyed fashion shows and martial arts. These activities taught her self-expression, how to dress powerfully and professionally, and how to defend herself. She eventually used these skills and attitudes to be a more creative, confident, and assertive problem solver in her job. These leisure activities increased her self-efficacy and competence in the workplace.

FAVORITE SAYING

Favorite sayings represent self-advice in the form of the best counsel one has for dealing with life's problems. Favorite sayings or mottos remind clients how to deal with their problems and become more complete. People are drawn to certain quotes or sayings on the basis of how well these statements resonate with them personally. Autotherapeutic mottos serve as reminders of how to deal with problems and live a personally meaningful life. For example, one client's motto, "You miss 100% of the shots you don't take," served to remind her that taking risks yields opportunities. Another client liked the words "If you stand for nothing, you'll fall for anything," because they reminded him to express his opinions and hold firm to his beliefs so as not to be manipulated. If clients have difficulty identifying a motto, the counselor asks for a phrase or quote they recall hearing. Regardless of the sayings and their origins, meaning derives from clients using them to deal with their central life problems and to become more complete (Savickas, 1989, 1998, 2009b, 2011a).

SCHOOL SUBJECTS

A client's favorite and least favorite school subjects indicate where the client achieved early experiences of success in the form of good grades and satisfaction in the form of enjoyed topics (Savickas, 1989, 1998, 2009b, 2011a). School subjects, like occupations, have relatively distinct requirements. Thus, classrooms in middle and high school are, in effect, mini work environments. For instance, mathematics differs from English, which, in turn, differs from biology. Each subject in the curriculum constitutes a distinct work setting and requires specific tasks. These preferred early work environments provide opportunities for exploring and cultivating abilities, aptitudes, and achievements that translate to work. At the same time, disliked subjects indicate what does not fit one's abilities, interests, and personality. In this way, interacting with the educational environment hones the self. Reflecting on these experiences indicates clients' preferred work environments and associated tasks as well as what environments and tasks they wish to avoid as they consider occupational alternatives.

Liked and disliked school subjects reveal what self-lessons clients learned that remain salient today. For example, a young man liked history, not for memorizing dates and events but because it concerns people's stories, triumphs, and failures. At the same time, he hated science because it dealt in "cold, hard facts" and "lacked a human element." The counselor helped the client concentrate on how work may be most meaningful when it involves using his ability and skill to engage in or with people's stories. The client, in fact, did not want to be a history teacher or historian but wanted to be a writer who could learn about and help people tell their own stories.

When inquiring about favorite school subjects, counselors distinguish between content and teachers. This is particularly relevant in cases where the reported favorite subjects do not seem to fit with the client's overall narrative. For example, a client may report that she enjoyed art because the teacher was humorous, charismatic, and an easy grader. Even though teachers can be admired for many reasons, the primary interest in counseling is in the content and tasks associated with the school subject that defined the client's selection.

EARLY MEMORIES

At the conclusion of the CCI, counselors ask clients for three stories from their early childhood. Early memories provide the most precise and clear indication of the client's central life problem, preoccupation, and pain—or hole in the heart (Savickas, 2011a). From the countless possible events that can be recalled, the client typically selects those most relevant to their current situation (Mosak & Di Pietro, 2006). The focus of exploration is not to determine the historical facts of the stories but rather to understand a person's self-perceptions and patterns of interacting with the world.

Early recollections contain reported memories for specific events that happened before the age of 10 years. The reason for focusing on early childhood is that these stories were formed during a time when people define what the world is like and how to fit into it. Eliciting three stories increases the opportunity for clients to explore their preoccupations, and it produces a pattern. This pattern typically indicates the client's most pressing concern from the first early memory, an elaboration on it from the second memory, and a potential solution from the third memory (Savickas, 2011a). It is important to bear in mind that these stories center on specific events rather than reports of family routines or broad descriptions of early life experiences. The relevance of early recollections rests in their typical ability to depict self-perceptions and the client's worldview as articulated through the stories (Mosak & Di Pietro, 2006). Therefore, these recollections often provide insight into the client's central interests, problems, and preoccupations that guide their personal strivings (Adler, 1937). Early memories do not cause behavior. Rather, they tell about the future and what needs to be done to heal the hole in the heart.

As clients tell stories from early childhood, the counselor records them precisely to capture the meaning conveyed in the words used to describe the events. To clarify succinctly the meaning of each memory, the client gives a headline to the story as if it were to appear in a newspaper. The headline encapsulates the central theme of the story (Shulman & Mosak, 1988). In the headlines and the stories themselves, the counselor pays close attention to the verbs the client uses because they signal how the client moves through life. For example, a client may use words like *striving, fighting,* or *hiding.* The action conveyed by these words parallels the client's mistaken ideas about life and the central problem, preoccupation, and pain.

For example, an accountant in her mid-20s felt anxious and overwhelmed at work. A job she once entered enthusiastically had grown discouraging and dissatisfying. In counseling, she related the following early memory about an event that occurred on a family vacation when she was about 5 years old:

> My siblings and I were swimming at a lake where my family owned a cabin. My mother was yelling at us to come in for lunch. My brother and sister went inside, but I kept playing in the water. Not a good idea. I don't remember exactly how it happened, but I wound up going in way too deep and started drowning. I was really panicking. Fortunately, my mother sent my brother to come and get me, and he saw me struggling in the water. He jumped in and pulled me back to shore.

The headline she gave for this story was "Swimming Alone Causes Near Drowning." The headline clarified the meaning of the memory and provided a metaphor for her current relationship to her work and workplace.

Despite her family and friends admonishing her to seriously consider her workload and to slow down at work, she often eagerly volunteered (akin to "playing in the water"), unlike her coworkers, to take on additional assignments and projects beyond the scope of her job. The net effect left her feeling exhausted by the extra workload, afraid she would not be able to keep up, and isolated from her coworkers. She found herself "swimming alone" in waters of work "way too deep" for her to tread. She and her counselor considered how her initial enthusiasm for work accompanied by working closely with others waned when she set off on her own to take on additional assignments. Her swimming alone into deeper waters of work prompted "panic" as she "struggled" to complete all of her many assignments. Accordingly, she sought career counseling essentially to "save" her from going in too deep at work. She and the counselor narrated her life theme and project as "I need to learn to save myself and cooperate with authority." Eventually, she learned to set realistic work boundaries and goals with her supervisor who, like her brother, effectively served as a rescuer who would allow her to meet performance expectations without sacrificing and isolating herself in the process. She also engaged the authority of her family and friends for support and feedback about her progress. In the end, she saved herself by heeding the call of her heart that echoed to her the pain that results from disregarding others and taking too much risk.

CONSTRUCTING A LIFE PORTRAIT

Assembling the small stories told from the separate CCI questions into a larger narrative yields a life portrait that "reconstructs the client's character with greater agency and self-consciousness" (Savickas, 2002, p. 190). Counselor and client co-construct the life portrait from the client's CCI responses that coherently indicate the life theme. The process of co-constructing the life portrait moves systematically through a routine that attends to the client's (a) problems and preoccupations from early memories, (b) self and solutions for life's problems from role models, (c) settings from magazines and television shows, (d) scripts from books and movies, (e) successes and satisfactions from school subjects, (f) skills and attitudes from leisure activities, and (g) scenarios for action plans from favorite sayings. Co-constructing a life portrait always includes the client's calling. It tells the story of the calling, its origin, and its goal. Interested readers may consult Savickas (2011a) and his audiovisual recordings (APA, 2006, 2009), which describe and illustrate career construction counseling in full detail.

Evidence and Future Directions

Table 1.1 lists recommendations for fostering meaningful work and workplaces derived from career construction theory, practice, and research. The comprehensive nature of career construction theory and practice permits the understanding of vocational behavior from differential, developmental, and design perspectives. Of these three perspectives, the life-design perspective provides the most insight into how meaning in work can be construed (Savickas et al., 2009). The particular usefulness of this perspective stems from its emphasis on increasing an individual's ability to narrate his or her life story through the use of counseling methods such as the CCI. The CCI offers a method for identifying life themes by ascribing meaning to past recollections, current experiences, and future prospects. Accordingly, the identification of life themes and subsequent self-understanding contribute to meaningfulness in work (Pratt & Ashforth, 2003).

Through a number of published case studies, the CCI has been demonstrated to be a useful career intervention. For example, the CCI has been found to be useful for assisting a client in selecting a college major (Savickas, 2005), fostering career decision making among adults (APA, 2006; Savickas, 2009a; Taber, Hartung, Briddick, Briddick, & Rehfuss, 2011), and counseling an adult seeking career direction in the face of uncertainty as a contract worker (Taber & Briddick, 2011). The effectiveness of the CCI in these case studies underscores the usefulness of narrative interventions in helping people to create meaningful occupational futures (Bujold, 2004).

Qualitative research has also examined the usefulness of the CCI from client and counselor perspectives. A qualitative study with 18 client–counselor dyads using the CCI reported that as a result of the interventions, clients attained greater career awareness, self-confidence, sense of direction, and confirmation that they were on the right career path (Rehfuss, Del Corso, Galvin, & Wykes, 2011). Another qualitative study examined the usefulness of the CCI as a career counseling technique from the perspective of 34 counselors trained in conducting the interview (Rehfuss, Cosio, & Del Corso, 2011). The results indicated that counselors using the CCI found it helpful in working with clients to identify life themes and make meaningful career decisions. From the case studies and qualitative research conducted to date, the CCI shows promise for further and more systematic study.

Future research with the CCI should focus on empirical investigation of the extent to which it produces desirable outcomes. Research would do well to examine whether people who engage in a CCI, when compared with a no-treatment control group, achieve outcomes such as greater self-concept clarity (Campbell et al., 1996), increased career adaptability (Savickas, 1997), and a work life more reflective of a calling (Wrzesniewski, McCauley, Rozin, & Schwartz, 1997). Should the CCI prove to be effective in producing such outcomes, research should then focus on which components of the CCI seem to be most effective in producing the desirable effects. For instance, one finding from the Rehfuss, Del Corso, et al. (2011) study indicated that the majority of clients found consideration of role models most meaningful to them, followed by exploration of early recollections. Given this finding, it would seem important to determine whether role models and early memories also have the greatest impact on clients in terms of effecting desirable outcomes. Using dismantling research methods (Heppner, Wampold, & Kivlighan, 2008), researchers could investigate the separate and combined effects of the CCI components to determine the most useful interview strategy. Counseling process research with the CCI would also be useful in this regard.

Fundamentally, research must concentrate on how career construction helps workers develop uniquely rather than simply as versions of other people, such as those presented in the RIASEC types. The differential and developmental aspects of career construction have been well-studied using primarily individual differences methods. Examining career construction's basis in the emerging tradition of life design and its efficacy as a counseling scheme requires qualitative and case study methods such as those used in psychotherapy research. Such methods emphasize life narratives and stories rather than numbers and test scores to provide enriched, contextualized explanations of human behavior and development.

Conclusion

Today's pervasive search for purpose and meaning in the workplace comes from a world that has dramatically changed. Unstable work makes for insecure workers who increasingly question their place in a highly uncertain world. Life in a 21st-century digital age of tremendous global interconnectivity yields the sad ironic consequence of workers left feeling ever more alienated and disconnected from work and workplaces. Traditional emphases on matching self to jobs and managing self across an occupational career now give way to an emphasis on making meaning through work. Career construction assists in this meaning-making process by helping workers to shape their identities and construct certainty and confidence within themselves. Using components of the CCI in whole or in part offers a useful scheme for empowering workers to coherently tell, hear, and retell with deeper clarity their life-career stories and identify ways to enact them in work. Meaningful work means making a meaningful life by heeding the call of the heart.

TABLE 1.1

Focus on the Workplace: A Career Construction Perspective

Recommendation	Tested in practice	Derived from theory	Supported by research
Encourage individuals to construct meaning within themselves and navigate a fluctuating, complex, and uncertain world and workplace by learning to be self-directed.[a]	✓	✓	✓
Increase work's meaning by assisting individuals to comprehend how they may use it to enact their life-career stories.	✓	✓	
Offer individuals a comprehensive understanding of work from three perspectives: job, career, and calling.[b,c,d]	✓	✓	✓
Assist individuals to know their traits (e.g., interests, abilities, and personality) and preferred environments (settings). Then they may align themselves with analogous job characteristics and requirements to successfully fit into the workplace.[e,f]	✓	✓	✓
Clearly communicate work tasks and requirements, and support employees so that they may complete them successfully. Then employees may feel empowered to fit work into their lives and promote their own career progression.[g]	✓	✓	✓
Emphasize career adaptability as a key to managing work across the life span.		✓	
Facilitate understanding of how participation in various life roles can provide avenues for meaning in life outside the work role.	✓	✓	
Clarify vocational self-concepts by focusing on personal meanings and life themes to make meaningful vocational choices.	✓	✓	✓
Assist individuals in reflecting on self, setting, skills, and self-advice for workplace success.	✓	✓	

Note. [a]Briscoe, Hall, & DeMuth (2006). [b]Bunderson & Thompson (2009). [c]Hall & Chandler (2005). [d]Wrzesniewski, McCauley, Rozin, & Schwartz (1997). [e]Holland (1997). [f]Lofquist & Dawis (1991). [g]Super (1990).

References

Adler, A. (1931). *What life should mean to you*. Boston, MA: Little, Brown.

Adler, A. (1937). Significance of early recollections. *International Journal of Individual Psychology, 3*, 283–287.

American Psychological Association. (Producer). (2006). *Career counseling* [DVD]. Available from http://www.apa.org/pubs/videos/4310737.aspx

American Psychological Association. (Producer). (2009). *Career counseling over time* [DVD]. Available from http://www.apa.org/pubs/videos/4310872.aspx

Amundson, N. E. (2003). *Active engagement: Enhancing the career counseling process*. Richmond, Canada: Ergon Communications.

Arthur, M. B., & Rousseau, D. M. (1996). Introduction: The boundaryless career as a new employment principle. In M. B. Arthur & D. M. Rousseau (Eds.), *The boundaryless career: A new employment principle for a new organizational era* (pp. 3–20). New York, NY: Oxford University Press.

Baumeister, R. F. (1999). Self-concept, self-esteem, and identity. In V. J. Derlega, B. A. Winstead, & W. H. Jones (Eds.), *Personality: Contemporary theory and research* (2nd ed., pp. 339–375). Belmont, CA: Wadsworth.

Bellah, R. N., Madsen, R., Sullivan, W. M., Swidler, A., & Tipton, S. M. (1985). *Habits of the heart*. New York, NY: Harper & Row.

Blustein, D. L. (2006). *The psychology of working: A new perspective for career development, counseling, and public policy*. Mahwah, NJ: Erlbaum.

Briscoe, J. P., Hall, D. T., & DeMuth, R. L. F. (2006). Protean and boundaryless careers: An empirical exploration. *Journal of Vocational Behavior, 69*, 30–47. doi:10.1016/j.jvb.2005.09.003

Bujold, C. (2004). Constructing career through narrative. *Journal of Vocational Behavior, 64*, 470–484. doi:10.1016/j.jvb.2003.12.010

Bunderson, J. S., & Thompson, J. A. (2009). The call of the wild: Zookeepers, callings, and the double-edged sword of deeply meaningful work. *Administrative Science Quarterly, 54*, 32–57. doi:10.2189/asqu.2009.54.1.32

Campbell, J. D., Trapnell, P. D., Heine, S. J., Katz, I. M., Lavallee, L. F., & Lehman, D. R. (1996). Self-concept clarity: Measurement, personality correlates, and cultural boundaries. *Journal of Personality and Social Psychology, 70*, 141–156.

Cochran, L. (1997). *Career counseling: A narrative approach*. Thousand Oaks, CA: Sage.

Erikson, E. H. (1963). *Childhood and society* (2nd ed.). New York, NY: Norton.

Gibson, D. E. (2004). Role models in career development: New directions for theory and research. *Journal of Vocational Behavior, 65*, 134–156. doi:10.1016/S0001-8791(03)00051-4

Hall, D. T. (1976). *Careers in organizations.* Glenview, IL: Foresman.

Hall, D. T., & Chandler, D. E. (2005). Psychological success: When the career is a *calling. Journal of Organizational Behavior, 26,* 155–176. doi:10.1002/job.301

Heppner, P. P., Wampold, B. E., & Kivlighan, D. M. (2008). *Research design in counseling* (3rd ed.). Belmont, CA: Brooks/Cole.

Holland, J. L. (1997). *Making vocational choices* (3rd ed.). Odessa, FL: Psychological Assessment Resources.

Lofquist, L. H., & Dawis, R. V. (1991). *Essentials of person–environment correspondence counseling.* Minneapolis: University of Minnesota Press.

Mosak, H. H., & Di Pietro, R. (2006). *Early recollections: Interpretive method and applications.* New York, NY: Routledge.

Parsons, F. (1909). *Choosing a vocation.* Boston, MA: Houghton Mifflin.

Pratt, M. G., & Ashforth, B. E. (2003). Fostering meaningfulness in working and in work. In K. S. Cameron, J. E. Dutton, & R. E. Quinn (Eds.), *Positive organizational scholarship: Foundations of a new discipline* (pp. 309–327). San Francisco, CA: Barrett-Koehler.

Rehfuss, M., Cosio, S., & Del Corso, J. (2011). Counselors' perspectives on using the Career Style Interview with clients. *The Career Development Quarterly, 59,* 208–218. doi:10.1002/j.2161-0045.2011.tb00064.x

Rehfuss, M., Del Corso, J., Galvin, K., & Wykes, S. (2011). Impact of the Career Style Interview on individuals with career concerns. *Journal of Career Assessment, 19,* 405–419. doi:10.1177/1069072711409711

Richardson, M. S., Meade, P., Rosbruch, N., Vescio, C., Price, L., & Cordero, A. (2009). Intentional and identity processes: A social constructionist investigation using student journals. *Journal of Vocational Behavior, 74,* 63–74. doi:10.1016/j.jvb.2008.10.007

Savickas, M. L. (1989). Career style assessment and counseling. In T. Sweeney (Ed.), *Adlerian counseling: A practical approach for a new decade* (3rd ed., pp. 289–320). Muncie, IN: Accelerated Development Press.

Savickas, M. L. (1997). Career adaptability: An integrative construct for life-span, life-space theory. *The Career Development Quarterly, 45,* 247–259. doi:10.1002/j.2161-0045.1997.tb00469.x

Savickas, M. L. (1998). Career style assessment and counseling. In T. Sweeney (Ed.), *Adlerian counseling: A practitioner's approach* (4th ed., pp. 329–360). Philadelphia, PA: Accelerated Development Press.

Savickas, M. L. (2002). Career construction: A developmental theory of vocational behavior. In D. Brown (Ed.), *Career choice and development* (4th ed., pp. 149–205). San Francisco, CA: Jossey-Bass.

Savickas, M. L. (2005). The theory and practice of career construction. In S. Brown & R. Lent (Eds.), *Career development and counseling: Putting theory and research to work* (pp. 42–70). New York, NY: Wiley.

Savickas, M. L. (2009a). Career studies as self-making and life designing. *Career Research and Development, 24,* 15–17.

Savickas, M. L. (2009b). Career-style counseling. In T. J. Sweeney (Ed.), *Adlerian counseling and psychotherapy: A practitioner's approach* (5th ed., pp. 183–207). New York, NY: Routledge.

Savickas, M. L. (2011a). *Career counseling.* Washington, DC: American Psychological Association.

Savickas, M. L. (2011b). The self in vocational psychology: Object, subject, and project. In P. J. Hartung & L. M. Subich (Eds.), *Developing self in work and career: Concepts, cases, and contexts* (pp. 17–33). Washington, DC: American Psychological Association. doi:10.1037/12348-002

Savickas, M. L., & Baker, D. B. (2005). The history of vocational psychology: Antecedents, origins, and early development. In W. B. Walsh & M. L. Savickas (Eds.), *Handbook of vocational psychology* (3rd ed., pp. 15–50). Mahwah, NJ: Erlbaum.

Savickas, M. L., Nota, L., Rossier, J., Dauwalder, J., Duarte, M. E., Guichard, J., . . . van Vianen, A. E. M. (2009). Life designing: A paradigm for career construction in the 21st century. *Journal of Vocational Behavior, 75,* 239–250. doi:10.1016/j.jvb.2009.04.004

Shulman, B. H., & Mosak, H. H. (1988). *Manual for life style assessment.* Bristol, PA: Accelerated Development Press.

Sullivan, S. E. (2011). Self-direction in the boundaryless career era. In P. J. Hartung & L. M. Subich (Eds.), *Developing self in work and career: Concepts, cases, and contexts* (pp. 123–140). Washington, DC: American Psychological Association. doi:10.1037/12348-008

Super, D. E. (1957). *The psychology of careers: An introduction to vocational development.* New York, NY: Harper & Row.

Super, D. E. (1990). A life-span, life-space approach to career development. In D. Brown & L. Brooks (Eds.), *Career choice and development: Applying contemporary theories to practice* (2nd ed., pp. 197–261). San Francisco, CA: Jossey-Bass.

Taber, B. J., & Briddick, W. C. (2011). Adlerian-based career counseling in an age of protean careers. *Journal of Individual Psychology, 67,* 107–121.

Taber, B. J., Hartung, P. J., Briddick, W. C., Briddick, H., & Rehfuss, M. (2011). Career Style Interview: A contextualized approach to career counseling. *The Career Development Quarterly, 59,* 274–287. doi:10.1002/j.2161-0045.2011.tb00069.x

Wrzesniewski, A., McCauley, C., Rozin, P., & Schwartz, B. (1997). Jobs, careers, and callings: People's relations to their work. *Journal of Research in Personality, 31,* 21–33. doi:10.1006/jrpe.1997.2162

Jo-Ida C. Hansen

A Person–Environment Fit Approach to Cultivating Meaning

2

E. K. Strong Jr. was a psychologist of the dustbowl empiricist persuasion. His labor of love, measuring vocational interests, remains one of the most important and influential contributions to vocational psychology and psychological testing, yet one never hears or reads about Strong's theory of interests because his empirical work was not theoretically driven and because he did not articulate the aggregation of his substantial scientific knowledge in a theory of his own. Nonetheless, Strong's work exemplified classic person–environment fit (P-E fit) research long before the term was coined. His research constructing the Strong Vocational Interest Blank assumed that a match between interests and jobs would lead to meaningful work and to more productive and happier employees (Strong, 1943). The method of test construction that he used—and, may I say, perfected—was the atheoretical and empirical method of contrast groups. To this day, Occupational Scales on the Strong Interest Inventory are constructed using this method of scale development.

http://dx.doi.org/10.1037/14183-003
Purpose and Meaning in the Workplace, B. J. Dik, Z. S. Byrne, and M. F. Steger (Editors)

Since Strong's early work, hundreds of studies have been conducted to explore the relation between P-E fit and a multitude of criteria. This work has generated theories, fit and congruence indices, assessment instruments, conflicting results, controversy, and intellectual arguments about the veracity of P-E fit. However, the terms *meaning in work* and *meaningful work* are not commonly used in P-E fit research. Rather, the outcomes assessed in P-E fit research typically include criterion variables such as satisfaction, feelings of accomplishment, performance, and psychological well-being. Steger and Dik (2010) are among the few to connect P-E fit and its outcomes to meaning. They noted that their definition of the construct of *comprehension,* a primary component of meaning of life, "resembles person–environment fit theories that predict work satisfaction in terms of how well a worker's abilities, interests, and needs match the requirements and reinforcers of an organization" (Steger & Dik, 2010, p. 133).

Frank Parsons—who was, it is interesting to note, an attorney, not a psychologist—is often credited as one of the originators of P-E fit models of career counseling. His work with poor immigrants was designed to assist them in finding meaningful work through their own self-understanding, analysis of job requirements, and the match of their strengths with the requirements of the work environment (Hansen, in press). D. G. Paterson's work at the University of Minnesota in the 1940s also used P-E fit theories to promote, through empirically derived methods of selection in industry and education, job placements that resulted in meaningful work for the unemployed after the first Great Depression in the 1930s and for returning veterans after World War II in the 1940s (Erdheim, Zickar, & Yankelovich, 2007). Fast forwarding to the present, people continue to seek meaningful work, and P-E fit theories provide a useful tool for vocational psychologists, career counselors, and human resource specialists who are engaged with clients and employees in the process of discovering individual strengths and job requirement matches that increase the probability that a person engages in meaningful work.

This chapter first provides an overview of four P-E fit theories—each of which has a slightly different emphasis—that predict vocational outcomes contributing to self-perceptions of being engaged in meaningful work. Integrative overviews of each of these theories—the theory of vocational personality types (Holland, 1997), the theory of work adjustment (Dawis & Lofquist, 1984), person–environment fit stress theory (Edwards, Caplan, & Harrison, 1998), and multidimensional P-E fit theory (Jansen & Kristof-Brown, 2006)—have provided evidence for many of the theories' postulates and hypothesized constructs. The discussion of these theories that follows is laden with traditional work predictor and outcome terminology. What the reader will find missing in this review of P-E fit theories and research is reference to an empirical assessment of meaning because, to date, such an assessment has not been used in P-E fit outcome research. However, the essence of meaning in work or meaningful work is captured by meta-analyses that provide evidence of the relation between fit, congruence, and correspondence and various criteria (e.g., satisfaction, internal motivation, career stability, psychological and physical well-being, self-efficacy; Assouline & Meir, 1987; Dawis, 2005; Edwards et al., 1998; Kristof-Brown, Zimmerman, & Johnson, 2005; Spokane & Cruza-Guet, 2005; Steger & Dik, 2010; Vogel & Feldman, 2009).This chapter also presents applications of P-E fit models for career counseling, organizational development, unemployment counseling, retirement counseling, and cultural fit. Finally, Table 2.1 provides six examples of the way in which extant P-E fit models can provide a foundation for developing interventions to enhance meaningfulness in educational, work, and community service settings.

Translating meaningful work definitions and theories into P-E fit models highlights conventional predictors and conventional outcomes (or criterion variables) of P-E fit research. For example, some of the foundations of meaning in life—such as personal control, autonomy, group importance, individualistic experience, collective experience, intrinsic motivation, affective commitment, and strengths (interests, abilities, values, personality)—overlap directly with predictors of work satisfaction and employee satisfactoriness (Dik, Steger, Fitch-Martin, & Onder, in press; Steger & Dik, 2010). Congruence between an individual's values and behaviors and the world of work is hypothesized to predict meaningfulness, and job characteristics such as variety, autonomy, and task significance are hypothesized to correlate with meaningfulness (Steger & Dik, 2010). Meaningfulness itself is said to be reflected in outcomes such as satisfaction, few work absences, self-perceived congruence between personal characteristics and job demands, and feelings of positive work experience and significant contributions (Dik et al., in press; Steger & Dik, 2010).

Theory of Vocational Personality Types

John L. Holland's 1959 paper, which was his first article to describe his now popular theory, slightly predated the early work of Lloyd Lofquist and René Dawis, who conceived the theory of work adjustment. In many ways, Holland followed the lead of E. K. Strong Jr. when he developed his theory of vocational personality types, linking interests to congruent environments, primarily vocational and educational environments. However, in addition to developing hypotheses around interest–environment congruence, Holland also articulated definitions of interests and their relations to one another. Embedded in his definition of six vocational interest types—realistic, investigative, artistic, social, enterprising, and conventional, collectively referred to as RIASEC—are hypotheses about the relation of each interest type to abilities, values, and personality. Holland drew on the earlier empirical work of John G. Darley (1938), E. K. Strong Jr. (1943), Leona E. Tyler (1951), B. R. Forer (1953), J. P. Guilford (Guilford, Christensen, Bond, & Sutton, 1954), and Anne Roe (1956) to formulate his definitions of the six interest types (i.e., realistic, investigative, artistic, social, enterprising, conventional) as well as to hypothesize the hexagonal relation among the six types (e.g., the six types can be arranged in RIASEC order on the points of a hexagon; types adjacent to one another are more closely related than are types diametrically opposite to each other). Holland also categorized work environments (i.e., occupations, jobs) into the same six types or some combination of the six types and hypothesized that the degree of congruence between the individual's type and the environment's type predicted satisfaction with and success at work (Holland, 1997).

After defining the six types and hypothesizing their hexagonal relationship, Holland's congruence construct probably is his next most well-known contribution. Numerous indices have been developed to measure levels of interest–environment congruence (e.g., FL–Hex, C-Index, K–P Index, Sb Index, Hexagon Congruence Index, Modified C-Index), some of which are more complicated to calculate than others (Hoeglund & Hansen, 1999). The tricky aspect (i.e., validity) of these indices or any attempt to measure fit is the extent to which the environment is accurately portrayed. Interests can be measured directly, but some inference takes place in most environment coding schemes, including those developed by Gottfredson and Holland (1989). One exception is Holland codes assigned to occupations represented on the Strong Interest Inventory. For these occupations, ample empirical data are available for determining their Holland types (Hansen, 1992). The difficulty in assessing or characterizing the environment is a persistent problem in P-E fit research; this is frequently referenced as an explanation for lower than expected correlations between congruence indices (predictors) and outcomes (criteria).

Theory of Work Adjustment

The *theory of work adjustment* (TWA; Dawis & Lofquist, 1984), as updated by Dawis (2005), is a theory of P-E fit and P-E interaction. *Fit*, of course, refers to the extent to which a person's characteristics correspond to characteristics of the environment. *Interaction* refers to the give and take that occurs between P and E. The criteria of TWA are worker satisfaction and worker satisfactoriness, which in combination lead to a third criterion, tenure. *Satisfaction* is the result of a person's needs being met. In other words, the environment reinforces the worker's need. *Satisfactoriness* of the person is the result of the environment's requirements, which are capabilities or skills, being met. In other words, satisfactoriness is the extent to which a person has the set of skills needed to do a job.

TWA stipulates both a predictive model and a process model. The congruence, or *correspondence* as it is labeled in TWA, between the environment's reinforcers and the person's needs (reinforcer requirements) predicts the person's satisfaction. In parallel, the correspondence of the person's skills (or abilities) to the environment's skill requirements predicts the person's satisfactoriness. Satisfaction is hypothesized to lead to a person's decision to remain in a job and satisfactoriness leads to retaining the person; in combination, the decisions to remain and to retain lead to tenure.

The *TWA predictive model* (i.e., fit model) can help people identify careers, jobs, and work environments that will bring them satisfaction and can help identify where they will perform satisfactorily. However, the TWA fit model does not address the real-world process of work adjustment that allows the person and environment to find correspondence (i.e., congruence or fit) when it is lacking. The *TWA process model* fills that gap, conceptualizing a cycle that begins when the person is dissatisfied and seeks adjustment or change to reduce that dissatisfaction. TWA proposes the individual difference of *flexibility* as a primary determinant of the length of time a person can tolerate discorrespondence before dissatisfaction occurs and the subsequent need for change increases to the point that action is taken. People who are flexible can tolerate discorrespondence longer than can those who are not flexible.

Once a person initiates change or adjustment, the person can adjust by trying to change the environment's reinforcers and/or the environment's skill requirements. TWA terms this an *active* approach to adjustment. Another approach, one during which the person attempts to change her or his own needs or skills, is labeled *reactive*. A final construct in the TWA process model is *perseverance*, or the length of time a person will continue to try to reduce discorrespondence and dissatisfaction before leaving the job or work environment.

Person–Environment Fit Stress Theories

P-E fit theories prominent in occupational stress research, which now is in the domain of occupational health psychology (OHP), tend to incorporate many of the basic elements found in TWA (Dawis & Lofquist, 1984). Edwards et al. (1998) described a model of theoretical relationships between job stress and health that captures the work of various theorists. Stress is assumed to arise from the absence of fit or lack of congruence between the person and the environment. The criteria, then, in P-E fit stress theories are strains that, in turn, can lead to illness. A recent trend in OHP work is to also look at positive outcomes (e.g., meaningfulness, happiness; Eggerth & Cunningham, 2012). Similar to TWA, the predictors for P include abilities and needs and for E include demands (required skills) and supplies (reinforcers). However, OHP P-E fit theories add an element of objective versus subjective (perceived) fit that is not articulated specifically in TWA. The element of perceived fit has received some attention in the industrial and organizational literature as well (Edwards, Cable, Williamson, Lambert, & Shipp, 2006; Piasentin & Chapman, 2006).

As is the case in TWA, OHP fit theories require that person and environment constructs refer to the same content dimensions. In other words, the measurement of the needs of the person should be commensurate with the measurement of the supplies of the environment. *Stress,* in these models, is defined as the degree of subjective misfit between P and E. Strain outcomes (or criteria) include dissatisfaction, dysphoria, anxiety, elevated blood pressure or serum cholesterol, and compromised immune functioning. The cumulative experience of strains over time, in turn, can lead to mental and physical illness (e.g., chronic depression, hypertension, heart disease, ulcers, cancer). Within OHP models, coping is hypothesized as one way to improve P-E fit, by changing either the environment or the person; this is analogous to TWA active or reactive adjustment.

One interesting twist to OHP P-E fit theories is the hypothesis that both over- and undersupply and insufficient or excessive ability can lead to misfit. In other words, as supplies increase to match needs, strain decreases, but at some point, when supplies exceed needs, the additional supplies have little effect on the continued reduction of strain. In those cases, *carryover* (i.e., use of excess supply to bring about changes in other areas) or *conservation* (i.e., excess supplies are saved for future use) may occur. On some occasions, excessive supplies (i.e., too much of a good thing) can actually increase strain. An analogous process is hypothesized for abilities that are insufficient for or exceed demand. Excessive ability may lead to increased strain (e.g., boredom, lack of motivation), but insufficient ability to meet demands also can increase strain (e.g., anxiety, exhaustion).

Multidimensional Theory of Person–Environment Fit

Attempts have been made to integrate various P-E fit theories as well as to extend extant theories to provide more specification. For example, several researchers have integrated Holland's (1997) theory of vocational personality, which emphasizes the P-E fit of interests to vocation, with Dawis and Lofquist's (1984) TWA, which emphasizes the fit of P's abilities and E's requirements and P's values and E's reinforcers (Lubinski & Benbow, 2000; Ton & Hansen, 2001; Tziner & Meir, 1997). Integrating Holland's model with the TWA framework provides a more multidimensional approach than does either theory alone for understanding the intricacies of P-E fit and the relation of congruence to outcome criteria. These integrated models capture multiple dimensions of the person that share a small amount of variance but are not redundant (e.g., interests, values, and abilities).

Jansen and Kristof-Brown (2006) have proposed a multidimensional theory of P-E fit that takes into account multiple dimensions of the environment. They argued that focusing on single aspects of the environment (e.g., job or organization) oversimplifies the P-E fit concept. Thus, they recommended an approach that combines multiple environments to "create an overall experience of PE fit" (Jansen & Kristof-Brown, 2006, p. 195). They identified five dimensions of E typically experienced simultaneously by workers: vocation (V), organization (O), group (G), job (J), and person (P). An important ingredient in their model is salience—specifically, salience of the E dimension for both the person and the environment. For them, the construct of salience (a) generates propositions related to personality and (b) values individual differences: Agreeable individuals will find P-P and P-G more salient than P-J and P-V; conscientious individuals will find person–job and person–vocation more salient than P-P or P-G; high-achievement individuals will find P-J and P-V more salient than P-P or P-G; individuals who have social values will find P-P and P-G more salient than P-J and P-V. They also proposed environmental differences in organizational culture and in the formality of the hierarchical structure of the organization: Strong organizational cultures reflect high organizational (O) salience; weak organizational cultures reflects high group (G) salience; a lack of group norms may lead to high person (P) salience; strong vocational identity leads to high vocation (V) salience; and the larger the organization and the more formal the hierarchy, the more likely the job (J) or group (G) has more salience than does the organization (O). Finally, they also acknowledged that the salience of various aspects of E may change during temporal stages of a person's career.

Tests of Person–Environment Fit Theories

One popular approach to P-E fit research examined the efficacy of the congruence of occupational interests with college majors or occupations for predicting satisfaction. Some of these studies were designed to test the predictive validity of occupational scales on the Strong Interest Inventory or Self-Directed Search (Holland, 1970) or Vocational Preference Inventory (Holland, 1953), scales that measure Holland's six types. In general, these studies showed that the match between interest inventory scores and college major selection or occupational selection is substantial; the majority of people in these studies expressed satisfaction with their choices (Hansen & Dik, 2005; Hansen & Lee, 2007; Hansen & Tan, 1992; Tracey & Hopkins, 2001). Another approach looked at the extent to which interests or personality predicts subjective or perceived person–vocation and person–job fit. Interests appeared to be the more powerful predictors (Ehrhart & Makransky, 2007). Generally, then, researchers conducting studies that have examined vocational interest–environment congruence find positive relations with outcomes such as educational and vocational stability as well as satisfaction, adjustment, and achievement (Assouline & Meir, 1987; Harms, Roberts, & Winter, 2006; Porter & Umbach, 2006; Smart & Feldman, 1998; Spokane, 1996).

Another large body of research on P-E fit supported the relation of components of person–organization congruence or fit to satisfaction, organizational commitment, and tenure. Meta-analysis results showed that both person–job and person–organization fit predict job satisfaction and organizational commitment. Person–supervisor (P-S) congruence also predicted job satisfaction (Kristof-Brown & Guay, 2011; Kristof-Brown et al., 2005). A moderator of these results is the way in which fit is assessed: Perceived (i.e., subjective) fit predicts positive outcomes better than does objective fit (Kristof-Brown & Guay, 2011). Research on the relation between P-E fit and performance has been less compelling. Regardless of the way in which performance is assessed (e.g., overall performance, task performance), the way in which fit is defined (perceived fit or direct measures), the time frame of the prediction (e.g., concurrent or predictive), or the type of fit (e.g., P-J, P-G, P-S), the effect sizes are small (Arthur, Bell, Villado, & Doverspike, 2006; Kristof-Brown et al., 2005).

Another trend in P-E fit research has been to narrow the search for fit to specific aspects of the person, the environment, and the outcome criterion. This line of research, designed to tease apart complex theoretical models to test discrete postulates, has provided rich opportunities for translational research in applied psychology. Other streams of research in this direction have used generic P-E fit as a model for the research design without declaring allegiance to a specific P-E fit theory that drives the research. Researchers using this approach have integrated many other P and E predictors and outcome variables into P-E fit models. For example, person predictor constructs, beyond those stated most frequently in theoretical models (e.g., skills and abilities, personality, interests, work values), include creativity (Livingstone, Nelson, & Barr,

1997), rural values (Little & Miller, 2007), empowerment (Laschinger, Wong, & Greco, 2006), volunteerism (Van Vianen, Nijstad, & Voskuijl, 2008), leisure interests (Melamed, Meir, & Samson, 1995), public service motivation (Steijn, 2008), work–home segmentation (Kreiner, 2006), intolerance of inequity (Ahmad, 2010), cognitive style (Cools, Van den Broeck, & Bouckenooghe, 2009), job complexity (Wilk & Sackett, 1996), and marital roles (Ton & Hansen, 2001). Examples of other outcomes (i.e., criteria) that have been studied and have real world applications for enhancing meaning in work include job involvement (Blau, 1987), burnout (or lack thereof; Laschinger et al., 2006), career certainty (Durr & Tracey, 2009), withdrawal behavior (Tak, 2011), and subjective well-being (Gottfredson & Duffy, 2008).

Applications of Person–Environment Fit Models

This section describes four ways in which P-E fit theories and translational research apply to interventions. Evidence of support for the first three applications—career counseling, organizational interventions, and unemployment counseling—is easily drawn from earlier discussions in this chapter, and the reader is directed to the cited references for elaboration. The use of P-E fit models in retirement counseling has been empirically tested less often and the body of work surrounding this application is smaller. Nonetheless, P-E fit research does generalize sufficiently to retirement counseling to allow the development of reasonable hypotheses to be tested.

CAREER COUNSELING

Career counseling has a long history of applying P-E fit to the process of vocational choice. Even early efforts to guide career selection focused on choice as a vehicle for increased meaning in a worker's life (Parsons, 1909). The current trend is to conceptualize the opportunity for choice as an important process, regardless of economic status, ethnicity, culture, or ability (Fouad & Kantamneni, 2008). The process of career counseling, in the trait-and-factor or P-E fit tradition, often relies heavily on assessment to identify P attributes that then can be matched to E requirements.

The career counseling setting may occur within an educational framework such as a high school or college, within other institutions such as prisons and hospitals, or even in the workplace itself. One primary client goal, of course, is vocational choice, but for some clients, the exploration process that leads to understanding the match between self and the work environment is as much about personal understanding and development as it is about making a choice. At a minimum, career interventions typically include assessment of interests. More elaborate schemes include the assessment of abilities, values, and personality, all of which have been demonstrated to be ingredients in predicting P-E fit.

ORGANIZATIONAL DEVELOPMENT

Within organizations, attention to identifying commensurate P and E fit variables that lead to positive affect (e.g., meaning, happiness, satisfaction, well-being) appears to provide the most promising direction for application. Large organizations often have the luxury of employee assistance programs that provide the necessary science-to-application translation. Implementation of such programs at the individual level provides opportunities for discovering areas of discorrespondence or mismatch, determining whether the mismatch may lead to reduced meaning for the worker, and then developing strategies for reducing the gap either through organizational change or individual self-development. Occasions amenable to P-E fit diagnosis that may prompt an intervention include but certainly are not limited to complaints about lack of challenge, feelings of burnout, dissatisfaction with the reward system, work–family imbalance, and interpersonal difficulties with coworkers or supervisors. One might think of these broadly as adjustment problems. These problems often are related to client perceptions related to actual work experiences.

The role of the counselor or employee assistance program professional is to determine with the employee the situations (E) that may contribute to lack of meaning for the employee, to determine whether the negative feelings have a factual basis, and then to work with the employee to develop an understanding of self and to determine whether the employee or the environment can be changed. If reducing the discorrespondence is not an option, then alternative strategies such as designing a plan to compensate through other activities (e.g., leisure or volunteer) or planning for a job change may be explored. In addition to individual approaches to facilitating work adjustment, organizations can also use P-E fit models to identify adjustment concerns prevalent within the organization and then develop group-level interventions or self-development programs. Modes of training and intervention might also be informed by P-E fit models. For example, individuals with strong social interests and values might respond well to group interactions, whereas those who value autonomy may be more satisfied with individual initiatives.

UNEMPLOYMENT COUNSELING

The effect of job loss is widely acknowledged as having a serious psychological impact that diminishes and calls into question the possibility of meaning through work. Similar to career counseling for vocational decision making, unemployment counseling can use a P-E fit model to help individuals understand their potential for reemployment (Dawis & Lofquist, 1984). Assessing the client's satisfaction and satisfactoriness in previous jobs may be a first step. If both were high, the search might focus on jobs that have similar requirements and rewards. However, if satisfaction was high and satisfactoriness was not, the client might pursue positions with different ability requirements or consider additional training. If satisfactoriness was adequate but satisfaction was not, then the intervention might assess interests and values to determine new options for vocation and/or organization.

RETIREMENT COUNSELING

Retirement adjustment is another area that may be amendable to implementation of P-E fit models. Retirement requires planning for both economic and psychological adjustment or for enhancing meaning. However, most retirement programs focus on factors such as health insurance, retirement distributions, and investment options rather than on strategies for psychological adjustment. Leaving work may mean many losses: loss of social status, loss of identity, and loss of social support, to name a few. Principles of P-E fit can be used to identify lost reinforcers and rewards from the work environment and to develop strategies for identifying replacements (Dawis & Lofquist, 1984) through interactions with family and friends, leisure activities, volunteer activities, and possibly part-time employment. Hobbies that have had meaning for a person in the past may also assume increased importance in retirement. Advanced planning for retirement in the context of P-E fit models allows time to identify environments that correspond to a person's interests and values as well as time to develop new skills if necessary. Additional research is needed within this area of application of P-E fit. For example, one obstacle to implementing this process may be lack of information on the characteristics of nonwork environments. Thus, comprehensive surveys on nonwork and avocational environments are needed to understand the environment requirements. One way to think about this taxonomy is to cluster activities (a) according to saliency of Holland's six types (RIASEC) or (b) according to people, data, or things intersecting with ability levels. Research also is needed to understand how adjustment styles might contribute to correspondence in the event that nonwork environments do not perfectly fit the interests and values of the person.

Future Directions

A line of P-E fit exploration that looks at cultural fit is emerging in international, cross-cultural, and diversity research. One stream of research is exploring the extent to which P-E fit theories, the most enduring of which have been developed with an eye toward American and other Western cultures, apply to diverse populations (e.g., ethnic groups; lesbians and gays; developing countries; European, Asian, Middle Eastern, and African populations). Recent results have suggested that this type of cross-cultural research will contribute to the generalizability and application of P-E fit models to many populations (Iplik, Kilic, & Yalcin, 2011; Lyons, Brenner, & Fassinger, 2005; Lyons & O'Brien, 2006; Phillips, Cheng, Yeh, & Siu, 2010). Another stream of research has focused on the fit between organizational practices and national culture. This line of research has taken into consideration the values, beliefs, and assumptions of national cultures and has hypothesized that environments that are congruent with national cultural or ethnocultural expectations will lead to positive outcomes for employees (e.g., meaningful work) and for the organization (Aycan, Kanungo, & Sinha, 1999; Hutz, Martin, & Beitel, 2007; Newman & Nollen, 1996).

A variety of factors may contribute to smaller than expected relations between predictor congruence and outcomes (e.g., range restriction for both congruence and criterion variables inadequacy of the measurement of the environment, serendipity, inability to control the effect of extraneous variables, the dynamic nature of P-E fit). A frequently suggested hypothesis for the mixed results in congruence–outcome studies is that the relation between congruence and outcomes is a more robust predictor for some people than for others. Some evidence has suggested that job involvement, intrinsic motivation, control in the work setting (Dik & Hansen, 2011), group importance (Vogel & Feldman, 2009), need for cognitive closure (Guan, Deng, Bond, Chen, & Chan, 2010), and levels of core self-evaluation (Park, Monnot, Jacob, & Wagner, 2011) moderate various levels of P-E fit (e.g., person–job, person–vocation, or person–organization fit). However, only the tip of the iceberg has been studied in congruence moderator research, and a plethora of variables wait to be tested for their moderating effect (e.g., personality traits; adjustment styles; demographic variables such as gender, race and age; interest types; situational moderators).

TABLE 2.1

Focus on the Workplace: A Person–Environment (P-E) Fit Perspective

Recommendation	Tested in practice	Derived from theory	Supported by research
Integrate college major and career decision-making counseling. Guide students to explore matches of their interests, values, and abilities with college major and occupational requirements. Hold job placement seminars that translate skills, knowledge, and interests of specific majors into job requirements.[a,b,c,d]	✓	✓	✓
Use job analysis and employee assessment to determine P-E correspondence of interests, values, abilities, knowledge, skills, and attitudes with lateral and promotional job opportunities.[a,b,c,e]	✓	✓	✓
Develop mentoring programs for new employees. Look for protégé–mentor match on personality, interests, values, and commitment to the mentoring process and experience.[a,b,c,f]	✓	✓	✓
Promote volunteer activities using P-E fit models to match volunteer interests, values, abilities, personalities, and motives for volunteering to the volunteer organization's mission, activities, and volunteer opportunities.[a,b,c,g]	Partially tested	✓	Some evidence
Evaluate person–organization congruence on variables such as power distance, uncertainty avoidance, individualism, masculinity, and abstract versus associative thinking. Modify Western management practices to reduce discorrespondence and to increase meaningfulness.[h,i]	Partially tested	✓	Some evidence
Use leadership and management practices (e.g., promote autonomy, encourage participative decision making and policy making, display confidence in employees) designed to increase empowerment and employee perception of P-E fit on work life variables (e.g., workload, control, reward, community, values, fairness).[j,k]	Partially tested	✓	✓

Note. [a]Dawis (2005). [b]Dawis & Lofquist (1984). [c]Holland (1997). [d]Porter & Umbach (2006). [e]Jansen & Kristof-Brown (2006). [f]Allen & Eby (2007). [g]Van Vianen, Nijstad, & Voskuijl (2008). [h]Newman & Nollen (1996). [i]Aycan, Kanungo, & Sinha (1999). [j]Kanter (1993). [k]Laschinger, Wong, & Greco (2006).

Conclusion

The impact of work-related factors on psychological and physical well-being has a long history of empirical evidence. A noticeable trend is for individuals and organizations to share the responsibility to optimize meaning. Interventions may be targeted at changing the environment as well as helping the individual adapt. One challenge is the development of interventions that are based on the available scientific evidence. Actual applications of P-E fit models tend to focus on small, specific components of theories that are amenable to translation of research into practice or policy and practical problem solving.

Table 2.1 provides six examples of the way in which the predictors and criteria of P-E fit models can be used in a variety of settings with the goal of cultivating meaning. These suggestions vary widely in terms of their current application as well as in the level of research reported in the literature that directly supports each application. However, all examples are driven by theory and are amenable to outcome evaluation research.

References

Ahmad, K. Z. (2010). Person–environment fit approach to intolerance of equity and free-riders. *International Business Research, 3*, 35–42.

Allen, T. D., & Eby, L. T. (Eds.). (2007). *Blackwell handbook of mentoring.* Oxford, England: Blackwell. doi:10.1111/b.9781405133739.2007.x

Arthur, W., Jr., Bell, S. T., Villado, A. J., & Doverspike, D. (2006). The use of person–organization fit in employment decision making: An assessment of its criterion-related validity. *Journal of Applied Psychology, 91*, 786–801. doi:10.1037/0021-9010.91.4.786

Assouline, M., & Meir, E. I. (1987). Meta-analysis of the relationship between congruence and well-being measures. *Journal of Vocational Behavior, 31*, 319–332. doi:10.1016/0001-8791(87)90046-7

Aycan, Z., Kanungo, R. N., & Sinha, J. B. P. (1999). Organizational culture and human resource management practices. *Journal of Cross-Cultural Psychology, 30*, 501–526. doi:10.1177/0022022199030004006

Blau, G. J. (1987). Using person–environment fit model to predict job involvement and organizational commitment. *Journal of Vocational Behavior, 30*, 240–257. doi:10.1016/0001-8791(87)90003-0

Cools, E., Van den Broeck, H., & Bouckenooghe, D. (2009). Coping styles and person–environment fit: Investigating the consequences of cognitive (mis)fit. *European Journal of Work and Organizational Psychology, 18*, 167–198.

Darley, J. G. (1938). A preliminary study of relations between attitude, adjustment, and vocational interest tests. *Journal of Educational Psychology, 29*, 467–473. doi:10.1037/h0061063

Dawis, R. V. (2005). The Minnesota theory of work adjustment. In S. D. Brown & R. W. Lent (Eds.), *Career development and counseling* (pp. 3–24). Hoboken, NJ: Wiley.

Dawis, R. V., & Lofquist, L. H. (1984). *A psychological theory of work adjustment.* Minneapolis: University of Minnesota Press.

Dik, B. J., & Hansen, J. C. (2011). Moderation of P-E fit–job satisfaction relations. *Journal of Career Assessment, 19,* 35–50. doi:10.1177/1069072710382613

Dik, B. J., Steger, M. F., Fitch-Martin, A. R., & Onder, C. C. (in press). Cultivating meaningfulness at work. In C. Routledges & J. Hicks (Eds.), *The experience of meaning in life: Classical perspectives, emerging themes, and controversies.* New York, NY: Springer.

Durr, M. R., II, & Tracey, T. J. G. (2009). Relation of person–environment fit to career certainty. *Journal of Vocational Behavior, 75,* 129–138. doi:10.1016/j.jvb.2009.05.003

Edwards, J. R., Cable, D. M., Williamson, I. O., Lambert, L. S., & Shipp, A. J. (2006). The phenomenology of fit: Linking the person and environment to the subjective experience of person–environment fit. *Journal of Applied Psychology, 91,* 802–827. doi:10.1037/0021-9010.91.4.802

Edwards, J. R., Caplan, R. D., & Harrison, E. V. (1998). Person–environment fit theory: Conceptual foundations, empirical evidence, and directions for future research. In C. L. Cooper (Ed.), *Theories of organizational stress* (pp. 28–67). Oxford, England: Oxford University Press.

Eggerth, D. E., & Cunningham, T. R. (2012). Counseling psychology and occupational health psychology. In E. M. Altmaier & J. C. Hansen (Eds.), *The Oxford handbook of counseling psychology* (pp. 752–799). New York, NY: Oxford University Press.

Ehrhart, K. H., & Makransky, G. (2007). Testing interests and personality as predictors of person–vocation and person–job fit. *Journal of Career Assessment, 15,* 206–226. doi:10.1177/1069072706298105

Erdheim, J., Zickar, M. J., & Yankelovich, M. (2007). Remembering Donald G. Paterson: Before the separation between industrial–organizational and vocational psychology. *Journal of Vocational Behavior, 70,* 205–221. doi:10.1016/j.jvb.2006.09.001

Forer, B. R. (1953). Personality factors in occupational choice. *Educational and Psychological Measurement, 13,* 361–366. doi:10.1177/001316445301300301

Fouad, N. A., & Kantamneni, N. (2008). Contextual factors in vocational psychology: Intersections of individual, groups, and societal dimensions. In S. D. Brown & R. W. Lent (Eds.), *Handbook of counseling psychology* (pp. 408–425). Hoboken, NJ: Wiley.

Gottfredson, G. D., & Duffy, R. D. (2008). Using a theory of vocational personalities and work environments to explore subjective well-being. *Journal of Career Assessment, 16,* 44–59. doi:10.1177/1069072707309609

Gottfredson, G. D., & Holland, J. L. (1989). *Dictionary of Holland occupational codes* (2nd ed.). Odessa, FL: Psychological Assessment Resources.

Guan, Y., Deng, H., Bond, M. H., Chen, S. X., & Chan, C. C. (2010). Person–job fit and work-related attitudes among Chinese employees: Need for cognitive closure as moderator. *Basic and Applied Social Psychology, 32,* 250–260. doi:10.1080/01973533.2010.495664

Guilford, J. P., Christensen, P. R., Bond, N. A., Jr., & Sutton, M. A. (1954). A factor analysis study of human interests [Special issue]. *Psychological Monographs, 68*(4).

Hansen, J. C. (1992). *User's guide for the Strong Interest Inventory.* Stanford, CA: Stanford University Press.

Hansen, J. C. (in press). Personality and vocational behavior. In R. Tett & N. Christensen (Eds.), *Handbook of personality at work.* New York, NY: Routledge.

Hansen, J. C., & Dik, B. (2005). Evidence of 12-year predictive and concurrent validity for SII occupational scale scores. *Journal of Vocational Behavior, 67,* 365–378. doi:10.1016/j.jvb.2004.08.001

Hansen, J. C., & Lee, W. V. (2007). Evidence of concurrent validity of SII scores for Asian American college students. *Journal of Career Assessment, 15,* 44–54. doi:10.1177/1069072706294514

Hansen, J. C., & Tan, R. N. (1992). Concurrent validity of the 1985 Strong Interest Inventory for college major selection. *Measurement and Evaluation in Counseling and Development, 25,* 53–57.

Harms, P. D., Roberts, B. W., & Winter, D. (2006). Becoming the Harvard man: Person–environment fit, personality development, and academic success. *Personality and Social Psychology Bulletin, 32,* 851–865. doi:10.1177/0146167206287720

Hoeglund, T. J., & Hansen, J. C. (1999). Holland-style measures of congruence: Are complex indices more effective predictors of satisfaction? *Journal of Vocational Behavior, 54,* 471–482. doi:10.1006/jvbe.1998.1675

Holland, J. L. (1953). *The Vocational Preference Inventory.* Odessa, FL: Psychological Assessment Resources.

Holland, J. L. (1959). A theory of vocational choice. *Journal of Counseling Psychology, 6,* 35–45. doi:10.1037/h0040767

Holland, J. L. (1970). *The Self-Directed Search.* Odessa, FL: Psychological Assessment Resources.

Holland, J. L. (1997). *Making vocational choice: A theory of vocational personalities and work environments* (3rd ed.). Odessa, FL: Psychological Assessment Resources.

Hutz, A., Martin, W. E., Jr., & Beitel, M. (2007). Ethnocultural person–environment fit and college adjustment: Some implications for college counselors. *Journal of College Counseling, 10,* 130–141. doi:10.1002/j.2161-1882.2007.tb00013.x

Iplik, F. N., Kilic, K. C., & Yalcin, A. (2011). The simultaneous effects of person–organization and person–job fit on Turkish hotel managers.

International Journal of Contemporary Hospitality Management, 23, 644–661. doi:10.1108/09596111111143386

Jansen, K. J., & Kristof-Brown, A. (2006). Toward a multidimensional theory of person–environment fit. *Journal of Managerial Issues, 18,* 193–212.

Kanter, R. M. (1993). *Men and women of the corporation.* New York, NY: Basic Books.

Kreiner, G. E. (2006). Consequences of work–home segmentation or integration: A person–environment fit perspective. *Journal of Organizational Behavior, 27,* 485–507. doi:10.1002/job.386

Kristof-Brown, A. L., & Guay, R. P. (2011). Person–environment fit. In S. Zedeck (Ed.), *APA handbook of industrial and organizational psychology* (Vol. 3, pp. 3–50). Washington, DC: American Psychological Association.

Kristof-Brown, A., Zimmerman, R. D., & Johnson, E. C. (2005). Consequences of individual's fit at work: A meta-analysis of person–job, person–organization, person–group, and person–supervisor fit. *Personnel Psychology, 58,* 281–342. doi:10.1111/j.1744-6570.2005.00672.x

Laschinger, H. K., Wong, C. A., & Greco, P. (2006). The impact of staff nurse empowerment on person–job fit and work engagement/burnout. *Nursing Administration Quarterly, 30,* 358–367.

Little, P. S., & Miller, S. K. (2007). Hiring the best teachers? Rural values and person–organization fit theory. *Journal of School Leadership, 17,* 118–158.

Livingstone, L. P., Nelson, D. L., & Barr, S. H. (1997). Person–environment fit and creativity: An examination of supply-value and demand-ability versions of fit. *Journal of Management, 23,* 119–146.

Lubinski, D., & Benbow, C. P. (2000). States of excellence. *American Psychologist, 55,* 137–150. doi:10.1037/0003-066X.55.1.137

Lyons, H. Z., Brenner, B. R., & Fassinger, R. E. (2005). A multicultural test of the theory of work adjustment: Investigating the role of heterosexism and fit preparations in the job satisfaction of lesbian, gay, and bisexual employees. *Journal of Counseling Psychology, 52,* 537–548. doi:10.1037/0022-0167.52.4.537

Lyons, H. Z., & O'Brien, K. M. (2006). The role of person–environment fit in the job satisfaction and tenure intentions of African American employees. *Journal of Counseling Psychology, 53,* 387–396. doi:10.1037/ 0022-0167.53.4.387

Melamed, S., Meir, E., & Samson, A. (1995). The benefits of personality–leisure congruence: Evidence and implications. *Journal of Leisure Research, 27,* 25–40.

Newman, K. L., & Nollen, S. D. (1996). Culture and congruence: The fit between management practices and national culture. *Journal of International Business Studies, 27,* 753–779. doi:10.1057/palgrave. jibs.8490152

Park, H. I., Monnot, M. J., Jacob, A. C., & Wagner, S. H. (2011). Moderators of the relationship between person–job fit and subjective well-being among Asian employees. *International Journal of Stress Management, 18,* 67–87. doi:10.1037/a0021854

Parsons, F. (1909). *Choosing a vocation.* Boston, MA: Houghton Mifflin.

Phillips, D. R., Cheng, K. H. C., Yeh, A. G. O., & Siu, O.-L. (2010). Person–environment (P–E) fit models and psychological well-being among older persons in Hong Kong. *Environment and Behavior, 42,* 221–242. doi:10.1177/0013916509333426

Piasentin, K. A., & Chapman, D. S. (2006). Subjective person–organization fit: Bridging the gap between conceptualization and measurement. *Journal of Vocational Behavior, 69,* 202–221. doi:10.1016/j.jvb.2006.05.001

Porter, S. R., & Umbach, P. D. (2006). College major choice: An analysis of P–E fit. *Research in Higher Education, 47,* 429–449. doi:10.1007/s11162-005-9002-3

Roe, A. (1956). *The psychology of occupations.* New York, NY: Wiley. doi:10.1037/13192-000

Smart, J. C., & Feldman, K. A. (1998). "Accentuation effects" of dissimilar academic departments: An application and exploration of Holland's theory. *Research in Higher Education, 39,* 385–418. doi:10.1023/A:1018737303291

Spokane, A. R. (1996). Holland's theory. In D. Brown & L. Brooks (Eds.), *Career choice and development* (3rd ed., pp. 33–74). San Francisco, CA: Jossey-Bass.

Spokane, A. R., & Cruza-Guet, M. C. (2005). Holland's theory of vocational personalities in work environments. In S. D. Brown & R. W. Lent (Eds.), *Career development and counseling: Putting theory and research to work* (pp. 24–41). Hoboken, NJ: Wiley.

Steger, M. F., & Dik, B. J. (2010). Work as meaning: Individual and organizational benefits of engaging in meaningful work. In P. A. Linley, S. Harrington, & N. Page (Eds.), *Handbook of positive psychology and work* (pp. 131–142). Oxford, England: Oxford University Press.

Steijn, B. (2008). Person-environment fit and public service motivation. *International Public Management Journal, 11,* 13–27. doi:10.1080/10967490801887863

Strong, E. K., Jr. (1943). *Vocational interests of men and women.* Stanford, CA: Stanford University Press.

Tak, J. (2011). Relationships between various person–environment fit types and employee withdrawal behavior: A longitudinal study. *Journal of Vocational Behavior, 78,* 315–320. doi:10.1016/j.jvb.2010.11.006

Ton, M., & Hansen, J. C. (2001). Using a person-environment fit framework to predict satisfaction and motivation in work and marital roles. *Journal of Career Assessment, 9,* 315–331. doi:10.1177/106907270100900401

Tracey, T. J. G., & Hopkins, N. (2001). Correspondence of interests and abilities with occupational choice. *Journal of Counseling Psychology, 48,* 178–189. doi:10.1037/0022-0167.48.2.178

Tyler, L. E. (1951). The relationships of interests to abilities and reputation among first grade children. *Educational and Psychological Measurement, 11,* 255–264. doi:10.1177/001316445101100209

Tziner, A., & Meir, E. I. (1997). Work adjustment: Extension of a theoretical framework. In C. L. Cooper & I. T. Robertson (Eds.), *International review of industrial and organizational psychology* (Vol. 12, pp. 96–114). Hoboken, NJ: Wiley.

Van Vianen, A. E. M., Nijstad, B. A., & Voskuijl, O. F. (2008). A person–environment fit approach to volunteerism: Volunteer personality fit and culture fit as predictors of effective outcomes. *Basic and Applied Social Psychology, 30,* 153–166. doi:10.1080/01973530802209194

Vogel, R. M., & Feldman, D. C. (2009). Integrating the levels of person–organizational fit: The roles of vocational fit and group fit. *Journal of Vocational Behavior, 75,* 68–81.

Wilk, S. L., & Sackett, P. R. (1996). Longitudinal analysis of ability–job complexity fit and job change. *Personnel Psychology, 49,* 937–967.

Douglas T. Hall, Elana Feldman, and Najung Kim

Meaningful Work and the Protean Career

3

I n this chapter, we explore the relationship between the protean career orientation (PCO) and meaningful work. Branching out from the idea that the meaning of work is an individual's interpretation of what work means to her or him personally (Wrzesniewski, Dutton, & Debebe, 2003), we consider meaningful work to occur when individuals find their work to be personally purposeful and significant (Pratt & Ashforth, 2003) and/or valuable and worthwhile (Hackman & Oldham, 1976; Wrzesniewski & Dutton, 2001).

Specifically, we aim to understand how people who are *protean*—that is, self-directed and self-managed (Hall, 2002, 2004a; Hall & Associates, 1996)—in their career orientations seek, maintain, create, and change the meaningfulness of their work, both at a given, single point in time and throughout their careers.[1] We argue that because people with a strong PCO, by definition, are more self-directed and driven by personal values than are people with a low protean orientation

---

[1]In this discussion, we use the terms protean individual and individual *with a strong PCO* interchangeably.

http://dx.doi.org/10.1037/14183-004
Purpose and Meaning in the Workplace, B. J. Dik, Z. S. Byrne, and M. F. Steger (Editors)

(Briscoe & Hall, 2006), they are more likely to change organizations, jobs, or occupations to achieve meaning in work (Hall, 1976, 2002). In the sections that follow, we revisit these core protean career concepts within the context of meaningful work. First, we discuss how the PCO may act as a moderator between personal choices and the outcome of meaningful work. Second, we examine how the protean metacompetencies may influence a person's achievement of meaningful work. Third, we adopt a life-span perspective to consider how the protean orientation affects meaningfulness over a lifelong career. Finally, we address workplace applications and key boundary conditions.

Meaningfulness of Work and Sources of Meaning in Work

It is important to distinguish between the sources of work meaning and the degree of meaningfulness in work that a person experiences. The meaning-of-work literature identifies two major sources from which meaning can be derived: what I do and with whom I do it. *What I do* suggests the individual finds meaning related to her or his job and task. *With whom I do it* indicates that an individual finds meaning through interaction or connections with coworkers, leaders, family, social groups, organizations, and/or other communities (Pratt & Ashforth, 2003).

Although there are certainly interindividual differences, we argue, following the thinking of Baumeister and colleagues (Baumeister, 1991; Baumeister & Vohs, 2002; Baumeister & Wilson, 1996) that people seek to find meaningfulness in life on the basis of four basic needs; indeed, the degree of meaningfulness that one experiences may depend on these four needs. The four needs are (a) the need for *purpose,* based on objective goals and subjective fulfillment; (b) the need for *efficacy,* which allows individuals to make a difference in society and to have a sense of control by changing the external environment (primary control) and/or changing their self and subjective perceptions (secondary or interpretive control); (c) the need for *justification through values* that individuals hold on to; and (d) the need for *self-worth,* based on one's position within the firm social hierarchy, as gained by individual achievement or group membership. When the needs for purpose and efficacy are met, individuals are likely to find their work meaningful because of its purposefulness and significance (Pratt & Ashforth, 2003). Similarly, work may be perceived as "generally meaningful, valuable, and worthwhile" (Hackman & Oldham, 1976, p. 256) when individuals' needs for self-worth and value are both met. The needs for purpose and efficacy touch on an individual's proactive efforts to think of what she or he can do to contribute to the society on the basis of both objective and subjective experiences of work, whereas the needs for value or justification and self-worth deal with an individual's defensive efforts to be appreciated by the society.

Toward a More Holistic View of the Individual

Although Baumeister (2005) wrote about meaningfulness in life, we argue that the same process he described also applies to perceived meaningfulness in work. Work is a major determinant of a person's overall identity, especially in Western cultures (Hall, 2002), so we would expect that the degree of meaningfulness that a person achieves in life would be highly or at least somewhat correlated with that which one experiences in work. By embracing this perspective, we take a holistic view of the individual, in which it is not possible to view a person's nonwork life as separate from work. In fact, the more a person grows and develops, the more her or his identity grows, the more the sense of identity becomes at once both more integrated with yet distinct from the specific life roles the person occupies (Erikson, 1963; Kegan, 1982).

One way to think about the relationship between work and life is to think of work as a piece or a fractal of life. A *fractal* is a "shape for which any suitably chosen part is similar in shape to a given larger or smaller part when magnified or reduced to the same size" ("Fractal," 2012; see also Mandelbrot, 1982). This characteristic property of the part resembling the whole is referred to as *self-similarity*. When one looks at a fractal, one sees all of the same elements that make up the whole entity. In a parallel way, one role from a person's life has certain elements in common with all other roles in that person's life—and, thus, with the person's entire identity.

Empirical data that support the connection between the meaning of work and the overall meaning of life can be found in the "5C" global study of careers (Chudzikowski et al., 2009; Demel, Shen, Las Heras, Hall, & Unite, 2010). In this broad international study spanning 11 countries, an extremely thorough qualitative analysis process identified three universal factors that represent career success: achievement, job satisfaction, and the work itself. These factors can be linked to Baumeister's elements of meaning, as follows: Achievement contributes to the need for purpose (reflecting goal attainment and subjective fulfillment) and to self-worth (if one's achievements lead to a certain position in a social hierarchy). In addition, job satisfaction contributes to the need for purpose based on attainment of job-related goals; there may also be justification through personal values if the person values job rewards. Finally, work itself, when properly designed to have significance and social impact, may permit the person to demonstrate efficacy and make a difference in the world while providing for self-worth if the work is associated with a respected position within a social hierarchy.

Before we elaborate how the PCO relates to the aforementioned sources of meaning of work and Baumeister's four needs that may drive meaningfulness in work, in the following section, we briefly discuss key concepts from the protean career literature (Baumeister, 1991; Baumeister & Vohs, 2002; Baumeister & Wilson, 1996).

The Protean Career Orientation: A Review of Key Concepts

The PCO is distinct from more traditional, organization-centered career orientations in several ways. Whereas in a traditional career, the organization directs the employee's career, in the protean career, the individual manages her or his own path (Hall, 2002, 2004a; Hall & Associates, 1996). Second, traditional career success is measured by external, objective criteria (e.g., position, income), but protean career success is gauged by more internal, subjective criteria (e.g., psychological success). (See Hall, 1976, for a detailed description of the difference between protean and traditional careers.)

The PCO is a mind-set rather than a set of particular behaviors (Briscoe & Hall, 2006). Specifically, it is "an attitude toward the career that reflects freedom, self-direction, and making choices based on one's personal values" (Briscoe & Hall, 2006, p. 6). Given this definition, there are two career management qualities that are at the heart of the PCO: self-direction and values-driven behavior. *Self-direction* implies autonomy and self-determination in career planning, and *values-driven behavior* means reliance on personal values to evaluate choices and career success (Briscoe & Hall, 2003). To be deemed protean, a person must be both self-directed and values driven (Briscoe & Hall, 2003); however, people can possess these qualities at higher or lower levels (Briscoe & Hall, 2006), thus creating a protean orientation continuum, with weakly protean individuals at one end of the spectrum and strongly protean individuals at the other end.

Two career metacompetencies are central to the PCO: *self-awareness*, which is a clear sense of one's personal identity, and *adaptability*, which is the capacity to change (Briscoe & Hall, 2003; Hall, 2002, 2004a; Hall & Associates, 1996; Harrington & Hall, 2007). These metacompetencies, which are key outcomes of the PCO, are the result of the values-driven and self-directed nature of individuals with a PCO (Briscoe &

Hall, 2003). Possessing one metacompetency without the other can be highly problematic. For instance, high adaptability without high self-awareness can lead to reactive behavior, wherein a person follows a path other than her or his own self-selected course (Hall, 2004a). Similarly, high self-awareness without adaptability would make it difficult for a person to alter her or his career course on the basis of shifting life priorities and/or identity changes.

Theoretically, the link between a PCO and meaningful work seems clear. Yet, to our knowledge, perhaps due to the obviousness of this link, little empirical work specifically explores this link. Therefore, we address this lack of research further when we discuss directions for additional research later in the chapter.

Moderating Effects of Protean Career Orientation on the Search for Meaningful Work

How might the protean orientation affect people's likelihood of finding meaning in their work? One straightforward argument is that the higher a person's PCO (i.e., the more self-directed and the more values-driven the person is), the more likely the person is to make choices that would lead to meaningful work. The reasoning for this argument is that the more aware people are of their values, the more they make choices that are aligned with those values.

Value is a drive that creates meaning in one's life (Baumeister, 1991), and knowing one's values increases the chance of clarifying what meaningful work actually means for a particular person. Some studies on the relationship between person–job fit and meaningful work indirectly support the positive effect of a protean career on one's meaningful work (Scroggins, 2008). This support implies a moderated relationship between personal choices and the outcome of meaningful work, as shown in Figure 3.1. The process is initiated by people's appraisal of how much meaning and/or sense of purpose is in their work. Then, if a person is self-directed and values-driven, one would expect to see the person adapt in some way that would make the work more meaningful, through processes such as job crafting or job change. This adaptation might also change the person's identity, because she or he would perceive more proactivity and competence in influencing the work environment.

What would the process look like if the person was low in the PCO? With low self-direction, the person would not be likely to make adaptations. In addition, if the person was not values-driven, she or he would not have a "values compass" that would help assess the degree

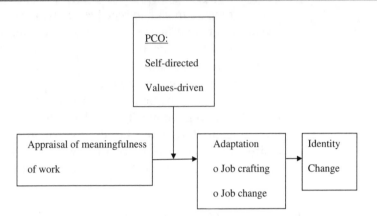

The moderating effects of the protean career orientation (PCO). A strong PCO affects a person's career adaptation. Those who are high in self-direction and values drive will be more likely to see opportunities to craft their job and make other changes in their assignment to fit with their personal values. Those with low PCOs will be less likely to see opportunities to make the work fit with their passions. Those who do make work adaptations to improve fit with personal passions could come to see themselves in a new, more confident way.

of person–values fit in the job, and she or he would also be deprived of inner signals that indicate the job may lack meaning. Either way, the person would not be motivated to make adaptations, and there would be no change.

There is, however, another interesting possibility for what might happen if the person had an unusually high protean orientation: These individuals might, in fact, be less likely to find meaning in work. Why? Strongly protean individuals tend to have values that are stronger and clearer than those of the average person, and they may have higher expectations for how work should align with personal values. Because of these high expectations, highly protean individuals might see every alternative career move that they might make as being deficient in some way; this could lead to dissatisfaction with every other option. This dissatisfaction may lead them to reject other courses of action and ultimately lead to nonadaptation or paralysis. (To our knowledge, there has been no research on this interesting possibility.)

Another variant of this less expected situation would be a person who was extremely values driven and self-directed. Such a person might enter into an overreactive, out-of-control cycle. With a "hyper-PCO," the person would tend to be extremely sensitive to internal signals about lack of meaning in work and would have a hair-trigger response tendency; thus, she or he would be "hyper-willing" to make changes. Therefore, at the first sign of poor fit on meaning, the person would move to recraft the job or to switch jobs. As a consequence, if the adaptation resulted in anything short of a perfect fit, it would lead to another change, and the result would be hyperadaptation. For instance, an empirical study on highly educated research and development professionals (Chang, Choi, & Kim, 2008) found that those with high intrinsic work values are more likely to leave the job. The notion of intrinsic work values in this study included the desire for learning, growth, autonomy, and achievement of something valuable; this notion is similar to the self-directed and values-driven nature of PCO. Thus, the person would be in a constant positive feedback loop, which would manifest itself as highly unstable job change behavior.

Moderating Effects of Career Metacompetencies in the Search for Meaning

As described earlier, the protean orientation is associated with two meta-competencies: self-awareness and adaptability (Briscoe & Hall, 2003; Hall, 2004a). We suggest that, similar to the functioning of the PCO itself, these two metacompetencies influence whether an individual finds meaningful work. Specifically, we posit that an individual who possesses high levels of both self-awareness and adaptability is more likely to achieve meaningfulness in work than would an individual who does not have high levels of both metacompetencies.

The coexistence of the two metacompetencies is critical because finding meaningful work requires paying attention to both internal (personal) and external (environmental and contextual) factors (Briscoe & Hall, 2003). Although self-awareness facilitates attention to the internal, subjective reality by helping an individual discern whether her or his work is meaningful—and if it lacks meaning, to identify what work characteristics are more likely to yield meaningfulness—adaptability facilitates attention to external realities, thus allowing the individual to make appropriate changes (e.g., job crafting, job switching) to gain greater meaning.

The importance of self-awareness and adaptability can also be considered within the context of Baumeister's four needs for meaning (purpose, values, efficacy, and self-worth; Baumeister, 1991). An individual who is self-aware and adaptable is more likely to derive sufficient meaning from her or his work because she or he may be able to more successfully reconsider and potentially make changes in her or his life until all four needs for meaning are fulfilled (Baumeister, 1991). In other words, someone who possesses high levels of both metacompetencies should be well equipped to consider her or his current work activities in light of future goals and to behave in ways that are consistent with her or his values. This allows the person to feel that the work is valid, to assess whether the work is making a difference, and to have a clear sense of the areas of work in which she or he may excel relative to others.

Figure 3.2 illustrates how an individual's level of the two protean metacompetencies can increase or decrease an individual's likelihood of achieving meaningful work. If a person possesses only low levels of each metacompetency, she or he is likely to remain immobile, with little chance of moving toward meaningful work (unless she or he stumbles on it by chance). Because of the low self-awareness, she or he cannot detect whether the work is meaningful and may be unsure about what different work characteristics might yield greater meaningfulness. Furthermore, because of the low adaptability, an immobile individual is unlikely to make changes to the situation, even if she or he is dissatisfied with the work.

Individuals who are low in self-awareness but high in adaptability will face similar obstacles to identifying whether the work is meaningful and/or what work characteristics might yield greater meaningfulness; yet, because of their high adaptability, they will likely make changes

FIGURE 3.2

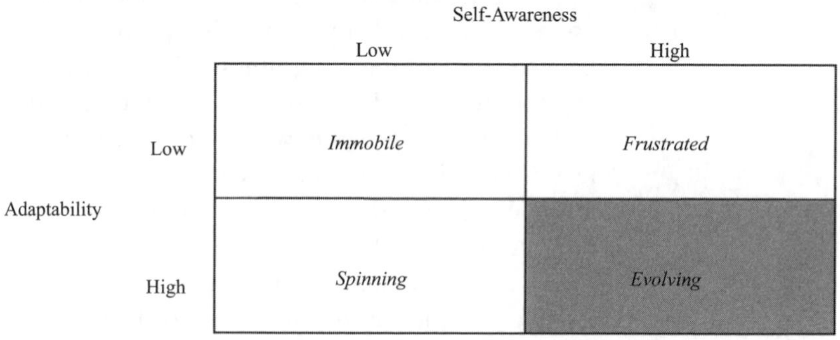

Influence of metacompetencies on achievement of meaningful work ("grid"). The chart depicts how varying levels of the two protean metacompetencies (self-awareness and adaptability) can increase or decrease an individual's likelihood of achieving meaningful work.

when generally dissatisfied with the work situation. However, these changes are unlikely to be aligned with their identity (because they are not clear on their identity) and therefore will probably not make the work more meaningful. Such individuals may be characterized as spinning, because they may make frequent, unhelpful changes, never gaining traction in the direction that is most important to them.

In contrast, an individual who is high in self-awareness but low in adaptability may be frustrated. Despite recognition that the work is not meaningful and despite knowing what kind of work might yield greater meaning, these individuals are unlikely to engage in behavior that would add greater meaning to the work; either they will not make any changes to (or within) the job or the changes may be unaligned with their sense of identity.

Finally, an individual who is high in both self-awareness and adapt-ability may be seen as evolving. Not only can such individuals discern whether their current work is meaningful but also, if it is not, they likely will have a clear sense of what work characteristics might yield greater meaningfulness. Furthermore, if they confront a work situation low in (or devoid of) meaning, they are likely to make changes that— because the changes are aligned with their sense of identity—should bring them closer to achieving meaningful work.

Meaning in Career and Identity Over the Life Span

An increasing number of people hold multiple sequential jobs through-out their careers (Gabriel, 2003), and individuals go through a series of shorter learning cycles over the course of their work life (Harrington & Hall, 2007). Depending on one's career orientation, the degree of meaningfulness that one finds in work may differ over time. The effect of developmental stages on the importance of meaningful work in one's overall life (Baumeister, 1991) may be applicable to people with all career orientations, but the degree of meaningfulness one needs throughout one's career and the way one experiences meaningfulness in work may depend on one's level of PCO.

Individuals with a strong PCO possess high self-awareness, so changes in their careers are more likely to trigger a meaning-making process for them than might be the case for less protean individuals. This difference between protean-oriented people and those without this orientation may not be significant when the change is positive. When the career change is positive, one may rely on increased self-worth and self-efficacy—two of the four needs of meaning (Baumeister, 1991)—to find meaningfulness in work. However, when the change is negative (e.g., traumatic experiences), individuals with a PCO are more likely to foster meaningfulness in work that is drawn from their purpose and value in work (the other two needs of meaning). The meaning that they find in their work can be a buffer against frustrations and job stress but, at the same time, can act as a source of an integral view of their lives (Baumeister & Vohs, 2002).

One of the protean metacompetencies—self-awareness—increases the chance of being persistent in finding meaning in work and hence allows an individual to be more resilient and adaptable when faced with changes. Any career change, whether it is negative or positive, is disruptive (Farjoun, 2010), and the degree of meaningfulness one finds in work may be stronger for people with a protean orientation. Protean people not only have high self-awareness to begin with but thanks to their self-reflective natures, are also more likely to develop self-awareness as they progress in their careers.

Therefore, we suggest that the meaningfulness one finds in work over time, throughout a series of career cycles, is higher for those with a PCO than for those without this orientation (see Figure 3.3). Furthermore, as people switch jobs, they are more likely to experience a high degree of meaningfulness in work if they go through a constant process of self-reflection with a PCO. Hence, each career change is a step of a stairway that leads to more purposeful and more significant meaning in work. However, if an individual lacks self-awareness, the meaningfulness of work is likely to be highly contingent on the objective success the person experiences in each job, potentially causing the overall perceived meaningfulness of work to fluctuate over the course of a person's work life.

Boundary Conditions

In the following sections, we address two potential boundary conditions for our arguments linking the protean career and meaningful work. Specifically, we discuss the role of the economic and social–political context and the nature of one's personal values.

WHAT IS THE ROLE OF THE ECONOMIC AND SOCIAL–POLITICAL CONTEXT?

Do people need to have a lot of financial and educational resources to be protean and to experience meaningful work? Not necessarily. Individuals who are less well-endowed with such resources might be forced to develop greater self-direction and personal agency to over-

FIGURE 3.3

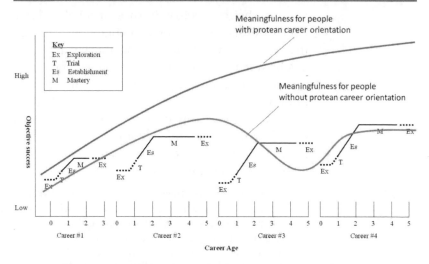

Changes in meaning as a function of protean career orientation (PCO) over the life span. This graph suggests the possible longitudinal paths of the degree of meaningfulness for people with a PCO and those without a PCO. The black line indicates the degree of objective success experienced by people as they change to different careers over time. Although the change in objective success is the same, people are expected to experience varying degrees of meaningfulness. The top line depicts the approximate change in the degree of meaningfulness for people with a PCO over the course of their careers. The line below depicts the possible change in the degree of meaningfulness for people without a PCO. From *The Career Is Dead—Long Live the Career: A Relational Approach to Careers* (p. 34), by D. T. Hall and Associates, 1996, San Francisco, CA: Jossey-Bass. Copyright 1996 by Jossey-Bass. Adapted with permission.

come their disadvantaged situations. In fact, we sometimes see the obverse in the experiences of people from highly privileged backgrounds who never develop the necessary drive and passion to launch satisfying careers. For example, one recent study has found that students from affluent backgrounds were less likely to take risks as adults and live their lives fully, whereas students from poorer backgrounds were more likely to do so (Griskevicius, Delton, Robertson, & Tybur, 2011).

Perhaps a more likely boundary condition would be the extent to which the economic and social context allows for and rewards individual initiative. Protean qualities such as self-direction and being values driven do not do a person much good if the environment does not have room for personal choice. That is, if the societal or political context does not permit freedom of action or if economic conditions are so extremely limited that there are no rewards for such agentic behavior, then there is likely no link between protean behaviors and meaning-related outcomes.

However, even distressed economic conditions can produce counter-intuitive support for finding one's calling. Hall and Chandler (2005) discussed a study of unemployed workers in Australia that showed that the job search requirements of the unemployment insurance system forced people to explore many different kinds of work. As a result, some of them discovered work activities that felt like a calling to them:

> In fact, several of these people have reported that it was not until their resources ran out, when they "reached bottom," that they were able to discern what they described as their true calling. In a discussion with a group of unemployed professionals there was consensus that having resources can in some cases be a barrier to discovering a calling, as that removes a source of motivation to self-explore and try out different kinds of work. (Hall & Chandler, 2005, p. 167)

DOES THE NATURE OF THE VALUES MATTER?

Yes! Although it is important to find one's own values in work to experience a high degree of meaningfulness in work, one must remember the danger of having a personal value that is misaligned with societal or moral values. For instance, a chief financial officer whose value is extrinsic monetary gain may have found her or his calling for earning money, but her or his financial success may hurt other people in society by destabilizing the economy. There are many historical examples of how self-oriented beliefs were detrimental to the larger society (e.g., Bernie Madoff), and these underline the importance of reflecting on how one's personal values and subjective definition of success may contribute to or detract from the common good.

Implications for Organizations and Managers

Protean individuals can be easy to please if the organization allows them to find their own meaning in and at work. However, they can be difficult to satisfy if they find no meaning in their work and/or find few personal connections between their work and their own identity.

Therefore, organizations can benefit from considering and developing multiple ways to provide resources to facilitate the development of customized "meaningfulnesses" by the various individuals they employ. As noted earlier, even in economically distressed situations, individuals are capable of finding meaning through constant self-reflection. When organizations help individuals to develop their self-reflection skills and self-awareness, people may become better at gaining clarity on and therefore pursuing their path with a heart (Shepard, 1984), thereby finding more meaning in work. Examples of what steps organizations might take include providing workshops that provide self-assessment exercises, coaching through mentoring and developmental networks, and implementing developmental career planning conversations with supervisors (who would receive the appropriate skills training).

Although it may be true that some jobs offer more room for individual discretion due to the nature of the work, it is in an organization's best interest to hire and retain employees who have a strong PCO. Strongly protean individuals are valuable assets because of their high levels of self-awareness and adaptability, which help them grow and learn as required by changes in their role, the organization, and/ or the external market. For instance, it has been suggested that having more adaptable managers results in a more flexible organization (Karaevli & Hall, 2006). Also, individuals with a strong PCO have high employability and are thus more readily redeployed to meet changing organizational requirements as business conditions change (McArdle, Waters, Briscoe, & Hall, 2007).

However, an organization cannot realistically expect to fill all of its positions—even its most critical ones—with individuals who are at high levels of both protean metacompetencies, although it is possible to help people develop higher levels of self-awareness and adaptability, as we discuss shortly.[2] One strategy might be to consider how people who possess lower levels of self-awareness and/or adaptability could be good contributors to the organization's effectiveness while they pursue their own satisfaction at the same time. For instance, returning to Figure 3.2, the positive side of the immobile employee—someone who is low on both metacompetencies—is that she or he could be highly committed to a certain area of work. For example, she or he might be a high-performing professional specialist. The organization's career management approach for such a person might be to provide sufficient technical and professional training to keep her or him at the forefront of her or his field. If continuously learning and developing, this individual will most likely also be stimulated and engaged.

---

[2]In fact, many organizations, such as the U.S. Army, focus on developing the metacompetencies as an important part of their leadership development processes.

People who are *spinners*—individuals who are high on adaptability but low on self-awareness—could occasionally be given special assignments to help build new entrepreneurial projects or ventures within the firm. Or they might be assigned to temporary projects outside the firm (e.g., working with partner organizations on emerging technologies and markets). These would be ways of tapping their adaptive capacities.

For those in the frustrated group (who are low on adaptability but high on self-awareness), if the cause of the dissatisfaction is an inability to mobilize and change, the organization could intervene and reassign them. This would best be done by a sensitive supervisor who knows the person's interests and values and who puts some effort into identifying job openings that would let the person express these interests and values. In this way, the frustration may be reduced. And perhaps as a result of the externally imposed job move, these employees might learn that job shifts are less difficult and more rewarding than they had expected; thus, they might be more willing to self-initiate a move in the future (i.e., they might learn to be more adaptable).

Another approach would be for organizations and managers to help those employees who are not evolvers (i.e., not strongly protean) become more self-aware and adaptable. Not only should encouraging development of the metacompetencies benefit the organization (e.g., by increasing its flexibility; Karaevli & Hall, 2006) but it would also likely help employees who begin with lower levels of self-awareness and adaptability achieve greater meaning in their work and increase their employability (Fugate, Kinicki, & Ashforth, 2004; McArdle et al., 2007).

TIPS FOR EMPLOYERS: INCREASING ADAPTABILITY AND SELF-AWARENESS

If an employer does opt to follow this strategy of helping employees build and develop their metacompetencies, what might be some ways to accomplish this? In the following tips for creative managers (summarized in Table 3.1), we start with some ideas for increasing adaptability and then consider strategies for growing self-awareness.[3]

- To increase adaptability, follow the "Mae West" principle. Mae West was a sex symbol in the early days of the U.S. film industry. One of her classic lines was, "When choosing between two evils, I always like to try the one I've never tried before." Assign employees not to the same types of jobs that they have held before but to jobs in new areas, jobs that stretch and push them in new directions. People learn adaptability through novel experiences.

---

[3]These suggestions are adapted from Hall (2004b).

- To increase adaptability, provide wings and roots. From attachment theory (Bowlby, 1969), we know that people need two conditions for psychological growth: psychological safety (roots), so that the risks and fears of failure are not too great, and freedom and encouragement or challenge (wings) to aspire higher to new goals and achievements (Kahn, 1996).
- To increase self-awareness, use self-assessment tools and processes. A variety of exercises and processes are available to help people engage in self-reflection and deepen their understanding of the self. (A chapter on tips for reflection is found in Hall, 2002. See also Harrington & Hall, 2007.)
- Consciously use relational methods and developmental networks. It is becoming increasingly clear that career development is facilitated through high-quality relationships (Hall & Associates, 1996; Higgins & Kram, 2001; Ragins & Kram, 2007). It appears that for career development, informal, emergent relational processes such as mentoring and peer coaching work better than formal programs do. To increase the likelihood of good helping relationships arising naturally, we recommend a two-pronged approach: (a) create conditions for high-quality relationships to occur naturally, such as networking events, long breaks with refreshments at conferences and work meetings, formal gatherings, and "on-boarding" events to welcome newcomers, and (b) identify and reward good developmental relationships when they happen naturally. Reward supervisors for subordinate development. Create award programs to provide recognition for leaders who are great developers of leaders.
- Use 360-degree feedback processes. Feedback from sources above and below and from peers, family, and those external to the organization can be powerful and highly motivational. This feedback method is usually most effective when combined with good coaching (see the point on relational methods discussed earlier).
- Use formal ceremonies to mark identity passages. When a person moves from one status to another (e.g., promotion, major cross-boundary transfer, entry, exit), create a special event and invite many people to celebrate the change. Ask coworkers, clients, former managers, friends, and family members to share the experiences and strengths of the person and invite members of the setting to which the person is moving to describe what the person's new role will be and what she or he is expected to contribute there.
- Create organizational holding environments to facilitate greater self-awareness. From Kegan (1982), we know that it is important to create sources of support and safe places for learning where a person can experiment with new behaviors without feeling threatened or overly evaluated. Examples of such holding environments are support groups of various kinds, recovery groups (e.g.,

Alcoholics Anonymous), men's groups, women's groups, affinity groups (based on social identity), in-work organizations, job search groups, career change groups, and "alumni" groups of former employees. Such groups create a container where the members can feel safe and confront difficult, growth-inducing situations away from everyday work stressors. Here, they may focus on growth and development of the self, rather than on performance.

These steps could be taken either separately or in conjunction with one another. As big changes often grow from small initial steps (Ibarra, 2003), we hypothesize that trying some of these actions could potentially create an ongoing change process that could result in a markedly stronger developmental culture in the organization (Hall & Mirvis, 1996).

IMPLICATIONS FOR ENCORE CAREERS

An *encore career* is a career that people hold after they retire from their main career (Freedman, 2007). People with a PCO are more likely to find meaning in later stages of their lives because they can adapt and navigate better. Yet we need to consider not only those who seek meaningful work for social, personal, and generative reasons but also those who seek only jobs that meet needs other than meaning, such as money or daily structure, to explore the link between age, the PCO, and the meaning of work changes. One extension of our earlier discussions of Figure 3.2 and later ideas on the implications for managers and organizations is that the protean orientation might be a useful tool for predicting which workers would want a job after retirement versus which ones would likely seek meaningful work. Another difference between these two types of encore workers might be in the source of meaning that is salient to them. For older people, the main source of meaning in seeking a job might be coworkers with whom they are working. For people seeking a higher purpose in their later life work, the source of meaning could be derived from the work itself and the significance that the work has in the society.

Another useful selection or self-assessment tool for older workers (and indeed for employees of all ages) might be a yet-to-be-developed instrument that would help employees understand the basic four needs of meaning and assess which need is most important to them. Then, if the employer had a list of available jobs organized in terms of the four needs, staffing specialists could provide coaching to job applicants to help them move into job areas that best fit their needs.[4] This suggests

---

[4]Developing such a list would not be a trivial activity. It would entail training human resources staff members or psychologists in the Baumeister (1991) model and developing a scoring protocol to code the extent to which jobs allow for meeting each of the four needs. However, the result could be an extremely useful career counseling resource.

a new way to frame jobs: in terms of their capacity for triggering need gratification and, thus, meaningfulness.

Future Directions for Theory, Research, and Practice

Given the lack of empirical studies linking meaningful work and the PCO, we recommend that future research efforts be directed toward testing the models we propose in this chapter (i.e., the moderating effects of the PCO and the moderating effects of the protean metacompetencies on the search for meaningful work, illustrated in Figures 3.1 and 3.2, respectively). In addition, studies that explore the direct relationship between the protean career and meaningful work are needed. As we previously noted, career development theories have suggested that people with a strong PCO may be more likely to find meaningful work in their careers (Mitchell, Levin, & Krumboltz, 1999; Savickas, 1997, 2000), yet this argument is supported by little empirical evidence. For instance, it is still not known which elements of the PCO increase the chance of having or crafting meaningful work or, furthermore, if this relationship actually withstands empirical testing. Considering the potential conflict between being protean and committing to an organization (Chang et al., 2008), it is important to determine which characteristics of people with a PCO actually increase the chance of achieving meaningful work versus which characteristics may decrease the chance of leaving the organization. This set of potential studies could increase the understanding of both the organizational and the career-developmental implications of the protean career–meaningfulness relationship. Moreover, it may be possible that the reverse relationship is also valid: Meaningful work might actually increase the chance of developing a PCO. Just as Park (2009) studied how a calling orientation increases the likelihood of following a protean career path, it may also be true that the experience of doing meaningful work could lead a person to develop a stronger PCO.

Conclusion

Following Baumeister (1991), we argue that work must satisfy four key needs if a person is to experience work as being meaningful: purpose, based on objective goals and subjective fulfillment; efficacy, in which the person sees that she or he has made a difference; justification of the work through personal values; and self-worth, which comes from

TABLE 3.1

Focus on the Workplace: A Protean Career Perspective

Recommendations	Tested in practice	Derived from theory	Supported by research
Take steps, as employers, managers, and career counselors, to boost protean metacompetencies (self-awareness and adaptability) to increase likelihood that individuals will have or find meaning (e.g., create a career center that is connected to multiple employment agencies and organizations and that develops individuals' self-awareness and adaptability).		✓	
Create a workplace environment that offers individuals opportunities to find or have meaningful work (e.g., offer greater discretion or leeway).		✓	
Use the grid[a] to assess level of each employee's protean metacompetencies and create individual career development plans that customize individual meaningfulness of work (from recruiting to exiting).		✓	
When possible, retain protean individuals through targeted challenges but prepare your organization for their potential departure (e.g., communication channels, documentation) and be willing to welcome them back at a later point in time.[b]	✓	✓	✓
Create "smart jobs" (Hall & Las Heras, 2010) that provide constant high-quality feedback to help employees expand their self-awareness, as well as requirements for change or learning (to increase their adaptability).	✓	✓	
Allow for greater internal job mobility to make it easier for people to find a job that has greater personal meaningfulness while remaining within the organization.		✓	
Develop formal relations with networks outside the organization to help individuals create developmental networks (the structure of relationships that the organization possesses can be a source of multiple developmental networks for individuals).		✓	

Note. [a]See Figure 3.2 for the grid. [b]Research on the first part of this idea, providing challenging assignments to retain growth-oriented employees, is found in job design research (e.g., Hackman & Oldham, 1976) and in research in the old AT&T (Howard & Bray, 1988), as well as in Schneider's attraction–selection–attrition research (e.g., Schneider, Goldstein, & Smith, 1995). Lawler and O'Toole (2006) reported that firms such as IBM, Capitol One, Deloitte & Touche, and UTC are using technology-based job assignment and career development processes that apply the protean concepts of self-direction based on personal interests and values. The practice of welcoming employees back is one that Douglas T. Hall has observed in some organizations, such as HP, but we are not aware of research on this practice.

individual achievement or attainment of group membership. In the workplace, these needs can be drawn from two sources of meaning: what I do and with whom I do it. Because the PCO entails working in a way that is driven by a person's most highly prized values and is self-directed, we see a positive relationship between the protean orientation and the experience of meaningfulness in work.

A protean person is more likely than other people to make choices that would lead to more meaningful work. Thus, the PCO can serve as a moderator of the relationship between job design characteristics and the experience of meaningfulness in work. Specifically, two metacompetencies linked to the protean orientation, self-awareness and adaptability, can affect the person's likelihood of achieving meaningful work. On the basis of these metacompetencies, which can be developed, and on the basis of the two components of the protean career, which can also be developed and/or more effectively deployed, we suggest a number of recommendations for employers who wish to help employees experience more meaningful work. None of these ideas are especially difficult to implement, nor are they resource intensive, so we are optimistic that these changes would be quite feasible in many organizations.

References

Baumeister, R. (2005). *The cultural animal: Human nature, meaning, and social life.* New York, NY: Oxford University Press.

Baumeister, R. F. (1991). *Meanings of life.* New York, NY: Guilford Press.

Baumeister, R. F., & Vohs, K. D. (2002). The pursuit of meaningfulness in life. In C. R. Snyder & S. J. Lopez (Eds.), *The handbook of positive psychology* (pp. 608–618). New York, NY: Oxford University Press.

Baumeister, R. F., & Wilson, B. (1996). Life stories and the four needs for meaning. *Psychological Inquiry, 7,* 322–325.

Bowlby, J. (1969). *Attachment and loss.* New York, NY: Basic Books.

Briscoe, J. P., & Hall, D. T. (2003). *Being and becoming protean: Individual and experiential factors in adapting to the new career.* Unpublished technical report, Department of Management, Northern Illinois University, DeKalb.

Briscoe, J. P., & Hall, D. T. (2006). The interplay of boundaryless and protean careers: Combinations and implications. *Journal of Vocational Behavior, 69,* 4–18. doi:10.1016/j.jvb.2005.09.002

Chang, J. Y., Choi, J. N., & Kim, M. U. (2008). Turnover of highly educated R&D professionals: The role of pre-entry cognitive style, work values and career orientation. *Journal of Occupational and Organizational Psychology, 81,* 299–317. doi:10.1348/096317907X204453

Chudzikowski, K., Demel, B., Mayrhofer, W., Briscoe, J. P., Unite, J., Milikic, B. B., . . . Zikic, J. (2009). Career transitions and their causes: A country comparative perspective. *Journal of Occupational and Organizational Psychology, 82,* 825–849. doi:10.1348/096317909X474786

Demel, B., Shen, Y., Las Heras, M., Hall, D. T., & Unite, J. (2010). *Career success and influencing factors in career success.* Unpublished manuscript.

Erikson, E. H. (1963). *Childhood and society.* New York, NY: Norton.

Farjoun, M. (2010). Beyond dualism: Stability and change as a duality. *Academy of Management Review, 35,* 202–225. doi:10.5465/AMR.2010.48463331

Fractal. (2012). In *Merriam-Webster's online dictionary.* Retrieved from http://www.merriamwebster.com/dictionary/fractal

Freedman, M. (2007). *Encore: Finding work that matters in the second half of life.* New York, NY: PublicAffairs.

Fugate, M., Kinicki, A. J., & Ashforth, B. E. (2004). Employability: A psycho-social construct, its dimensions, and applications. *Journal of Vocational Behavior, 65,* 14–38. doi:10.1016/j.jvb.2003.10.005

Gabriel, P. E. (2003, September). An examination of occupational mobility among full-time workers. *Monthly Labor Review, 126,* 32–36. Retrieved from http://www.bls.gov/opub/mlr/2003/09/art2full.pdf

Griskevicius, V., Delton, A. W., Robertson, T. E., & Tybur, J. M. (2011). Environmental contingency in life history strategies: The influence of mortality and socioeconomic status on reproductive timing. *Journal of Personality and Social Psychology, 100,* 241–254. doi:10.1037/a0021082

Hackman, J. R., & Oldham, G. R. (1976). Motivation through the design of work: Test of a theory. *Organizational Behavior and Human Performance, 16,* 250–279. doi:10.1016/0030-5073(76)90016-7

Hall, D. T. (1976). *Careers in organizations.* Santa Monica, CA: Goodyear.

Hall, D. T. (2002). *Careers in and out of organizations.* Thousand Oaks, CA: Sage.

Hall, D. T. (2004a). The protean career: A quarter-century journey. *Journal of Vocational Behavior, 65,* 1–13. doi:10.1016/j.jvb.2003.10.006

Hall, D. T. (2004b). Self-awareness, identity, and leader development. In D. V. Day, S. J. Zaccaro, & S. Halpern (Eds.), *Leader development for transforming organizations: Growing leaders for tomorrow* (pp. 153–176). Mahwah, NJ: Erlbaum.

Hall, D. T., & Associates. (1996). *The career is dead—Long live the career: A relational approach to careers.* San Francisco, CA: Jossey-Bass.

Hall, D. T., & Chandler, D. E. (2005). Psychological success: When the career is a calling. *Journal of Organizational Behavior, 26,* 155–176. doi:10.1002/job.301

Hall, D. T., & Las Heras, M. (2010). Reintegrating job design and career theory: Creating not just good jobs but *smart* jobs. *Journal of Organizational Behavior, 31,* 448–462. doi:10.1002/job.613

Hall, D. T., & Mirvis, P. H. (1996). The new protean career. In D. Hall & Associates, *The career is dead—Long live the career: A relational approach to careers* (pp. 15–45). San Francisco, CA: Jossey-Bass.

Harrington, B., & Hall, D. T. (2007). *Career management & work/life integration: Using self-assessment to navigate contemporary careers.* Thousand Oaks, CA: Sage.

Higgins, M. C., & Kram, K. E. (2001). Reconceptualizing mentoring at work: A developmental network perspective. *Academy of Management Review, 26,* 264–288.

Howard, A., & Bray, D. W. (1988). *Managerial lives in transition: Advancing age and changing times.* New York, NY: Guilford Press.

Ibarra, H. (2003). *Working identity: Unconventional strategies for reinventing your career.* Boston, MA: Harvard Business School Press.

Kahn, W. E. (1996). Secure base relationships at work. In D. T. Hall & Associates, *The career is dead—Long live the career: A relational approach to careers* (pp. 158–179). San Francisco, CA: Jossey-Bass.

Karaevli, A., & Hall, D. T. (2006). How career variety promotes the adaptability of managers: A theoretical model. *Journal of Vocational Behavior, 69,* 359–373. doi:10.1016/j.jvb.2006.05.009

Kegan, R. (1982). *The evolving self: Problem and process in human adult development.* Cambridge, MA: Harvard University Press.

Lawler, E. E., & O'Toole, J. (Eds.). (2006). *America at work: Choices and challenges.* New York, NY: Palgrave Macmillan.

Mandelbrot, B. B. (1982). *The fractal geometry of nature.* New York: Freeman.

McArdle, S., Waters, L., Briscoe, J. P., & Hall, D. T. (2007). Employability during unemployment: Adaptability, career identity and human and social capital. *Journal of Vocational Behavior, 71,* 247–264. doi:10.1016/j.jvb.2007.06.003

Mitchell, K. E., Levin, S. A., & Krumboltz, J. D. (1999). Planned happenstance: Constructing unexpected career opportunities. *Journal of Counseling & Development, 77,* 115–124. doi:10.1002/j.1556-6676.1999.tb02431.x

Park, Y. (2009). An integrative empirical approach to the predictors of self-directed career management. *Career Development International, 14,* 636–654. doi:10.1108/13620430911005690

Pratt, M. G., & Ashforth, B. E. (2003). Fostering meaningfulness in working and at work. In K. S. Cameron, J. E. Dutton, & R. E. Quinn (Eds.), *Positive organizational scholarship* (pp. 309–327). San Francisco, CA: Berrett-Koehler.

Ragins, B. R., & Kram, K. E. (Eds.). (2007). *The handbook of mentoring at work: Theory, research, and practice.* Thousand Oaks, CA: Sage.

Savickas, M. L. (1997). Career adaptability: An integrative construct for life-span, life-space theory. *The Career Development Quarterly, 45,* 247–259. doi:10.1002/j.2161-0045.1997.tb00469.x

Savickas, M. L. (2000). Renovating the psychology of careers for the twenty-first century. In A. Collin & R. A. Young (Eds.), *The future of career* (pp. 53–68). Cambridge, England: Cambridge University Press. doi:10.1017/CBO9780511520853.004

Schneider, B., Goldstein, H. W., & Smith, D. B. (1995). The ASA framework: An update. *Personnel Psychology, 48,* 747–773. doi:10.1111/j.1744-6570.1995.tb01780.x

Scroggins, W. A. (2008). Antecedents and outcomes of experienced meaningful work: A person–job fit perspective. *Journal of Business Inquiry: Research, Education and Application, 7,* 68–78.

Shepard, H. A. (1984). On the realization of human potential: A path with a heart. In M. B. Arthur, L. Bailyn, D. J. Levenson, & H. A. Shepard (Eds.), *Working with careers* (pp. 25–46). New York, NY: Columbia University School of Business.

Wrzesniewski, A., & Dutton, J. E. (2001). Crafting a job: Revisioning employees as active crafters of their work. *Academy of Management Review, 26,* 179–201.

Wrzesniewski, A., Dutton, J. E., & Debebe, G. (2003). Interpersonal sensemaking and the meaning of work. *Research in organizational behavior, 25,* 93–135 doi:10.1016/S0191-3085(03)25003-6

MEANING MAKING ON THE JOB II

Justin M. Berg, Jane E. Dutton, and Amy Wrzesniewski

Job Crafting and Meaningful Work

4

T he design of employees' jobs can significantly shape how they experience the meaningfulness of their work (Grant, 2007; Hackman & Oldham, 1980). A *job design* consists of the tasks and relationships assigned to one person in an organization (Ilgen & Hollenbeck, 1991). However, research suggests that job designs may be starting points from which employees introduce changes to their tasks and relationships at work, and such changes are captured by the concept of *job crafting*. Specifically, job crafting is the process of employees redefining and reimagining their job designs in personally meaningful ways (Wrzesniewski & Dutton, 2001). These changes, in turn, can influence the meaningfulness of the work. By *meaningful work,* we refer to work that employees believe is significant in that it serves an important purpose (Pratt & Ashforth, 2003). We use the term *meaningfulness* to capture the amount or degree of significance employees believe their work possesses (Rosso, Dekas, & Wrzesniewski, 2010). Meaningfulness is associated with numerous work-related benefits, including increased job satisfaction, motivation,

http://dx.doi.org/10.1037/14183-005
Purpose and Meaning in the Workplace, B. J. Dik, Z. S. Byrne, and M. F. Steger (Editors)

and performance (Grant, 2007; Hackman & Oldham, 1980; Rosso et al., 2010). Although we recognize that meaningful work may come with negative side effects (e.g., Berg, Grant, & Johnson, 2010; Bunderson & Thompson, 2009), for our purposes in this chapter, we follow the trend in the literature and treat meaningfulness as a generally positive or beneficial outcome for individuals and organizations.

Job crafting is a way to think about job design that puts employees in the driver's seat in cultivating meaningfulness in their work. Job crafters can proactively reshape the boundaries of their jobs using three categories of job crafting techniques: task, relational, and cognitive. *Task crafting* involves employees altering the set of responsibilities prescribed by a formal job description by adding or dropping tasks; altering the nature of tasks; or changing how much time, energy, and attention are allocated to various tasks (e.g., a tech-savvy customer service representative offering to help her colleagues with their IT issues). *Relational crafting* involves changing how, when, or with whom employees interact in the execution of their jobs (e.g., a software engineer forming a collaborative relationship with a marketing analyst). And finally, *cognitive crafting* involves employees changing the way they perceive the tasks and relationships that make up their jobs (e.g., a ticket salesperson seeing the job as an essential part of providing people with entertainment, not just processing orders).

By using any combination of these three types of job crafting techniques, employees become job crafters, altering the boundaries of their jobs in ways that change their experience of the meaningfulness of their work. Job crafting is not an isolated, one-time event. On the contrary, job crafting is a continuous process that is likely influenced by where employees are in their career trajectories (Fried, Grant, Levi, Hadani, & Slowik, 2007) and the social context in which they work (Berg, Wrzesniewski, & Dutton, 2010). A core feature of job crafting is that employees initiate and carry out alterations in their jobs from the bottom up, rather than managers directing changes from the top down, as in many job redesign interventions. This enables employees to leverage the unique knowledge they have of their jobs and themselves to craft their jobs in ways that create more meaningfulness. For example, a history teacher with a longtime passion for performing music could incorporate music into his curriculum (task crafting), collaborate with the music teacher in his school (relational crafting), and draw parallels between the act of teaching in front of a classroom and the experience of performing music (cognitive crafting). By crafting his job in these ways, this teacher is able to incorporate musical performance and the experience of being a musician—which are valued parts of his identity—into his life at work, thus bringing new meaningfulness into his work (Berg, Grant, & Johnson, 2010).

Job crafting is particularly critical as a path to meaningfulness in modern work contexts (Wrzesniewski, Berg, & Dutton, 2010). The idea of employees working from a fixed job description is becoming less common over time. In a rapidly changing knowledge economy, organizations place a premium on employee proactivity (Grant & Ashford, 2008). Instead of reacting to a set of job responsibilities, employees' personal initiatives in shaping their jobs often deliver benefits to organizations by fostering innovativeness and adaptability (Frese & Fay, 2001). Freedom to take initiative opens up opportunities for employees to create meaningful experiences for themselves through job crafting.

In addition, job crafting is an especially important process for cultivating work engagement and satisfaction in a workforce that is experiencing increasing dissatisfaction with work (The Conference Board, 2010) and retiring later in life (Johnson, Butrica, & Mommaerts, 2010). At the same time, many members of Generations X and Y hold the view that they can "be anything they want to be" (Twenge, 2006, p. 72) and thus have strong expectations for the meaningfulness they would like to derive from their careers. These demographic and employment trends contribute to pressure for employees to stay in less than ideal jobs for longer periods of time, making it more likely that employees will need to reengineer their jobs from within as a way to find increased meaningfulness or foster engagement. From an organization's perspective, these trends produce similar pressures to keep productive employees in their jobs. Thus, both employees and organizations stand to benefit from job crafting as a way of sparking new meaningfulness or rekindling old meaningfulness in long-held jobs.

In this chapter, we aim to explain how job crafting can be a powerful process for cultivating meaningful work experiences. We begin by summarizing insights from theory and research in the growing literature on job crafting, then give recommendations for how job crafting can be used in organizations, and conclude with promising areas for future research and practice on job crafting.

Theoretical and Empirical Literature

The literature on job crafting is relatively new but has been expanding rapidly over the past few years. Wrzesniewski and Dutton (2001) established the theoretical framework of job crafting, including the three forms described earlier. Their model was based on insights from previous research on how hairdressers, engineers, nurses, chefs, and hospital cleaners crafted their jobs, often without support or recognition from their organizations or from higher-ups. A key theoretical insight from their original conceptual piece was that employees construct their own experiences of the meaningfulness in their work by thinking about and performing their jobs in particular ways. Thus, the job design that is formally prescribed to an employee from the top down is only part of how the meaningfulness of the job is constructed; the other part is initiated and driven by the employee through job crafting (see Figure 4.1).

Several scholars have elaborated on Wrzesniewski and Dutton's (2001) original job crafting framework. In a study of salespersons, Lyons (2008) found that employees' cognitive ability, quality of self-image, perceived level of control, and readiness to change all predicted the extent to which they engaged in job crafting, such that employees who were rated higher in these measures engaged in more job crafting. Consistent with these findings, Clegg and Spencer (2007) theorized that employees would be more likely to engage in job crafting when they are performing well and perceived by themselves and others as competent and trustworthy.

In a study of early childhood educators, Leana, Appelbaum, and Shevchuk (2009) introduced the idea of *collaborative job crafting,* in which employees work together to collectively redesign their jobs. They found that educators who engaged in collaborative job crafting tended to perform better than did those who did less collaborative crafting, especially when the educators were less experienced. In addition to higher performance, job crafting has also been associated with increased levels of resilience in the face of adversity at work (Ghitulescu, in press) and increased emotional well-being (French, 2010).

Using a qualitative study of employees in the for-profit and nonprofit sectors, Berg, Wrzesniewski, and Dutton (2010) uncovered how employees perceive and adapt to challenges in crafting their jobs and how these processes differ for employees in relatively high- versus low-ranking jobs in organizations. Specifically, they discovered that high-ranking employees perceived the challenges in job crafting as located in their own expectations of how they should use their time, and they adapted to these challenges by settling for only the opportunities to job craft that were readily available to them. In contrast, low-ranking employees saw the challenges in job crafting as located in others' expectations of them and adapted to these challenges by winning others' support in ways that created new opportunities to job craft. Thus, high-ranking employees seemed to feel more constrained with respect to their freedom to job craft, whereas low-ranking employees felt relatively more autonomy to proactively craft their jobs. These findings suggest that the level of formal autonomy and power within a prescribed job design does not necessarily have the impact on employees' perceptions of opportunities to craft their jobs that one would expect. Rather, greater formal autonomy and power may sometimes be associated with greater psychological constraint with respect to job crafting.

Also using a qualitative study, Berg, Grant, and Johnson (2010) examined how people craft their jobs to pursue unanswered occupational callings (i.e., occupations) other than their own that people feel

FIGURE 4.1

Job Design
(Top-down, One-size-fits-all)
Manager-initiated structure that shapes
employees' experience of meaningfulness
through task identity, variety, and significance.

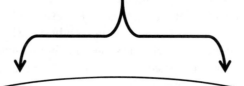

Meaningfulness Derived from Job

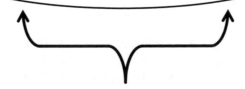

Job Crafting
(Bottom-up, Individualized)
Employee-initiated process that shapes one's
own experience of meaningfulness through
proactive changes to the tasks, relationships,
and perceptions associated with the job.

The interaction between job design and job crafting
in shaping employees' experience of meaningfulness.
Meaningfulness derived from a job is the result of an
interaction between top-down job design and bottom-
up job crafting.

drawn to pursue because they consider them to be intrinsically enjoyable and meaningful and an important part of who they are. They found that people use three job crafting techniques to pursue desired components of their unanswered callings within their current occupations: (a) *task emphasizing,* which involves allocating more time, energy, and attention to tasks that are related to an unanswered calling; (b) *job expanding,* which involves adding new tasks or projects related to an unanswered calling; and (c) *role reframing,* which involves mentally drawing connections between the purpose of one's current role and an unanswered calling. Using these job crafting techniques can bring about the enjoyable and meaningful experiences that people associate with pursuing their unanswered callings, but, at the same time, this process can have negative consequences. For example, engaging in job crafting to pursue an unanswered calling is stressful when it is difficult or frustrating to pursue. Furthermore, regret may result through reexposure to desirable but unattainable aspects of the unanswered calling that might otherwise be out of sight, out of mind. These effects highlight the sometimes double-edged sword of job crafting: It is not always positive and can produce unintended side effects, especially when it runs counter to the organization's goals.

Applications in the Workplace

The growing academic literature on job crafting has made it a ripe concept for practitioners to begin using as a tool to help employees enhance the meaningfulness they experience in their work. In addition to applying ideas and methods around job crafting that have already been developed, we see numerous promising opportunities for practitioners to experiment with new methods of using job crafting that have not yet been extensively tested. Next, we discuss several possible ways of using job crafting in the workplace, all of which are inspired by existing theory and/or research but only some of which have been tested in practice.

JOB CRAFTING THROUGH CHANGING TASKS

Most jobs consist of tasks that can be altered to make the job more meaningful. Traditional job design theory states that tasks are more meaningful when they involve a greater variety of skills (*task variety*) and are seen as part of an identifiably whole piece of work (*task identity*; Hackman & Oldham, 1976, 1980). In addition, relational job design perspectives (Grant, 2007, 2008; Grant & Parker, 2009) highlight that when employees are able to see the impact that their tasks have on others (*task significance*), they experience their work as more meaningful, often leading to higher motivation and performance. Combining these job design theories with the job crafting techniques described by Berg, Grant, and Johnson (2010), we propose three ways employees can craft their tasks to cultivate greater task variety, identity, and significance, thereby enhancing the meaningfulness they are likely to derive from their work:

- *Adding tasks.* Employees can add whole tasks or projects that they find meaningful into their jobs. For example, a human resources recruiter with an interest in technology might add the task of using social media to attract and communicate with recruits. Adding this task would bring the application or development of new, desirable skills into the job and allow the recruiter to more easily track how her or his efforts are influencing recruiting results over time. The depth that these changes bring to the tasks of the job would likely spark feelings of deeper meaningfulness at work.
- *Emphasizing tasks.* Employees can take advantage of any tasks that they see as meaningful that are already part of their jobs by allocating more time, energy, and attention to them. For example, a dentist could spend more time educating patients on healthy dental habits. In this way, the dentist can better leverage an existing part of the job that is considered to be meaningful.
- *Redesigning tasks.* Especially when time constraints make adding or emphasizing tasks difficult, employees can find ways to reengineer existing tasks to make them more meaningful. For example, an experienced salesperson could bring a new colleague along on sales calls, so this task would involve both selling to clients and training the colleague. Helping the new colleague forge important connections and learn this part of the job might invigorate the salesperson by making a mundane task more meaningful.

JOB CRAFTING THROUGH CHANGING RELATIONSHIPS

In addition to crafting tasks, employees can craft their interactions with others at work in ways that foster meaningfulness through altering with whom and how they form connections and relationships. We use the term *connections* to denote short, momentary interactions with others that could evolve into or contribute to a longer term relationship. We know from a broad array of research about employee interactions that even short-term connections, particularly high-quality connections (where employees experience mutual trust, positive regard, and vitality), can be highly consequential (Dutton & Heaphy, 2003). High-quality connections between people are associated with more adaptability in jobs and careers (e.g., Ibarra, 2003), increased job commitment and more positive work attitudes (e.g., Chiaburu & Harrison,

2008), better physiological functioning (Heaphy & Dutton, 2008), and recovery from pain and suffering (Lilius et al., 2008). As well, relationships with others on the job provide key inputs to how employees make sense of the meaning of their work, the job, and themselves in the job (Wrzesniewski, Dutton, & Debebe, 2003). Thus, relationships—and the short-term connections that form them—are key sources of meaningfulness that can be unlocked through job crafting. We propose three main pathways through which crafting relationships can facilitate meaningfulness at work:

- *Building relationships.* Employees can craft their jobs to cultivate meaningfulness by forging relationships with others who enable them to feel a sense of pride, dignity, or worth. For example, we found that hospital cleaners increased the amount of interaction they had with patients and their families, because within these interactions, they experienced more appreciation and enacted a role of caregiver that elevated the sense of meaningfulness that they derived from their work (Wrzesniewski et al., 2003).

- *Reframing relationships.* Employees can craft their work relationships by changing the nature of each relationship to be about a new, more meaningful purpose. For example, a school principal might reframe what it means to have relationships with teachers to be about getting to know their individual work preferences and interests (and helping them understand the principal's) rather than just supervising or evaluating teachers' work. Approaching relationships in this way may change the nature and content of interactions with teachers by compelling the principal to ask more questions (as opposed to just giving directions) and explain the reasoning behind these actions, which may produce more high-quality connections with teachers and thus enhance the meaningfulness the principal and the teachers derive from their relationships (e.g., Gerstner & Day, 1997; Laschinger, Purdy, & Almost, 2007).

- *Adapting relationships.* Rather than changing the purpose of relationships or adding new ones, employees can craft their existing relationships to cultivate meaningfulness by providing others with valuable help and support in carrying out their jobs, thus encouraging others to give valuable help and support in return. These adaptations are likely to deepen and strengthen the relationships that comprise employees' jobs by fostering higher quality connections through increasing levels of mutual trust, positive regard, and vitality. In this way, employees can unlock meaningfulness from within their current relationships without having to form new relationships or change the purpose of relationships, which may be difficult or impossible if the job is highly structured or the organization is fairly small. For example, Fletcher (1998) found that engineers often interacted with others in adaptive ways that enabled them to be successful in their jobs. She called this way of interacting *mutual empowering*, and as a form of relational job crafting, it can foster meaningful relationships in which both parties readily give and receive valuable help and support. Similarly, employees may craft their jobs by adapting relationships with new or less experienced colleagues to focus on mentoring or coaching, which could be meaningful for both the mentor and the mentee (Ragins & Kram, 2007).

JOB CRAFTING THROUGH CHANGING PERCEPTIONS

Unlike crafting tasks and relationships, crafting perceptions does not involve changing anything physical or objective about the job, such as what tasks one is doing or who one is interacting with. Instead, changing perceptions—or *cognitive job crafting*—points to enhancements in meaningfulness than can arise from employees altering how they think about the tasks, relationships, or jobs as a whole. The potential power of this mental form of job crafting is supported by research on the power of mind-sets for changing how employees subjectively experience their work, without changing anything physical or objective about the job itself (e.g., Crum & Langer, 2007; Langer, 1989). We propose three ways in which employees may craft their perceptions of their jobs to experience more meaningfulness in their work. As mentioned earlier, this might involve employees reframing how they see their jobs—for example, a hospital cleaner seeing his or her work as healer or caregiver. Through rethinking the job and what it means—in a team, in an organization, or in society—job crafters are able to imbue their work (and themselves) with greater significance and value.

- *Expanding perceptions.* Employees can cultivate meaningfulness by broadening their perceptions of the impact or purpose of their jobs. This often takes the form of employees thinking about their jobs as a whole rather than a set of separate tasks and relationships. By keeping the holistic purpose of their jobs in mind, employees are able to better connect with the ultimate fruits of their labor and beneficiaries of their work (Grant, 2007) and thus experience their work as more meaningful and motivating (Hackman & Oldham, 1976, 1980). For example, Bunderson and Thompson (2009) found that many zookeepers—whose jobs involve mostly cleaning cages and feeding animals—often see their work as a moral duty to protect and provide proper care for animals, and this holistic view of their jobs is likely more meaningful and motivating to them than simply focusing on the individual tasks that make up their jobs.

- *Focusing perceptions.* In contrast to expanding perceptions, employees can also foster meaningfulness by narrowing their mental scope of the purpose of their job on specific tasks and relationships that are significant or valuable to them. This technique may be most useful for employees who dislike a substantial portion of the tasks and/or relationships that make up their jobs but do find some specific parts of their jobs to be meaningful. For example, software engineers who find meaningfulness in creating new ideas but not the actual coding involved in implementing their ideas could try to focus on and continually remind themselves that much of their job is about creating new ideas. By taking frequent steps back and mentally focusing on the creative aspects of the job that are most meaningful to them, they may be able to more effectively leverage the meaningful components of their jobs to bear the parts that seem less meaningful. In addition, by mentally breaking the job into two chunks—one that is more meaningful (creating new ideas) and one that is less (coding)—they can treat the more meaningful work as a future reward to help motivate them to get through the less meaningful work (e.g., Oettingen, Pak, & Schnetter, 2001).
- *Linking perceptions.* In addition to focusing perceptions, employees can take advantage of existing components of their jobs by drawing mental connections between specific tasks or relationships and interests, outcomes, or aspects of their identities that are meaningful to them. For example, a customer service representative who has a passion for stand-up comedy might draw a mental connection between the experience of performing comedy with the moments in the workday spent cracking jokes to build rapport with customers. Seeing the link between these two experiences may help the representative perceive such interactions with customers as more meaningful because it taps into a valued personal interest and an important aspect of identity (Berg, Grant, & Johnson, 2010).

CRAFTING A BETTER PERSON–JOB FIT: USING MOTIVES, STRENGTHS, AND PASSIONS

Research on person–job fit has suggested that when employees see more of a fit between themselves and their jobs, they are more likely to experience their work as personally meaningful and respond with enhanced job performance, satisfaction, and retention in their organizations (Caldwell & O'Reilly, 1990; Kristof-Brown, Zimmerman, & Johnson, 2005). The nine job crafting techniques described previously can all help employees reshape their jobs to better fit themselves. But this raises the question: Which aspects of themselves should employees focus on when crafting their jobs to better fit them? In reflecting on our research on job crafting and, in particular, how employees were able to successfully craft their jobs in ways that were meaningful to them and helpful to the organization, we identified three key categories of personal characteristics that employees used to guide their crafting efforts:

- *Motives.* Job crafting in ways that align with employees' key motives, or the specific outcomes that drive them to put forth effort and persistence (e.g., enjoyment, personal growth, friendship), can foster meaningfulness by enabling employees to pursue outcomes that they care about and deeply value (Ambrose & Kulik, 1999).
- *Strengths.* Job crafting in ways that enable employees to leverage their strengths, or areas of talent that can be productively applied at work (e.g., problem-solving skills, attention to detail, public speaking), can cultivate meaningfulness by helping employees leverage what they are naturally capable of doing well (Clifton & Harter, 2003).
- *Passions.* Job crafting in ways that create opportunities to pursue passions, or the activities and topics that spark deep interest (e.g., learning, teaching, using technology), can be a rich source of enjoyment, engagement, and meaningfulness (Csikszentmihalyi, 1990; Vallerand et al., 2003; Wrzesniewski, Rozin, & Bennett, 2002).

Where possible, if employees can achieve better fit between these three characteristics and the jobs they craft, they can make work more meaningful. Specifically, because employees' motives, strengths, and passions tap into valued personal desires and abilities, job crafting that facilitates the expression of motives, strengths, and passions is likely to cultivate greater meaningfulness. In essence, these three categories can provide a more systematic basis for helping employees think about which aspects of themselves they should try to craft their jobs to better fit.

ESTABLISHING A JOB CRAFTING MIND-SET: FOCUSING ON OPPORTUNITIES FOR SMALL WINS

All of the strategies we have identified could be enhanced if an employee has a *mind-set*—defined as a particular way of seeing and interpreting the world (e.g., Dweck, 2007; Langer, 1989)—that values and encourages this form of proactivity. Just as some people hold the mind-set that people's characteristics are fairly fixed and unchangeable and others believe that people can and do change substantially (Dweck, 1999), some employees tend to see their jobs as fixed and unchangeable, whereas others see their jobs as flexible and changeable. A job crafting mind-set starts with an underlying belief that job crafting is possible. In other words, job crafters must believe that their job is something that they can proactively shape, not a fixed entity that simply places unchangeable demands on them. Job crafting cannot occur without the belief that there are or could be opportunities to introduce changes to the job.

In addition to this underlying belief about the malleability of the job itself, a job crafting mind-set involves paying ongoing attention to where the opportunities are for crafting. Further, job crafting relies on a willingness to experiment with different aspects of the tasks and relationships the job comprises, as well as different ways of framing the significance of the work. Because making sizeable changes to one's job may be difficult, especially if these changes run counter to established norms or disrupt other people's work, a job crafting mind-set may be challenging to sustain over time as attempts at crafting fail or fall short of expectations. One strategy that may help sustain a job crafting mind-set is focusing on "small wins" (Weick, 1984). By defining success in terms of *small wins*—or relatively modest, incremental improvements— job crafters may avoid feeling frustrated or disillusioned and thus be able to better sustain their job crafting mind-set. In turn, as the small wins accrue over time, the incremental changes may grow into larger, more substantial changes to the job.

Finally, a job crafting mind-set might depend on something as simple as whether employees subscribe to the belief that change is positive or negative, appropriate or inappropriate. Employees with a job crafting mind-set believe they have the right to be the architect of their jobs, even in small ways, whereas other employees may instead feel that only managers or others in power have the freedom to suggest or introduce changes into the work. These beliefs about who has control over changing the job help to inform a mind-set that treats the job as either malleable or fixed; these beliefs may be reflected in whether employees see job crafting as positive or as breaking a set of unwritten rules. At its core, a job crafting mind-set grows from a frame of mind in which employees believe they have agency and that the exercise of their agency is desirable. Only then are employees likely to seize the opportunities for job crafting that they perceive or create.

PUTTING IT ALL TOGETHER: THE JOB CRAFTING EXERCISE

The *Job Crafting Exercise* is a tool that helps people identify opportunities to craft their jobs to better suit their motives, strengths, and passions. We developed this exercise on the basis of theory and qualitative empirical research on the ways in which employees are able to craft their jobs to cultivate meaningfulness, resulting in desirable outcomes for individuals and organizations. The exercise and all of the supplies needed to do it are sold as an instruction booklet by the Center for Positive Organizational Scholarship at the University of Michigan's Ross School of Business (see http://www.jobcrafting.org).

The main idea of the exercise is to have people think about their jobs as a flexible set of building blocks rather than just a fixed list of duties, as people tend to do once they settle into a job. By encouraging participants to think about their jobs in this flexible, visual way, the exercise fosters a job crafting mind-set, because participants come to see their jobs as more changeable. Participants begin by creating a *before sketch* to get a quick gauge of how they are currently spending their time, energy, and attention in their jobs. To do this, participants are asked to break their job into three categories of *task blocks:* Tasks that take up the most time, energy, and attention go into the largest blocks; tasks that take the least time, energy, and attention go in the smallest blocks; and tasks that fall somewhere in between go in medium-size blocks (see Figure 4.2). This first part of the exercise enables participants to see in a concise and clear way how they are allocating their personal resources at work.

Participants then move to the second part of the exercise, where they create an *after diagram* (see Figure 4.3). Whereas the before sketch depicts how participants currently do their jobs, the after diagram is supposed to represent a more ideal (but still realistic) version of their jobs. In this way, the after diagram serves as an image of opportunities for how participants can craft their jobs to be more meaningful and hence more engaging and fulfilling. To create the after diagram, participants begin by identifying the three aforementioned important aspects of themselves at work: their motives, strengths, and passions. With these three aspects in mind, participants then create a new set of task blocks to symbolize how they would like to spend their time, energy, and attention in the future. Participants use their motives, strengths, and passions as criteria for assessing how well each task included in their jobs suits them. The final step of creating the after diagram is drawing *role frames* around groups of tasks that participants see as serving a common purpose. Role frames are intended to help participants engage in

FIGURE 4.2

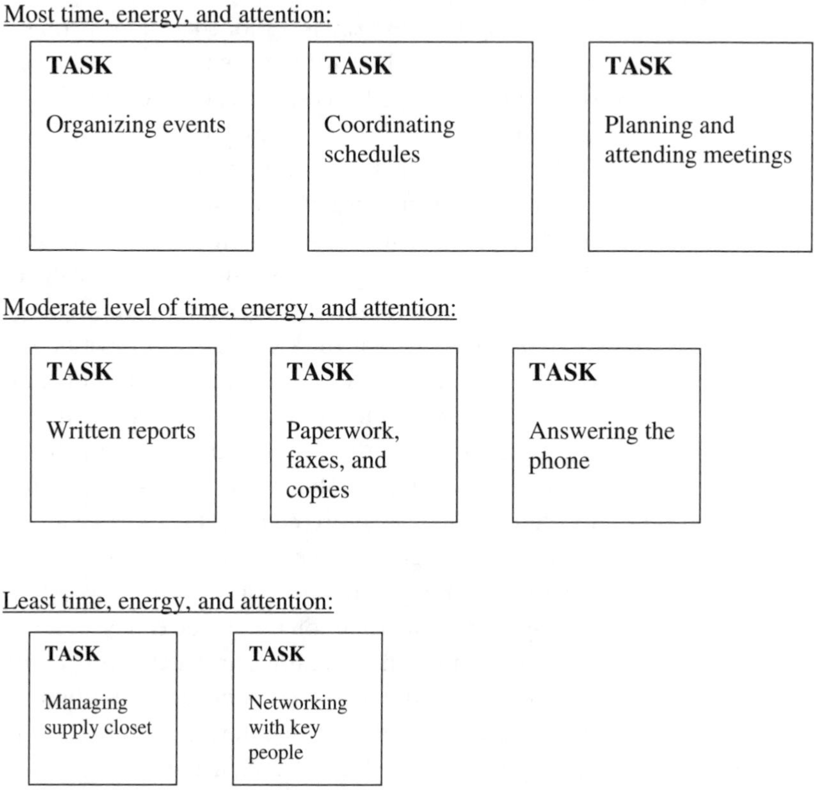

Most time, energy, and attention:

TASK	TASK	TASK
Organizing events	Coordinating schedules	Planning and attending meetings

Moderate level of time, energy, and attention:

TASK	TASK	TASK
Written reports	Paperwork, faxes, and copies	Answering the phone

Least time, energy, and attention:

TASK	TASK
Managing supply closet	Networking with key people

An administrative assistant's Before sketch (Part 1 of the Job Crafting Exercise). An example of how an administrative assistant approached her before sketch, which is the part of the Job Crafting Exercise that captures how one currently spends his or her time, energy, and attention on the job. Figure 4.3 depicts the administrative assistant's after diagram. From *Job Crafting Exercise*, by J. M. Berg, J. E. Dutton, and A. Wrzesniewski, 2008. Copyright 2008 by the Regents of the University of Michigan. Adapted with permission.

cognitive or perceptions crafting, because they help participants mentally label tasks in ways that are meaningful to them. Through arranging their after diagrams, participants reveal insights on how they can craft their jobs to enhance meaningfulness. The final step of the exercise is creating an action plan in which participants define specific goals and

FIGURE 4.3

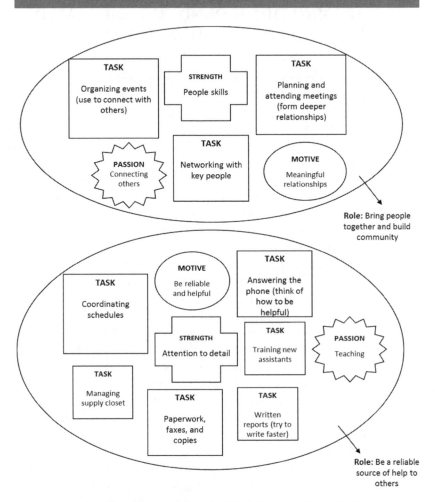

An administrative assistant's After diagram (Part 2 of the Job Crafting Exercise). The administrative assistant's after diagram represents a more ideal (but still realistic) allocation of her time, energy, and attention. The administrative assistant added the task of "Training new assistants," moved "Written reports" to a small block, and moved "Networking with key people" to a medium block. From *Job Crafting Exercise,* by J. M. Berg, J. E. Dutton, and A. Wrzesniewski, 2008. Copyright 2008 by the Regents of the University of Michigan. Adapted with permission.

strategies in the near and long terms for making the more ideal version of the their job depicted in their after diagram into a reality.

SEEDING THE GROUND FOR JOB CRAFTING: FROM JOB DESCRIPTIONS TO JOB LANDSCAPES

As discussed earlier, our research has suggested that simply giving employees formal autonomy and power within a formal job design does not necessarily ensure that they will experience autonomy to craft their jobs. Even employees with a great deal of formal autonomy and power can feel constrained when it comes to job crafting because they tend to feel stuck in the daily grind of their jobs and see the set of tasks and relationships that make up their jobs as rigid and fixed (Berg, Wrzesniewski, & Dutton, 2010). This presents a challenge to organizations that value innovation and rapid adaptation, because an organization is unlikely to change much if its employees treat their job designs as fixed entities. This raises the question of how jobs can be designed to seed the ground for job crafting over the long run.

Our research has hinted that one key to designing jobs that facilitate job crafting may be in finding the right balance between structure and freedom. In addition to finding that employees with plenty of formal autonomy and power could still feel constrained in terms of their opportunities to craft, we also found that employees with little formal autonomy and power had to put in a great deal of effort to create opportunities to craft (Berg, Wrzesniewski, & Dutton, 2010). However, despite the extra effort required, it was relatively easier for these employees to recognize opportunities for crafting, thanks to their more structured job designs. Because their jobs included tasks that had clear means and ends established (e.g., you should service this machine using the following steps, or you must enter these data in this way), it was easier for them to see the "white space" in their jobs—that is, where they could fit in new tasks or relationships or drop tasks and relationships that were not important. In contrast, the higher rank employees' job designs consisted in large part of end goals that they had to decide how to pursue on their own. This lack of structure, combined with the continuous pressure to pursue their end goals, seemed to make it more difficult for them to recognize opportunities to craft their jobs.

In other words, to color outside the lines of a job, one needs lines there in the first place. Thus, the challenge seems to be in creating job designs that provide employees with the right amount and type of structure so that they can recognize opportunities to craft but not have to put in too much effort to make the crafting happen. As a possible framework for striking this balance, we propose the idea of *job landscapes*. Traditionally, a job design (or job description) is a fixed list of duties and reporting relationships (Ilgen & Hollenbeck, 1991). A job landscape, however, includes two elements: (a) a list of general end goals assigned to an employee and (b) a set of interdependencies or ways in which these end goals overlap and relate to the end goals of other relevant employees or departments. By describing how one's own end goals are related to others' end goals, a job landscape creates a better understanding of how employees' work is interconnected with the work of those around them (e.g., a marketing employee's goals of creating and devising marketing strategies overlaps with research and development goals of creating and developing marketable products). Unlike a traditional job design, the focus of a job landscape is not necessarily on hierarchical relationships but rather on shared goals among individuals and units. However, job landscapes do not prescribe how these shared goals should be pursued—that is up to employees to decide in collaboration with those with whom they are interdependent.

Drawing from macro theories of landscape design (Levinthal & Warglien, 1999), interdependencies may provide the right balance between structure and freedom to enable job crafting; interdependencies make landscapes more rugged, meaning that the possible behavioral pathways available to individuals are constrained by the actions and responses of others, but they are also malleable in that all the parties can decide how to act on the basis of their unique knowledge of their situations rather than being controlled by a centralized body. By prescribing interdependencies and end goals but not how these goals should be pursued, job landscapes free the job from being a set of tasks and reporting relationships as in traditional job descriptions. Thus, although traditional job descriptions generally indicate a set of top-down, one-size-fits-all constraints on employees, job landscapes place employees in situations where they face both constraints as well as opportunities to work with others to customize their jobs from the bottom up. The key for job landscape designers is to make landscapes sufficiently rugged while not including interdependencies that are irrelevant or too numerous for employees to manage.

In addition to balancing structure and freedom in a way that may help enable task crafting, defining for employees how their work is interconnected with others' work may help provide them with raw materials for cultivating meaningfulness through cognitive and relational crafting. Because job landscapes make the relational interdependencies around the job holder clear, employees may have an easier time making sense of how their work has an impact on others in the organization, which may facilitate positive meaning making (Wrzesniewski et al., 2003) and foster increased motivation and performance (Grant, 2007, 2008).

In sum, job landscapes provide a different approach to designing jobs in organizations that value rapid innovation and adaptation, where job crafting is especially important. After all, an organization is unlikely to change much if the content of its employees' jobs stays the same. We hope scholars and practitioners explore the concept of job landscapes and build knowledge of how and when they can be used to foster beneficial job crafting (see Table 4.1).

Future Directions for Theory, Research, and Practice

Because the academic literature on job crafting is relatively new, many important yet unanswered questions remain about the triggers, moderators, and outcomes of job crafting as a way of cultivating meaningfulness in work. First, we still know relatively little about what individual, interpersonal, occupational, and organizational factors enable or limit job crafting (Morgeson, Dierdorff, & Hmurovic, 2010). Are certain personality traits associated with specific forms of crafting? Are there particular managerial behaviors or group dynamics or practices that foster beneficial job crafting? Can job crafting be contagious, meaning that when one person job crafts, it can set off a chain as others in the same network also engage in crafting? What is the role of organizational culture in enabling or constraining job crafting?

Second, despite the fact that job crafting is an ongoing, dynamic process rather than a single time event, little theory or research has addressed the role of time in job crafting. Future longitudinal studies could explore different job crafting trajectories. Are there patterns in

TABLE 4.1

Focus on the Workplace: A Job Crafting Perspective

Recommendations	Tested in practice	Derived from theory	Supported by research
Job crafting through changing tasks.[a,b]	✓	✓	✓
Job crafting through changing relationships.[a,c]	✓	✓	✓
Job crafting through changing perceptions.[a,c]	✓	✓	✓
Crafting a better person–job fit: Using motives[d], strengths[e], and passions.[a,f]	✓	✓	✓
Cultivating a job crafting mind-set.		✓	
Completing the Job Crafting Exercise.[a,g]	✓	✓	✓
Seeding the ground for job crafting: From job descriptions to job landscapes.		✓	

Note. [a]Berg, Grant, & Johnson (2010). [b]Leana, Appelbaum, & Shevchuk (2009). [c]Wrzesniewski, Dutton, & Debebe (2003). [d]Ambrose & Kulik (1999). [e]Clifton & Harter (2003). [f]Csikszentmihalyi (1990). [g]Berg, Wrzesniewski, & Dutton (2010).

when employees attempt to craft and when it is most beneficial or costly? Do longer tenured employees engage in more job crafting, or is job crafting more the province of newer employees who can see more possibilities in the job before they become habituated to the work?

Third, although some research has linked job crafting with particular outcomes related to performance and perceptions of the work (e.g., Berg, Grant, & Johnson, 2010; Leana et al., 2009), there seems to be a need for more theory and research that link specific forms of crafting to particular individual and organizational outcomes, both positive and negative. For example, when and how can job crafting become a source of innovation at the group or organization level? Under what conditions are certain forms of crafting costly or likely to produce negative side effects for individuals and organizations (e.g., burnout, stress, or decreased performance)?

Not all jobs and situations are equally conducive to job crafting. Researchers and practitioners should take seriously the boundary conditions that apply. For example, some job structures require strict rule compliance and adherence to rigid procedures—for example, jobs in high reliability organizations such as air traffic controllers, nuclear plant technicians, emergency room staff, and firefighters (Roberts, 1990)—that may limit task and relational crafting (but may not restrict cognitive crafting as extensively). Similarly, some employees find themselves in organizations or units that restrict or punish efforts to redefine or craft their jobs, because the colleagues with whom they are interdependent demand that work be done a certain way, their managers demand that their jobs be performed in a prescribed way, or a combination of both. These powerful social pressures constitute a strong situation (Mischel & Shoda, 1995), which is likely to limit employees' opportunities to craft their tasks and relationships. It may still be possible to craft perceptions in such strong situations, although the altered perceptions of the job may be difficult to sustain over time if they run counter to situational pressures and demands from colleagues, managers, or both. In these sorts of constrained contexts, employees may benefit from being vigilant about the psychological, interpersonal, and performance costs of job crafting. On the basis of their assessments, employees could determine whether and when restrictions on crafting might warrant giving up on crafting or, in cases in which employees are highly dissatisfied, leaving the job or organization altogether.

Although there are limits to job crafting, we see lots of opportunities for practitioners and managers to learn more about applying job crafting in organizations. First, practitioners and managers could explore different methods for fostering beneficial job crafting. Is it best to encourage job crafting in one-on-one coaching situations, in group workshops, or through personally setting an example? Second, because the Job Crafting Exercise is a relatively new tool, it has only been extensively tested with individuals doing the exercise by themselves. It may also be effective for some groups or teams to do together as a way to divide up work between one another or engage in collective job crafting (Leana et al., 2009) in which group members decide to change their jobs in agreed on ways. Third, although the Job Crafting Exercise can be useful for creating a plan to seize opportunities for job crafting, one of the challenges we most often hear from employees is implementing the plan they create during the exercise, because it is easy to fall back into old routines or get caught up in the day-to-day grind of the job and forget about job crafting. We invite practitioners and managers to experiment with various ways of helping employees carry out their job crafting intentions, such as helping employees strategize the best route to implementing their crafting and who to talk to about it, creating a program of incremental goals to create a more ideal version of the job, scheduling check-up meetings to discuss the employee's crafting progress, or setting aside time for pursing crafting intentions.

Conclusion

Whether in the academic or the practical realm, job crafting offers an exciting way to understand how jobs are reengineered from the bottom up by employees to create more meaningful work. A focus on job crafting reminds researchers and practitioners that jobs are inherently malleable in thought and in action. Job crafting brings our attention to employees' everyday—yet sometimes remarkable—efforts to be resourceful on the job. In a world where meaningfulness may be in short supply, job crafting can be an important process through which employees cultivate meaningfulness and, in so doing, create valuable outcomes for themselves and their organizations.

References

Ambrose, M. L., & Kulik, C. T. (1999). Old friends, new faces: Motivation research in the 1990s. *Journal of Management, 25,* 231–292. doi:10.1177/014920639902500302

Berg, J. M., Dutton, J. E., & Wrzesniewski, A. (2008). *Job Crafting Exercise.* Ann Arbor, MI: Regents of the University of Michigan.

Berg, J. M., Grant, A. M., & Johnson, V. (2010). When callings are calling: Crafting work and leisure in pursuit of unanswered occupational callings. *Organization Science, 21,* 973–994. doi:10.1287/orsc.1090.0497

Berg, J. M., Wrzesniewski, A., & Dutton, J. E. (2010). Perceiving and responding to challenges in job crafting at different ranks: When proactivity requires adaptivity. *Journal of Organizational Behavior, 31,* 158–186. doi:10.1002/job.645

Bunderson, J. S., & Thompson, J. A. (2009). The call of the wild: Zookeepers, callings, and the double-edged sword of deeply meaningful work. *Administrative Science Quarterly, 54,* 32–57. doi:10.2189/asqu.2009.54.1.32

Caldwell, D. F., & O'Reilly, C. A. (1990). Measuring person–job fit with a profile-comparison process. *Journal of Applied Psychology, 75,* 648–657. doi:10.1037/0021-9010.75.6.648

Chiaburu, D. S., & Harrison, D. A. (2008). Do peers make the place? Conceptual synthesis and meta-analysis of coworker effects on perceptions, attitudes, OCBs and performance. *Journal of Applied Psychology, 93,* 1082–1103. doi:10.1037/0021-9010.93.5.1082

Clegg, C., & Spencer, C. (2007). A circular and dynamic model of the process of job design. *Journal of Occupational and Organizational Psychology, 80,* 321–339.

Clifton, D. O., & Harter, J. K. (2003). Investing in strengths. In K. Cameron, J. Dutton, & R. Quinn (Eds.), *Positive organizational scholarship: Foundations of a new discipline* (pp. 111–121). San Francisco, CA: Berrett-Koehler.

The Conference Board. (2010). U.S. job satisfaction at lowest level in two decades [Press release]. Retrieved from http://www.conferenceboard.org/press/pressdetail.cfm?pressid=3820

Crum, A. J., & Langer, E. (2007). Mind-set matters: Exercise and the placebo effect. *Psychological Science, 18,* 165–171. doi:10.1111/j.1467-9280.2007.01867.x

Csikszentmihalyi, M. (1990). *Flow: The psychology of optimal experience.* New York, NY: Harper & Row.

Dutton, J., & Heaphy, E. (2003). The power of high-quality connections at work. In K. Cameron, J. Dutton, & R. E. Quinn (Eds.), *Positive organizational scholarship* (pp. 263–278). San Francisco, CA: Berrett-Koehler.

Dweck, C. S. (1999). *Self-theories: Their role in motivation, personality, and development.* Philadelphia, PA: Psychology Press.

Dweck, C. (2007). *Mindset: The new psychology of success.* New York, NY: Random House.

Fletcher, J. K. (1998). Relational practice: A feminist reconstruction of work. *Journal of Management Inquiry, 7,* 163–186. doi:10.1177/105649269872012

French, M. (2010). Job crafting. In R. Watkins & D. Leigh (Eds.), *Handbook of improving performance in the workplace: Vol. 2. Selecting and implementing performance interventions* (pp. 555–568). Hoboken, NJ: Wiley.

Frese, M., & Fay, D. (2001). Personal initiative: An active performance concept for work in the 21st century. *Research in Organizational Behavior, 23,* 133–187. doi:10.1016/S0191-3085(01)23005-6

Fried, Y., Grant, A., Levi, A., Hadani, M., & Slowik, L. (2007). Job design in temporal context: A career dynamics perspective. *Journal of Organizational Behavior, 28,* 911–927. doi:10.1002/job.486

Gerstner, C. R., & Day, D. V. (1997). Meta-analytic review of leader–member exchange theory: Correlates and construct issues. *Journal of Applied Psychology, 82,* 827–844. doi:10.1037/0021-9010.82.6.827

Ghitulescu, B. E. (in press). Making change happen: The impact of work context on adaptive and proactive behavior. *Journal of Applied Behavioral Science.*

Grant, A. M. (2007). Relational job design and the motivation to make a prosocial difference. *Academy of Management Review, 32,* 393–417. doi:10.5465/AMR.2007.24351328

Grant, A. M. (2008). The significance of task significance: Job performance effects, relational mechanisms, and boundary conditions. *Journal of Applied Psychology, 93,* 108–124. doi:10.1037/0021-9010.93.1.108

Grant, A. M., & Ashford, S. J. (2008). The dynamics of proactivity at work. *Research in Organizational Behavior, 28,* 3–34. doi:10.1016/j.riob.2008.04.002

Grant, A. M., & Parker, S. K. (2009). Redesigning work design theories: The rise of relational and proactive perspectives. *The Academy of Management Annals, 3,* 317–375. doi:10.1080/19416520903047327

Hackman, J. R., & Oldham, G. R. (1976). Motivation through the design of work: Test of a theory. *Organizational Behavior and Human Performance, 16,* 250–279. doi:10.1016/0030-5073(76)90016-7

Hackman, J. R., & Oldham, G. R. (1980). *Work redesign.* Reading, MA: Addison-Wesley.

Heaphy, E., & Dutton, J. (2008). Positive social interactions and the human body at work: Linking organizations and physiology. *Academy of Management Review, 33,* 137–162. doi:10.5465/AMR.2008.27749365

Ibarra, H. (2003). *Working identity: Unconventional strategies for reinventing your career.* Boston, MA: Harvard Business School Press.

Ilgen, D. R., & Hollenbeck, J. R. (1991). The structure of work: Job design and roles. In M. D. Dunnette & L. M. Hough (Eds.), *Handbook of industrial and organizational psychology* (2nd ed., Vol. 2, pp. 165–207). Palo Alto, CA: Consulting Psychologists Press.

Johnson, R. W., Butrica, B., & Mommaerts, C. (2010). *Work and retirement patterns for the G.I. Generation, Silent Generation, and Early Boomers: Thirty years of change* (Discussion Paper 10-04). Retrieved from Urban Institute website: http://www.urban.org/publications/412175.html

Kristof-Brown, A., Zimmerman, R., & Johnson, E. (2005). Consequences of individuals' fit at work: A meta-analysis of person–job, person–

organization, person–group, and person–supervisor fit. *Personnel Psychology, 58,* 281–342. doi:10.1111/j.1744-6570.2005.00672.x

Langer, E. J. (1989). *Mindfulness.* Reading, MA: Addison-Wesley.

Laschinger, H. K. S., Purdy, N., & Almost, J. (2007). The impact of leader–member exchange quality, empowerment, and core self-evaluation on nurse manager's job satisfaction. *The Journal of Nursing Administration, 37,* 221–229. doi:10.1097/01.NNA.0000269746.63007.08

Leana, C., Appelbaum, E., & Shevchuk, I. (2009). Work process and quality of care in early childhood education: The role of job crafting. *Academy of Management Journal, 52,* 1169–1192. doi:10.5465/AMJ.2009.47084651

Levinthal, D. A., & Warglien, M. (1999). Landscape design: Designing for local action in complex worlds. *Organization Science, 10,* 342–357. doi:10.1287/orsc.10.3.342

Lilius, J. M., Worline, M. C., Maitlis, S., Kanov, J., Dutton, J. E., & Frost, P. (2008). The contours and consequences of compassion at work. *Journal of Organizational Behavior, 29,* 193–218. doi:10.1002/job.508

Lyons, P. (2008). The crafting of jobs and individual differences. *Journal of Business and Psychology, 23,* 25–36. doi:10.1007/s10869-008-9080-2

Mischel, W., & Shoda, Y. (1995). A cognitive–affective system theory of personality: Reconceptualizing situations, dispositions, dynamics, and invariance in personality structure. *Psychological Review, 102,* 246–268. doi:10.1037/0033-295X.102.2.246

Morgeson, F., Dierdorff, E., & Hmurovic, J. (2010). Work design in situ: Understanding the role of occupational and organizational context. *Journal of Organizational Behavior, 31,* 351–360. doi:10.1002/job.642

Oettingen, G., Pak, H., & Schnetter, K. (2001). Self-regulation of goal setting: Turning free fantasies about the future into binding goals. *Journal of Personality and Social Psychology, 80,* 736–753. doi:10.1037/0022-3514.80.5.736

Pratt, M., & Ashforth, B. (2003). Fostering meaningfulness in working and at work. In K. Cameron, J. E. Dutton, & R. E. Quinn (Eds.), *Positive organizational scholarship: Foundations of a new discipline* (pp. 309–327). San Francisco, CA: Berrett-Koehler.

Ragins, B., & Kram, K. (2007). *The handbook of mentoring at work: Theory, research, and practice.* Thousand Oaks, CA: Sage.

Roberts, K. (1990). Some characteristics of one type of high reliability organization. *Organization Science, 1,* 160–176. doi:10.1287/orsc.1.2.160

Rosso, B., Dekas, K., & Wrzesniewski, A. (2010). On the meaning of work: A theoretical integration and review. *Research in Organizational Behavior, 30,* 91–127. doi:10.1016/j.riob.2010.09.001

Twenge, J. M. (2006). *Generation Me: Why today's young Americans are more confident, assertive, entitled—and more miserable than ever before.* New York, NY: Free Press.

Vallerand, R. J., Blanchard, C., Mageau, G. A., Koestner, R., Ratelle, C., Léonard, M., . . . Marsolais, J. (2003). Les passions de l'âme: On obsessive and harmonious passion. *Journal of Personality and Social Psychology, 85,* 756–767. doi:10.1037/0022-3514.85.4.756

Weick, K. E. (1984). Small wins: Redefining the scale of social problems. *American Psychologist, 39,* 40–49. doi:10.1037/0003-066X.39.1.40

Wrzesniewski, A., Berg, J. M., & Dutton, J. E. (2010, June). Turn the job you have into the job you want. *Harvard Business Review, 88,* 114–117.

Wrzesniewski, A., & Dutton, J. E. (2001). Crafting a job: Revisioning employees as active crafters of their work. *Academy of Management Review, 26,* 179–201.

Wrzesniewski, A., Dutton, J. E., & Debebe, G. (2003). Interpersonal sensemaking and the meaning of work. *Research in Organizational Behavior, 25,* 93–135. doi:10.1016/S0191-3085(03)25003-6

Wrzesniewski, A., Rozin, P., & Bennett, G. (2002). Working, playing, and eating: Making the most of most moments. In C. L. M. Keyes & J. Haidt (Eds.), *Flourishing: Positive psychology and the life well-lived* (pp. 185–204). Washington, DC: American Psychological Association. doi:10.1037/10594-008

William A. Kahn and Steven Fellows

Employee Engagement and Meaningful Work 5

T he concept of engagement was developed to explain what traditional studies of work motivation overlooked—namely, that employees offer up different degrees and dimensions of themselves according to some internal calculus that they consciously and unconsciously compute (Kahn, 1990). Traditional motivation studies implicitly assumed that workers were either on or off; that is, on the basis of external rewards and intrinsic factors, they were either motivated to work or not, and this was a relatively steady state that they inhabited (e.g., Taylor, 1911; Vroom, 1964). The engagement concept is framed on the premise that workers are more complicated than this. Like actors, they make choices about how much of their real selves they would bring into and use to inform their role performances (Kahn, 1990). They might truly express themselves, to the extent the role allows, or they might not, with varying degrees of expression in between. Rather than label workers as motivated or not, these personal movements

http://dx.doi.org/10.1037/14183-006
Purpose and Meaning in the Workplace, B. J. Dik, Z. S. Byrne, and M. F. Steger (Editors)

into or out of role performances could change a great deal as various conditions shift. The engagement concept captures the process of moving into and out of roles.

When people engage, they move toward that which matters to them. Indeed, the word itself conjures images of movement: We engage the clutch in a car, which moves it out of neutral and allows progression; we become engaged in marriage, betrothing ourselves to a life together with a partner; we engage in conversation, moving toward insight and connection with others. Engagement is thus movement; it is the bringing of one's self into something outside the self. This movement can be fleeting: An individual cares briefly about a task and engages in it and then recedes, falling back into a steady state of some partial role performance. Engagement can also be the steady state, punctuated by interludes of relative disengagement. Engagement at work can thus be the foreground in a worker's life, or it can be at the edges of that life, moving to the front only at particular moments that flicker and fade. The difference between where engagement resides in workers depends on the largeness of that which matters to them.

Individual purposes are the broader context in which to ground our understanding of engagement and meaningful work. Engagement that represents the foreground of a worker's role performances requires individuals to feel some connection between the work that they do and larger meanings and purposes to which they subscribe (Baumeister, 1991; Hackman, 2002). As the theologian Frederick Buechner (1993) wrote, vocation "is the place where your deep gladness and the world's deep hunger meet" (p. 95). This connection is a necessary condition, without which engagement is short-lived. But this sense of connection between the particular (job, role, tasks) and the general (vocational calling) is not sufficient to sustain employee engagement (Dik & Duffy, 2009). The particular nature of the organizational context matters. Vocations can be pursued from any number of roles and organizations, as individuals seek out settings in which they can most clearly and easily do what they are called to do in the world (Berg, Grant, & Johnson, 2010). Certain factors matter a great deal here, as they play out in the context of a worker's particular job, role, group, and organization.

In this chapter, we review the nature of employee engagement and then turn to the factors that shape the extent to which particular work settings offer necessary conditions for engagement to exist. Our discussion of these factors combines the theoretical and the practical. We discuss the relevant concepts and research and point to the ways in which those concepts shape what actually occurs in work settings.

What Engagement Looks Like

Imagine a police detective working a case. A jewelry store merchant has been robbed. The case is straightforward—no dead bodies, no ex-lovers turning up as suspects, no shadowy corporate deals in the background. Our detective is fine; this is not a story of his redemption from grief, drink, or idealism. It is just a large robbery and a competent detective.

The detective arrives at the diamond store. He moves thoughtfully through the store, noticing what there is to notice: the empty jewelry cases, unbroken glass, shattered video camera in the corner, nervous clerk, distraught store owner, muddy footprint near the backdoor exit. The detective directs a colleague to check for fingerprints, take a picture of the footprint, and see whether the video camera caught anything on tape. The detective moves toward the clerk, who nervously takes a step back until she is pressed against a display case. The detective smiles, asks whether she's OK, and is met with an unsure nod. The detective gently asks questions, nods encouragingly, takes notes, offers tissues when the clerk cries, reassures, asks more questions, hands her a card with his mobile number, and turns toward the store owner.

Our detective spends the rest of the day following up leads, considering various scenarios that might explain the ease with which the robbery occurred, with no witnesses, broken doors, and the theft of only the most valuable diamonds. He keeps replaying parts of the interview with the clerk in his mind, nagged by a certain feeling—a hunch—that he was being played, perhaps; that she was a shade too upset. He calls the store owner to ask for personnel records. He brings in another detective who knows the neighborhood in which the clerk had grown up before moving to a nicer section of the city. The detective's supervisor is unhappy with using two squad members on the case, but our detective insists, explaining his hunch. The supervisor nods his approval. Four days later, after much digging through arrest records, the two detectives piece together a possible trail linking the store clerk and a known criminal from her old neighborhood—a distant cousin, it turns out, with whom she had attended grade school before he graduated to armed robbery. One thing leads to another: The footprint places the subject at the store; the clerk, confronted, breaks into sobbing confession; and the detective makes the arrests. Our detective smiles and goes back to work.

This scenario offers us a way to think about engagement at work. Although we are not all detectives, we all have projects to do, problems to solve, and work that must get done. Across the vast array of industries and jobs, our engagement can look remarkably similar to that of our detective. Indeed, we know engagement mostly by what people actually do—the actions that they take when presented with tasks. The most clearly observable behaviors that suggest engagement are people's efforts. We believe that people are engaged when we see them working hard, putting in effort, and staying involved. They truly show up for their work. They remain focused on what they are doing while at work. They strive to move their work forward. They put energy into what they are doing. Our detective showed such behaviors. He worked hard on the case. He followed leads, interviewed witnesses, researched files, and made calls. He followed the evidence to where it led and kept trying to move the case ahead. We can be similarly engaged in other sorts of jobs. Programmers, bankers, teachers, consultants, project leaders—we all have tasks that we can focus on, put energy into, try and move forward, and work hard on (Bateman & Porath, 2003). We stay with our work and are not easily distracted. We keep plugging away at it. We work to solve whatever problems and puzzles are getting in the way.

Yet engagement is not simply about the vigor with which people work, their high levels of involvement. It is about putting ourselves— our real selves—into the work (Kahn, 1990, 1992). This begins but does not end with effort. Our real selves show up when we say what we think and feel, in the service of doing the work the best way that we know how. Our detective did this when he pushed on his supervisor to assign another detective to help him. When we deeply care about what we are doing and are committed to doing the best that we can, we feel compelled to speak rather than remain silent (Hirschman, 1970). We use our voices. Voice is part of engagement (Beugré, 2010). When we are engaged, we express that self rather than defend or withdraw it from view. An accountant tells her supervisor that she does not feel comfortable using a certain financial technique that seems to hide certain budgetary practices. A project manager tells a colleague that he is frustrated by the lack of communication across departments. A consultant tells a client that she feels like she is wasting her time and their money on a project that has no senior management support. These workers are expressing rather than hiding their thoughts and feelings.

We fully show up at work when we allow the full range of our senses to inform what we do. Our detective honored rather than dismissed a nagging feeling about the store clerk, in effect bringing all of his self to his work. This bringing of the self is different than following routines and procedures to go through required paces, processes that can require little of workers except their simply showing up at work and putting in their time (Ashforth & Fried, 1988). The detective placed his ideas, his hunches, and his feelings into the case that he was trying to solve. It mattered that it was this detective working on this case. It mattered that something about the situation—how the clerk was pressed against the unbroken jewelry case, a tightening of her face, her refusal to look at the store owner—flickered into a feeling and then a thought in the detective, which later turned into a hunch that he followed. When we are fully engaged, we bring to our tasks our personal connections to the work, our commitment to see tasks through to completion in ways that enliven and gladden us (Hall, 1993; Tulku, 1978). This matters to the work. For example, a line worker on the manufacturing floor senses that the wooden handles he creates on the lathe are smaller than usual in his hands. On a break, he checks the specifications on the machine and discovers that the settings are wrong. A bank clerk senses something odd in the manner of someone making a large wire transfer and takes an extra moment to examine paperwork that proves identity theft. These workers are bringing a depth of which they may not even be fully aware to bear on their work (Kahn, 1992).

What It Is Like to Be Engaged

Being present is not simply physical, although it begins with people showing up at work. Being present is psychological (Kahn, 1992). Such presence is experienced along four salient dimensions that describe people who are fully engaged: attentive, connected, integrated, and absorbed.

ATTENTIVE

When workers are engaged, they are alive to what is around them in their immediate surroundings. They pay attention (Langer, 1984). We might have seen this if we looked closely enough at the detective. His eyes were clear and focused; his gaze was steady on colleagues, witnesses, and suspects. He was absorbed in what he was discovering—the physical evidence in the jewelry store, the nervousness of the store clerk, his own unease about her story—and open to what he might find. He did not make the case routine. He remained open and attentive to whatever he could discover.

CONNECTED

Engaged workers feel joined with something outside themselves. They are connected to some larger mission or purpose, infusing them as they occupy roles and perform tasks (Bunderson & Thompson, 2009). They feel connected to others who are working toward similar ends. Such connections sustain people as they pursue their vocations (Dutton & Heaphy, 2003; Kahn, 1998). Our detective's engagement was thus partly a matter of feeling joined with others on a mission—solving a crime, seeking justice, repairing the world, or however he would have defined it—that offered him a sense of purpose. The sense of connection keeps such engagement a very real possibility for people as they go about their work.

INTEGRATED

Engaged workers make themselves—their thoughts, feeling, intuitions, energies—fully available to the work that they do. The detective took various pieces of information, gathered from the crime scene and from his own sense of unease, and followed them as he would a path. The path derived from his ability to piece together bits of information that he gleaned in various ways—from analysis, intuition, and feeling. This bringing together of multiple aspects of the self is an integrative process. People feel integrated rather than internally split off from their roles when they are able to bring into their work role performances whatever material they need to draw on (Wrzesniewski & Dutton, 2001). The lack of engagement involves the sense of standing apart and away from one's actions, as if observing some other person; energies are thus split between observing and acting (Kahn, 1992).

ABSORBED

Engaged workers also feel absorbed by and into the work that they are doing in ways that resemble the idea of flow (Csikszentmihalyi, 1990). It is as if they have set themselves on quests that constantly (pre)occupy them. Our detective was absorbed in such a fashion. Even as he worked on other cases, a part of him remained focused on the store robbery, sifting through information, reflecting on bits of information, acknowledging his hunch, and remaining optimistic. Such ongoing awareness is a matter of being absorbed by a situation, even as we work on other parts of our jobs (Rothbard, 2001). The lack of absorption is remaining distant and apart from a situation, an absenting of our selves.

Conditions for Engagement

Remaining present is not a simple matter. It requires a depth of intensity and focus that cannot be constantly sustained. Workers need intervals, moments of absence, of being away. They need space in which to recharge before their next engagements (Maslach, Schaufeli, & Leiter, 2001). The brief scenario of our detective did not show those moments—long lunches reading the sports pages, talking with his teen-ager about her use of the car, sitting through an interminable presentation at headquarters, flipping through a magazine while waiting to testify in another case. These moments are necessary, but they are not entirely sufficient. People do not become engaged simply because they get enough breaks, just as runners do not train simply by scheduling intervals of running and resting. Engagement is a far more delicate phenomenon, trickier to create and sustain.

We should note here that there are no guarantees about when individual workers will fully engage. There are some workers who may never become engaged and others who will do so easily and often. Such variations in engagement may be explained partly by individual differences. People's temperaments, life experiences, support systems, and aptitudes (to name a few) are important determinants of their level of engagement at a particular point in time (Macey & Schneider, 2008; Staw, Bell, & Clausen, 1986; Wildermuth, 2010). People's shifting needs and desires, related to phases in adult development and career progression, also shape the weights they place on the variables that determine the nature and extent of their engagements (Hall & Schneider, 1972; Levinson, Darrow, Klein, Levinson, & McKee, 1978). So too are deeply ingrained ways in which individuals experience and relate to their environments, manage relationships, and express themselves: personality dimensions that can close down or open up workers to the possibility of fully engaging in their tasks (Macey & Schneider, 2008; Rabinowitz & Hall, 1977; Wildermuth, 2010). Yet the extremes of individual differences, in which workers will never be able to engage because of their temperaments, are relatively rare. In truth, most workers are waiting, some optimistically and others pessimistically, for leaders to create the conditions under which it is more likely that they will choose to engage and feel as if they have made the right choice. The original research on engagement indicated three such conditions: meaningfulness, safety, and availability (Kahn, 1990).

In the remainder of this chapter, we focus on the first condition for employee engagement: the extent to which workers experience meaningfulness at work. In some respects, the other conditions are, like Herzberg's (1968) hygiene factors, necessary but not sufficient for motivation to exist. Workers need to be psychologically available if they are to engage. And they need to feel safe enough to say what they think and feel. But to be available and safe is not sufficient; there must also be the internal drive, the desire to engage. The sense of meaningfulness is that drive. It is, therefore, quite important for managers, researchers, consultants, counselors, coaches, and academics to know as much as possible about what factors are most likely to enable workers to feel a sense of meaningfulness.

Sources of Meaning

Research and theory point to various sources of meaning that are likely to influence people's choices to engage at work. These sources are of two types: *foundational,* which focus on the nature of the work role and its implications for workers; and *relational,* which focus on the relationships that workers build with others and the implications for their work experiences. This is not to suggest that all sources of meaning are neatly contained within one category or the other; after all, the way people construct the meaning of the tasks they perform is often the result of a collective understanding developed with coworkers (Wrzesniewski, Dutton, & Debebe, 2003). For ease of discussion, however, we address these sources of meaning according to the worker's perception of whether they reside primarily in the work itself or as part of associated interpersonal connections.

FOUNDATIONAL SOURCES OF MEANING

Attractive Identities

People value work roles by which they create identities that matter to them. An identity is a way to be known to oneself and to the world. Identities that matter to people are those that fit with how they wish to think about themselves and be thought of by others (Dutton, Dukerich, & Harquail, 1994; Ibarra, 1999). Our detective, for example, may gather meaning from his identity as a protector, as an officer of the law, or as serving the powerless and the wronged. This identity is meaningful because it allows him to act in accordance with his values and beliefs, such as the importance of lawfulness over lawlessness. Similarly, a computer programmer may derive meaning from her identity as a cutting-edge problem solver, reflecting her belief that technology can positively influence the world. Work identities that matter are those that enable us to see our lives as having meaning (Pratt & Ashforth, 2003).

Challenging Work

The actual tasks that workers perform can challenge them, forcing them to develop skills, deepen knowledge, and learn new behaviors. Or tasks can be routine, requiring little of people except to do, over and again, what they already know how to do. Researchers know a great deal about how to structure roles, tasks, and authority in ways that challenge workers to expand repertoires of knowledge and skills (Hackman & Oldham, 1976, 1980; Lawler & Hall, 1970). Routine tasks tend to dull our senses; they ask little of us other than to go through motions that we have already long mastered; they lead to boredom and disengagement. Yet tasks that are too complex and challenging lead to despair, for we have no hope of completing them. The work that challenges us is neither thoroughly boring nor impossible (Hackman, 2002; McClelland, 1985). It allows us to grow in ways that we have not yet grown. It calls on us to use different parts of ourselves in the way that a new sport calls on both familiar and unfamiliar movements. In that challenge lies meaning.

Clear Roles

People are more likely to find meaning in roles that are clear rather than ambiguous (Ivancevich & Donnelly, 1974). Our detective knew what his role was: He was the lead investigator on the robbery case, responsible for following police procedures in charging those responsible for a crime. He knew what his tasks were: to collect evidence and follow leads, narrow possibilities, develop a theory of the case borne out by facts, and act on that theory. He knew what his authority was and the decisions that he could make with and without consultation and permission. Such clarity—of role, tasks, authority—creates a clearly defined path down which the detective could walk. The lack of such clarity takes away from the meaning of our work. When people are not sure of what they are supposed to do, the steps that they need to take, or whether they have the authority to make decisions, they are less likely to bring their selves into their work (Rizzo, House, & Lirtzman, 1970). They hold themselves in reserve, unwilling to risk wasting their efforts.

Meaningful Rewards

Unavoidably, the meaning that people ascribe to their work is shaped by the rewards that they get from that work. Much organizational research over the years has explored the nature and impact of rewards on effort, motivation, and job performance (e.g., Herzberg, 1968; Kerr, 1975; Pfeffer & Lawler, 1980). We thus know a great deal about meaningful rewards. Workers need to feel that there is a clear and fair relation between the work that they do and the resulting extrinsic rewards, such as money, promotions, status, and visibility (Vroom, 1964). They also need a sense of intrinsic reward from the work that they do—that is, that the work feels good to do and complete, that they are recognized and valued by others, and that what they do makes a difference (Gagné & Deci, 2005; Herzberg, 1968). They need to feel that the measurement systems by which they are evaluated provide clear, sensible, and justifiable feedback and lead to fair outcomes (Hackman, 2002). When these dimensions are missing, it makes it difficult for people to see the meaning in what they do. If our detective felt that the rewards were few in his work—being passed over for promotion in favor of less deserving but better connected colleagues, receiving pay raises that did not keep up with costs of living, getting evaluations that focused on paperwork completed more than cases solved—he would be less likely to find the meaning in his work.

RELATIONAL SOURCES OF MEANING

Voices That Are Heard

People at work derive meaning from knowing that their voices matter. We use our voices to offer opinions, ideas, suggestions, warnings, agreements, and support (Beugré, 2010). Our detective used his voice. He said what he thought to his supervisor. He shared his developing theory of the case with his colleague. He instructed others to gather evidence. His ideas were taken seriously. When our voices are heard, we feel a sense of efficacy: a sense that what we say is valued and valuable, makes a difference to others and to our work, and has influence around us (Spreitzer, 1995). When people's voices are not heard, they react accordingly. They stop saying what they think and feel. They use their voices badly rather than well, with cynicism, rumors, and misinformation. People are remarkably adaptive. When their voices are dismissed, they stop wasting them, as one would stop talking to those clearly not listening (Martinko & Gardner, 1982; Peterson, Maier, & Seligman, 1993). When their voices are taken into account, they keep using them, to inform, help, and contribute. For example, the bank teller suggests a different way to exchange currency and is greeted with appreciation. The project manager warns of an impending conflict with a supplier and heads off a potential snafu. When people speak and are heard, they feel as if they matter; they feel meaningful (Axelrod, 2000).

Important Work Relationships

Work relationships serve a number of functions. Our colleagues can help us get work done. They can offer personal support (Kahn, 2001). They can provide mentoring (Kram, 1985). They can help us make sense of ambiguous situations (Weick, 1995). And they can help provide us with a sense of meaning (Wrzesniewski et al., 2003). Our work lives matter to us more when we feel connected to others at work and less when we feel isolated and alone (Baumeister & Leary, 1995; McClelland, 1985). Work has more meaning when we are joined with others—doing things together, spurring one another on, having fun, and learning about ourselves in relation to others (Dutton & Heaphy, 2003). It becomes meaningful as well when we are treated with a certain amount of dignity, respect, and appreciation by others with whom we work—particularly by supervisors and other figures of authority (Bandura, 1986; Kinch, 1963). Our detective seemed to experience this dignity in relation to colleagues who respect him and a supervisor who trusts him. Those relationships offered the space and the support in which he could do his job. Such relationships are an important source of meaning.

Competent Supervision

Workers' relations with their supervisors have a demonstrated impact on their experiences of their work (Sparrowe & Liden, 2005). Competent supervisors are trustworthy (Brower, Lester, Korsgaard, & Dineen, 2009), supportive (Rafferty & Griffin, 2006), evenhanded (Pillai, Schriesheim, & Williams, 1999), and thoughtful (Kegan, 1994). As supervisors give employees the space to pursue their own ideas—as the supervisor of our detective did—those employees are likely to feel challenged in their work, experience their voices as valued, and have their identities affirmed (Hackman, 2002). The lack of competent supervision undermines the meaning that employees find in their work. Supervisors who remain too close (micromanaging, untrusting, suffocating) and those who remain too distant (ignoring, unavailable, abandoning) in relation to their employees too often sap the meaning of the work from employees (Seltzer & Numerof, 1988). Competent supervision draws employees more tightly into their work, offering them an attachment figure to whom they can turn when they need support and insight and a sense of connectedness to the larger meaning of what they do (Podolny, Khurana, & Hill-Popper, 2004).

Useful Interventions

To the extent that these sources of meaning are present, they enable employees to answer positively the question that they pose to themselves, consciously or not: Is it worthwhile for me to fully engage at this moment, in the context of my role and this task? How individuals answer this question determines their willingness to put effort, energy, and focus into the enactments of their roles. When they are able to answer this question affirmatively, it is because they feel certain ways about themselves and their work: They feel useful and valued. They like who they are in their roles and what it reflects about them. They are challenged and stretched by their work. They like the results of their efforts. They feel appreciated, supported, and validated. They feel a sense of collaboration with their coworkers and that they are well led. When workers experience these things, it is more than likely that they are engaging fully in their roles at work.

The question, of course, is what supervisors, senior leaders, human resources staff, and consultants can do to ensure that employees experience these reasons to fully engage. We describe here two levels of useful interventions. The first set of interventions focuses on creating the contextual conditions under which it will become more rather than less likely that workers will perceive specific situations as worthy of their engagements. The second set of interventions focuses on ennobling individual workers—that is, engaging them in ways that call forth the deeper vocations and purposes that move them and can be expressed in the context of their roles. The first set of interventions works from the outside in, shaping the work context in ways that are inviting to workers. The second set of interventions works from the inside out, bringing forth the callings and purposes that give meaning to workers' lives and channeling these callings and purposes into the roles the workers perform. Both sets of interventions are crucial to an understanding of how engagement is created and sustained at work.

CREATING CONTEXTS

The sources of meaning described previously offer a reasonably clear outline for interventions that make it more likely that employees will engage in certain situations. They include structures that enable workers to have appropriate involvement in decisions, processes that help clarify their roles, team-based work, and effective reward systems that provide incentives for superior efforts and performances. Such structures and processes (see Table 5.1) are developed on behalf of organization members more generally. They make it more likely that all employees will move toward engaging in their roles.

The recommendations in Table 5.1 are made on the basis of the premise that the meaning workers ascribe to their role performances depends mostly on external conditions that can vary across leaders, situations, projects, and groups. Engagement is thus likely to be heavily situation based, depending on the extent to which these conditions exist. Although the recommendations are not simple to implement, they are within the realm of what supervisors, senior leaders, human resources staff, and consultants are often working on in the context of performance management processes.

ENNOBLING WORKERS

A different type of intervention involves ennobling the workers themselves—that is, treating them in ways that elevate and make noble the meanings of their work. These interventions involve calling forth the individual worker's self as it gets expressed and expanded in the course of work. This calling forth occurs in different ways (see Table 5.1). It involves bringing larger purposes—both those of workers themselves and those of their organizations—into conversations about what people are doing. This process of alerting employees to the larger purposes of their work raises people's sights up from the particular tasks that they perform and onto the larger meanings of those performances. When those meanings matter to people—when they resonate with how they wish to be in the world and how they wish to see themselves—their engagements are likely to be sustained. Their selves expand in the context of their work; work becomes the vehicle through which the selves are expressed. Workers feel as if they belong to something larger than themselves, in terms of larger missions or communities of others.

The interventions in Table 5.2 are made on the basis of the premise that the meaning that workers ascribe to their role performances depends mostly on their own willingness, abilities, and imaginations to connect what they do with who they are. Engagement in this regard is more likely to be located within individuals than in their situations. People who are more oriented toward work as a calling rather than as a job or career are more likely to make the deeper connections between their work and who they are—and thus understand their work as the context for sustained engagement (Bunderson & Thompson, 2009; Wrzesniewski, McCauley, Rozin, & Schwartz, 1997). Such workers have the capacity to frame their work as *quests*—pursuits of larger purposes in the world that give their lives a larger sense of meaning. Quests require companions. People lose their bearings; they lose their faith; they lose the larger perspective as daily events take them over. The role of supervisors, senior leaders, human resources staff, and consultants in this regard is to help keep people's quests alive. The recommended interventions are ways to do this. The interventions involve calling forth people, reminding them of who they wish to be and what they wish to accomplish in the world. The interventions ennoble workers, offering them ways to connect to and engage in being part of that which is larger than their individual selves.

Future Directions

This chapter contains implications for developing theoretical and practical knowledge about the relation between meaning and engagement. There is a great deal already known about what it means to design jobs, coordinate efforts, reward performance, and manage in ways that motivate workers. Less understood are the structures, processes, and behaviors by which the authentic selves of workers are called forth into the work that they perform. Engagement at work is not simply about the effort and vigor that people put forth. It is also about people fully employing their selves—calling forth and expressing their selves in the performance of their roles, as our detective did earlier in this chapter. For this to occur, workers' selves need to be called forth and welcomed into the contexts of their work. In considering future directions in the relation between meaning and engagement at work, we need to examine both parts of this process.

CALLING FORTH THE SELF

Calling forth the self in the context of work involves making the meaningfulness of what people do more evident as they go about their daily role performances (Pratt & Ashforth, 2003). There is more that needs to be understood, in theory and in practice, about how to actually do this. We have suggested in this chapter, for example, the importance of ongoing conversations at work that bring to the surface the identity-related dimensions of people's work. The premise is straightforward: The more that people talk about how their identities are or might be expressed through their work, the more mindful they will be about engaging meaningfully in their work. There are practical questions here related to how such conversations can be developed and sustained. There are theoretical questions as well, related to the relation between such identity conversations and the nature of performance management, career development, and mentoring.

It is also important to develop knowledge about a different sort of ongoing conversation by which workers are reminded of the meaning and impact of what they do in the world. It is through these conversations that workers are likely to expand the narrowed focus that they often adopt as they solve particular problems in specific situations. The questions here focus on the practical dimensions of creating and sustaining such conversations—who participates, in which settings, with what framing, and with what follow-up. There is also more research to be done in the promising area of job crafting, which focuses on expanding the task and relational dimensions of jobs in ways that create larger senses of meaning and impact for workers (Wrzesniewski & Dutton, 2001). It is through these efforts that we can increasingly develop knowledge about the nature of the conversations that sustain meaning and engagement.

WELCOMING THE SELF

Welcoming the self of the worker into the context of his or her work is necessary to sustain the meaning of that work and therefore engagement. This formulation goes against the implicit assumption that workers' orientation toward the work is a matter of individual temperament, histories, personality dimensions, and the like. Bellah, Madsen, Sullivan, Swidler, and Tipton (1985) identified three work orientations. People can view work as a *job*, focusing primarily on the material benefits of work; as a *career*, focusing on the rewards related to promotions; and as a *calling*, focusing on the fulfillment associated with doing the work. These three orientations are located within individuals and are relatively immutable, perhaps changing in the context of adult development but otherwise reasonably stable within individuals. It is possible, however, that there can be some movement here; that is, workers with job or career orientations might well be able to bring themselves into calling orientations and thereby find more meaning in their work (Wrzesniewski, 2003).

The shift toward the calling orientation is likely to involve coaxing forth, welcoming, and validating the moments when workers venture past the boundaries of their given roles and infuse their selves more deeply into their work. Any movement that individuals make toward self-expression, the enlarging of jobs and job crafting, and the conversations by which they seek to understand or explore the larger purposes and impact of their work must be encouraged and validated. How such positive reinforcement occurs, who provides it, and in what systematic structures and processes all need to be understood on a practical dimension. A theoretical question involves the extent to which supervisors, leaders, human resources personnel, and peers are the appropriate locus of intervention efforts, given the nature of their roles and the nuanced relationship between the individual development of workers and the management of their performance. The processes by which workers make sense of their work experiences, link their efforts to larger purposes, and create and sustain the deeper meanings of their work are inherently social (Wrzesniewski et al., 2003). How this occurs in practice is worth examining more closely.

Conclusion

Engagement at work is intimately related to the meaning of that work for people. People can work really hard at a job. They can show up regularly and put in long hours. But real engagement requires a sense that the work matters in some fashion, that it is deeply meaningful. Leaders and supervisors, consultants and human resources staff, and peers all have the potential to create the settings in which such deeper, larger meanings can surface in ways that inspire workers to explore their relations to such meanings. We have suggested in this chapter the nature of useful interventions—creating the contexts in which the

TABLE 5.1

Focus on the Workplace: Creating Contexts

Recommendations	Tested in practice	Derived from theory	Supported by research
Create structures and processes to link employees' roles and tasks to larger missions and purposes.[a]	✓	✓	✓
Develop and maintain clear expectations about employees' tasks, roles, and decision-making authority.[b]	✓	✓	✓
Create transparently fair processes to reward employees and encourage outstanding efforts.[c]	✓	✓	✓
Involve employees appropriately in diagnosing and solving problems, making decisions, and implementing ideas.[d]	✓	✓	✓
Create, authorize, and support small groups and teams to take on important, prominent assignments.[e]	✓	✓	✓
Invest prominently in selecting, training, evaluating, and rewarding highly competent supervisors and leaders.[f]	✓	✓	✓

Note. [a]Bunderson & Thompson (2009); Duffy & Sedlacek (2007); Emmons (2003); Pratt & Ashforth (2003). [b]House & Rizzo (1972); Ivancevich & Donnelly (1974); Rizzo, House, & Lirtzman (1970). [c]Blader & Tyler (2009); Tyler & Blader (2003). [d]Beugré (2010); Feldman & Khademian (2003); Spreitzer (1995). [e]Burpitt & Bigoness (1997); Hackman (2002); Richardson & West (2010); Wageman (1997). [f]Bass & Avolio (1990); Segers, De Prins, & Brouwers (2010).

TABLE 5.2

Focus on the Workplace: Ennobling Workers

Recommendations	Tested in practice	Derived from theory	Supported by research
Developmental reviews that allow for ongoing discussions with supervisors about employees' sense of purpose and meaning in relation to their work and roles.[a]	✓	✓	✓
Job crafting that enables workers to expand their sense of contributions to the larger world.[b]	✓	✓	✓
Validate and value workers through the regular practice of caring behaviors, appreciative inquiry, and celebrating efforts and achievements.[c]	✓	✓	✓
Build organizational communities that provide members with the sense of belonging, connectedness, and meaningful attachments.[d]		✓	✓

Note. [a]Clifton & Harter (2003); Kegan & Lahey (2009); Schaufeli & Salanova (2010). [b]Bakker (2010); Berg, Grant, & Johnson (2010); Wrzesniewski & Dutton (2001). [c]Gable, Gonzaga, & Strachman (2006); Gable, Reis, Impett, & Asher (2004); Kahn (1993, 2001). [d]Baumeister & Leary (1995); Dutton & Heaphy (2003); Gersick, Bartunek, & Dutton (2000); Grant (2008); Reis & Gable (2003).

meanings of work are likely to be enhanced and ennobling workers so they call forth and express their own deeper selves in the context of their work. Sustained engagement is a direct function of these types of interventions insofar as they excavate the hidden depths of the meaning beneath people's daily work.

References

Ashforth, B. E., & Fried, Y. (1988). The mindlessness of organizational behaviors. *Human Relations, 41*, 305–329. doi:10.1177/001872678804100403

Axelrod, R. H. (2000). *Terms of engagement.* San Francisco, CA: Berrett-Koehler.

Bakker, A. B. (2010). Engagement and "job crafting": Engaged employees create their own great place to work. In S. Albrecht (Ed.), *Handbook of employee engagement: Perspectives, issues, research and practice* (pp. 229–244). Northampton, MA: Edward Elgar.

Bandura, A. (1986). *Social foundations of thought and action: A social cognitive theory.* Englewood Cliffs, NJ: Prentice-Hall.

Bass, B. M., & Avolio, B. J. (1990). Developing transformational leadership: 1992 and beyond. *Journal of European Industrial Training, 14*(5), 21–27. doi:10.1108/03090599010135122

Bateman, T. S., & Porath, C. (2003). Transcendent behavior. In K. S. Cameron, J. E. Dutton, & R. E. Quinn (Eds.), *Positive organizational scholarship: Foundations of a new discipline* (pp. 122–137). San Francisco, CA: Berrett-Koehler.

Baumeister, R. F. (1991). *Meanings of life.* New York, NY: Guilford Press.

Baumeister, R. F., & Leary, M. R. (1995). The need to belong: Desire for interpersonal attachment as a fundamental human motivation. *Psychological Bulletin, 117*, 497–529. doi:10.1037/0033-2909.117.3.497

Bellah, R. N., Madsen, R., Sullivan, W. M., Swidler, A., & Tipton, S. M. (1985). *Habits of the heart.* New York, NY: Harper & Row.

Berg, J. M., Grant, A. M., & Johnson, V. (2010). When callings are calling: Crafting work and leisure in pursuit of unanswered occupational callings. *Organization Science, 21*, 973–994. doi:10.1287/orsc.1090.0497

Beugré, C. (2010). Organizational conditions fostering employee engagement: The role of "voice." In S. Albrecht (Ed.), *Handbook of employee engagement: Perspectives, issues, research and practice* (pp. 174–181). Northampton, MA: Edward Elgar.

Blader, S. L., & Tyler, T. R. (2009). Testing and extending the group engagement model: Linkages between social identity, procedural justice, economic outcomes, and extrarole behavior. *Journal of Applied Psychology, 94*, 445–464. doi:10.1037/a0013935

Brower, H. H., Lester, S. W., Korsgaard, M. A., & Dineen, B. R. (2009). A closer look at trust between managers and subordinates: Understanding the effects of both trusting and being trusted on subordinate outcomes. *Journal of Management, 35,* 327–347. doi:10.1177/0149206307312511

Buechner, F. (1993). *Wishful thinking.* New York, NY: HarperCollins.

Bunderson, J. S., & Thompson, J. A. (2009). The call of the wild: Zookeepers, callings, and the double-edged sword of deeply meaningful work. *Administrative Science Quarterly, 54,* 32–57. doi:10.2189/asqu.2009.54.1.32

Burpitt, W. J., & Bigoness, W. J. (1997). Leadership and innovation among teams: The impact of empowerment. *Small Group Research, 28,* 414–423. doi:10.1177/1046496497283005

Clifton, D. O., & Harter, J. K. (2003). Investing in strengths. In K. S. Cameron, J. E. Dutton, & R. E. Quinn (Eds.), *Positive organizational scholarship: Foundations of a new discipline* (pp. 111–121). San Francisco, CA: Berrett-Koehler.

Csikszentmihalyi, M. (1990). *Flow: The psychology of optimal experience.* New York, NY: Harper & Row.

Dik, B. J., & Duffy, R. D. (2009). Calling and vocation at work: Definitions and prospects for research and practice. *The Counseling Psychologist, 37,* 424–450. doi:10.1177/0011000008316430

Duffy, R. D., & Sedlacek, W. E. (2007). The presence of and search for a calling: Connections to career development. *Journal of Vocational Behavior, 70,* 590–601. doi:10.1016/j.jvb.2007.03.007

Dutton, J. E., Dukerich, J. M., & Harquail, C. V. (1994). Organizational images and member identification. *Administrative Science Quarterly, 39,* 239–263. doi:10.2307/2393235

Dutton, J. E., & Heaphy, E. D. (2003). The power of high-quality connections. In K. S. Cameron, J. E. Dutton, & R. E. Quinn (Eds.), *Positive organizational scholarship: Foundations of a new discipline* (pp. 263–278). San Francisco, CA: Berrett-Koehler.

Emmons, R. A. (2003). Personal goals, life meaning, and virtue: Wellsprings of a positive life. In C. L. M. Keyes & J. Haidt (Eds.), *Flourishing: Positive psychology and the life well-lived* (pp. 105–128). Washington, DC: American Psychological Association. doi:10.1037/10594-005

Feldman, M. S., & Khademian, A. M. (2003). Empowerment and cascading vitality. In K. S. Cameron, J. E. Dutton, & R. E. Quinn (Eds.), *Positive organizational scholarship: Foundations of a new discipline* (pp. 343–358). San Francisco, CA: Berrett-Koehler.

Gable, S. L., Gonzaga, G. C., & Strachman, A. (2006). Will you be there for me when things go right? Supportive responses to positive event disclosures. *Journal of Personality and Social Psychology, 91,* 904–917. doi:10.1037/0022-3514.91.5.904

Gable, S. L., Reis, H. T., Impett, E. A., & Asher, E. R. (2004). What do you do when things go right? The intrapersonal and interpersonal benefits of sharing positive events. *Journal of Personality and Social Psychology, 87,* 228–245. doi:10.1037/0022-3514.87.2.228

Gagné, M., & Deci, E. L. (2005). Self-determination theory and work motivation. *Journal of Organizational Behavior, 26,* 331–362. doi:10.1002/job.322

Gersick, C. J. G., Bartunek, J., & Dutton, J. E. (2000). Learning from academia: The importance of relationships in professional life. *Academy of Management Journal, 43,* 1026–1044. doi:10.2307/1556333

Grant, A. M. (2008). Does intrinsic motivation fuel the prosocial fire? Motivational synergy in predicting persistence, performance, and productivity. *Journal of Applied Psychology, 93,* 48–58. doi:10.1037/0021-9010.93.1.48

Hackman, J. R. (2002). *Leading teams: Setting the stage for great performances.* Boston, MA: Harvard Business School Press.

Hackman, J. R., & Oldham, G. R. (1976). Motivation through the design of work: Test of a theory. *Organizational Behavior and Human Performance, 16,* 250–279. doi:10.1016/0030-5073(76)90016-7

Hackman, J. R., & Oldham, G. R. (1980). *Work redesign.* Reading, MA: Addison-Wesley.

Hall, D. (1993). *Life work.* Boston, MA: Beacon Press.

Hall, D. T., & Schneider, B. (1972). Correlates of organizational identification as a function of career pattern and organizational type. *Administrative Science Quarterly, 17,* 340–350. doi:10.2307/2392147

Herzberg, F. (1968). One more time: How do you motivate employees? *Harvard Business Review, 46*(1), 53–62.

Hirschman, A. O. (1970). *Exit, voice, and loyalty: Responses to decline in firms, organizations, and states.* Cambridge, MA: Harvard University Press.

House, R. J., & Rizzo, J. R. (1972). Role conflict and ambiguity as critical variables in a model of organizational behavior. *Organizational Behavior and Human Performance, 7,* 467–505. doi:10.1016/0030-5073(72)90030-X

Ibarra, H. (1999). Provisional selves: Experimenting with image and identity in professional adaptation. *Administrative Science Quarterly, 44,* 764–791. doi:10.2307/2667055

Ivancevich, J. M., & Donnelly, J. H. (1974). A study of role clarity and need for clarity for three occupational groups. *Academy of Management Journal, 17,* 28–36. doi:10.2307/254768

Kahn, W. A. (1990). Psychological conditions of personal engagement and disengagement at work. *Academy of Management Journal, 33,* 692–724. doi:10.2307/256287

Kahn, W. A. (1992). To be fully there: Psychological presence at work. *Human Relations, 45,* 321–349. doi:10.1177/001872679204500402

Kahn, W. A. (1993). Caring for the caregivers: Patterns of organizational caregiving. *Administrative Science Quarterly, 38,* 539–563. doi:10.2307/2393336

Kahn, W. A. (1998). Relational systems at work. *Research in Organizational Behavior, 20,* 39–76.

Kahn, W. A. (2001). Holding environments at work. *Journal of Applied Behavioral Science, 37,* 260–279. doi:10.1177/0021886301373001

Kegan, R. (1994). *In over our heads: The mental demands of modern life.* Cambridge, MA: Harvard University Press.

Kegan, R., & Lahey, L. L. (2009). *Immunity to change: How to overcome it and unlock potential in yourself and your organization.* Boston, MA: Harvard Business Press.

Kerr, S. (1975). On the folly of rewarding A while hoping for B. *Academy of Management Journal, 18,* 769–783. doi:10.2307/255378

Kinch, J. W. (1963). A formalized theory of the self-concept. *American Journal of Sociology, 68,* 481–486. doi:10.1086/223404

Kram, K. E. (1985). *Mentoring at work: Developmental relationships in organizational life.* Glenview, IL: Scott Foresman.

Langer, E. J. (1984). *Mindfulness.* Reading, MA: Addison-Wesley.

Lawler, E. E., III, & Hall, D. T. (1970). Relationship of job characteristics to job involvement, satisfaction, and intrinsic motivation. *Journal of Applied Psychology, 54,* 305–312. doi:10.1037/h0029692

Levinson, D. J., Darrow, C. N., Klein, E. B., Levinson, M. H., & McKee, B. (1978). *The seasons of a man's life.* New York, NY: Knopf.

Macey, W. H., & Schneider, B. (2008). The meaning of employee engagement. *Industrial and Organizational Psychology: Perspectives on Science and Practice, 1,* 3–30. doi:10.1111/j.1754-9434.2007.0002.x

Martinko, M. J., & Gardner, W. L. (1982). Learned helplessness: An alternative explanation for performance deficits. *Academy of Management Review, 7,* 195–204.

Maslach, C., Schaufeli, W. B., & Leiter, M. P. (2001). Job burnout. *Annual Review of Psychology, 52,* 397–422. doi:10.1146/annurev.psych.52.1.397

McClelland, D. C. (1985). *Human motivation.* Glenview, IL: Scott Foresman.

Peterson, C., Maier, S. F., & Seligman, M. E. P. (1993). *Learned helplessness: A theory for the age of personal control.* New York, NY: Oxford University Press.

Pfeffer, J., & Lawler, J. (1980). Effects of job alternatives, extrinsic rewards, and behavioral commitment on attitude toward the organization: A field test of the insufficient justification paradigm. *Administrative Science Quarterly, 25,* 38–56. doi:10.2307/2392225

Pillai, R., Schriesheim, C. A., & Williams, E. S. (1999). Fairness perceptions and trust as mediators for transformational and transactional leadership: A two-sample study. *Journal of Management, 25,* 897–933. doi:10.1177/014920639902500606

Podolny, J. M., Khurana, R., & Hill-Popper, M. (2004). Revisiting the meaning of leadership. *Research in Organizational Behavior, 26,* 1–36. doi:10.1016/S0191-3085(04)26001-4

Pratt, M. G., & Ashforth, B. E. (2003). Fostering meaningfulness in working and at work. In K. S. Cameron, J. E. Dutton, & R. E. Quinn (Eds.), *Positive organizational scholarship: Foundations of a new discipline* (pp. 309–327). San Francisco, CA: Berrett-Koehler.

Rabinowitz, S., & Hall, D. T. (1977). Organizational research on job involvement. *Psychological Bulletin, 84,* 265–288. doi:10.1037/0033-2909.84.2.265

Rafferty, A. E., & Griffin, M. A. (2006). Refining individualized consideration: Distinguishing developmental leadership and supportive leadership. *Journal of Occupational and Organizational Psychology, 79,* 37–61. doi:10.1348/096317905X36731

Reis, H. T., & Gable, S. L. (2003). Toward a positive psychology of relationships. In C. L. M. Keyes & J. Haidt (Eds.), *Flourishing: Positive psychology and the life well-lived* (pp. 129–159). Washington, DC: American Psychological Association. doi:10.1037/10594-006

Richardson, J., & West, M. A. (2010). Engaged work teams. In S. Albrecht (Ed.), *Handbook of employee engagement: Perspectives, issues, research and practice* (pp. 323–340). Northampton, MA: Edward Elgar.

Rizzo, J. R., House, R. J., & Lirtzman, S. I. (1970). Role conflict and ambiguity in complex organizations. *Administrative Science Quarterly, 15,* 150–163. doi:10.2307/2391486

Rothbard, N. P. (2001). Enriching or depleting? The dynamics of engagement in work and family roles. *Administrative Science Quarterly, 46,* 655–684. doi:10.2307/3094827

Schaufeli, W. B., & Salanova, M. (2010). How to improve work engagement? In S. Albrecht (Ed.), *Handbook of employee engagement: Perspectives, issues, research and practice* (pp. 399–415). Northampton, MA: Edward Elgar.

Segers, J., De Prins, P., & Brouwers, S. (2010). Leadership and engagement: A brief review of the literature, a proposed model, and practical implications. In S. Albrecht (Ed.), *Handbook of employee engagement: Perspectives, issues, research and practice* (pp. 149–158). Northampton, MA: Edward Elgar.

Seltzer, J., & Numerof, R. E. (1988). Supervisory leadership and subordinate burnout. *Academy of Management Journal, 31,* 439–446. doi:10.2307/256559

Sparrowe, R. T., & Liden, R. C. (2005). Two routes to influence: Integrating leader-member exchange and network perspectives. *Administrative Science Quarterly, 50,* 505–535.

Spreitzer, G. M. (1995). Psychological empowerment in the workplace: Dimensions, measurement, and validation. *Academy of Management Journal, 38,* 1442–1465. doi:10.2307/256865

Staw, B. M., Bell, N. E., & Clausen, J. A. (1986). The dispositional approach to job attitudes: A lifetime longitudinal test. *Administrative Science Quarterly, 31,* 56–77. doi:10.2307/2392766

Taylor, F. W. (1911). *The principles of scientific management.* New York, NY: Harper Brothers.

Tulku, T. (1978). *Skillful means.* Berkeley, CA: Dharma.

Tyler, T. R., & Blader, S. L. (2003). The group engagement model: Procedural justice, social identity, and cooperative behavior. *Personality and Social Psychology Review, 7,* 349–361. doi:10.1207/S15327957PSPR0704_07

Vroom, V. H. (1964). *Work and motivation.* New York, NY: Wiley.

Wageman, R. (1997). Critical success factors for creating superb self-managing teams. *Organizational Dynamics, 26,* 49–61. doi:10.1016/S0090-2616(97)90027-9

Weick, K. E. (1995). *Sensemaking in organizations.* Thousand Oaks, CA: Sage.

Wildermuth, C. (2010). The personal side of engagement: The influence of personality factors. In S. Albrecht (Ed.), *Handbook of employee engagement: Perspectives, issues, research and practice* (pp. 197–208). Northampton, MA: Edward Elgar.

Wrzesniewski, A. (2003). Finding positive meaning in work. In K. S. Cameron, J. E. Dutton, & R. E. Quinn (Eds.), *Positive organizational scholarship: Foundations of a new discipline* (pp. 296–308). San Francisco, CA: Berrett-Koehler.

Wrzesniewski, A., & Dutton, J. E. (2001). Crafting a job: Revisioning employees as active crafters of their work. *Academy of Management Review, 26,* 179–201.

Wrzesniewski, A., Dutton, J. E., & Debebe, G. (2003). Interpersonal sensemaking and the meaning of work. *Research in Organizational Behavior, 25,* 93–135. doi:10.1016/S0191-3085(03)25003-6

Wrzesniewski, A., McCauley, C., Rozin, P., & Schwartz, B. (1997). Jobs, careers, and callings: People's relations to their work. *Journal of Research in Personality, 31,* 21–33. doi:10.1006/jrpe.1997.2162

Blake E. Ashforth and Glen E. Kreiner

Profane or Profound? Finding Meaning in Dirty Work

6

> The court officers consider us bleeding hearts. They look
> down on us. We're shat on, basically . . . because the
> DAs, the cops, the judges, all the courtroom personnel,
> they all think we work for the scum, the slime. We work
> with the evil people. We're closely equated with our
> clients, in that this person is evil and therefore you're
> defending evil. They seem to forget the whole civil rights
> argument, the whole Constitution, the idea that we
> might love our country because everyone has the right
> to a fair trial and counsel and all that.
> —*A social worker (Bowe, Bowe, & Streeter, 2000, p. 416)*

There are many occupations that society tends to view as
"physically, socially or morally" tainted (Hughes, 1958,
p. 122), from funeral directors to soldiers, hospice workers to
correctional officers, and pawnbrokers to defense attorneys.
Physically tainted occupations include those that are thought
to be associated with death, garbage, and so on, or to be
performed under dangerous or pernicious conditions; *socially
tainted* occupations include those perceived as involving servility or regular contact with individuals who are themselves
stigmatized; and *morally tainted* occupations include those
that are generally viewed as "somewhat sinful or of dubious
virtue" or as using methods that are "deceptive, intrusive,
confrontational, or that otherwise defy norms of civility"
(Ashforth & Kreiner, 1999, p. 415). Because society views

http://dx.doi.org/10.1037/14183-007
Purpose and Meaning in the Workplace, B. J. Dik, Z. S. Byrne, and M. F. Steger
(Editors)

dirtiness as bad and cleanliness as good (Douglas, 1966), occupations that are physically, socially, or morally dirty tend to become stigmatized, and the individuals who belong to them come to be socially defined as "dirty workers" (Ashforth & Kreiner, 1999; Hughes, 1962).[1]

Those in dirty work occupations thus face a vexing paradox. Like most individuals, they view their occupations as identity badges and look to society for affirmation that the work they are doing is valued. And yet, even though they are performing tasks that society itself has mandated, society tends to deny them that affirmation. Accordingly, individuals in such occupations often feel whipsawed by a demanding but condemning public. Acutely aware of the stigma their occupation faces, they may labor to find positive meaning in their efforts.

This chapter is about how people doing dirty work find edifying meaning when it is so problematic and thus quite poignant. We focus on occupations that face what we have referred to elsewhere as *pervasive stigma* (Kreiner, Ashforth, & Sluss, 2006) because meaningfulness is most problematic in such cases. In pervasive stigma, both the *breadth* of perceived dirtiness (the proportion of tasks that is dirty or the centrality of that dirt to the occupational identity) and the *depth* (the degree of dirtiness and the individual's direct involvement in the dirt) are high. These are the kinds of occupations mentioned previously. Conversely, in cases where the depth of taint is high but the breadth is low (e.g., corporate PR executives spinning a scandal), it is relatively easy to compartmentalize and dismiss the stigma (e.g., Emerson & Pollner, 1976). Similarly, in cases where the breadth of taint is high but the depth is low (e.g., auto mechanics work in an environment that is dirty but not extremely so), the stigma is diluted and therefore less threatening.

We begin by reviewing the literature on dirty work. We discuss what positive meaning entails in the context of dirty work and discuss various ideological practices that are often used to imbue such work with meaning. A key point is that because meaning is both subjective and socially constructed, individuals typically have wide latitude for discerning positive meaning. We then consider managerial applications to the workplace; we focus on how organizations can proactively shape the meaning that individuals construct so as to develop edifying understandings that are consistent with the missions of their occupations and organizations.

---

[1]As noted in Ashforth and Kreiner (1999), all dirty work is stigmatized in some way. Yet, as we note later, discourses regarding the meaning of dirt vary across contexts and over time. Thus, a given amount of dirt may be construed as more stigmatizing or less stigmatizing depending on the context and period. For example, Sudnow (1967) observed that a hospital's morgue attendant always changed out of his bloodstained gown before entering the staff cafeteria, whereas physicians did not, presumably because blood was associated with death in the former and with saving life in the latter. Thus, it should be borne in mind that there is not a perfect correlation between objective dirt and subjective stigma.

Theoretical and Empirical Literature

Following Pratt and Ashforth's (2003) literature review, we define *meaningful work* as that which is perceived "by its practitioners to be . . . purposeful and significant. . . . It helps answer the question, 'Why am I here?'" (p. 311; see also Rosso, Dekas, & Wrzesniewski, 2010).[2] The qualifier "by its practitioners" is important because meaningfulness is inherently subjective and socially constructed. The element of subjectivity suggests that the search for meaningfulness is not impartial; individuals are motivated to seek salutary meaning that resonates with their personal beliefs. Thus, individuals may derive self-serving meaningfulness from their work that outsiders would find questionable, such as pimps who contend that women want to be protected and controlled by men (Ritzer & Walczak, 1986).

The element of social construction indicates that individuals typically do not create meaningfulness alone (Rosso et al., 2010); it is to some degree co-constructed. In the context of dirty work jobs, outsiders and insiders are two particular kinds of audiences that play key—but often competing—roles. Occupational outsiders help shape the meaningfulness of work, but for dirty work occupations, they can play a rather adversarial role, reminding job incumbents of their stigma and differentness from those in nontainted jobs. Conversely, occupational insiders—coworkers, managers, and occupational members in other organizations—are motivated to facilitate positive meaning for work. Indeed, dirty work occupations often develop strong subcultures (to help shield the workers from the aspersions of outsiders) with well-developed ideologies that extol the nature and necessity of the work and the characteristics of its practitioners (Ashforth & Kreiner, 1999; Lucas & Buzzanell, 2004; Trice, 1993). The sense that other insiders share the derived meaning greatly reinforces its perceived validity. For instance, Purser (2009) studied two groups of immigrant day laborers and found that, despite their ostensible similarity, each group construed itself as morally superior to the other. Moreover, because individuals equate *shared* with *valid*, groups can sustain their necessarily biased beliefs better than can lone individuals. As Brewer (1991) surmised, "What is painful at the individual level becomes a source of pride at the group level—a badge of distinction rather than a mark of shame" (p. 481).

---

[2]We use the terms *meaningfulness* and *positive meaning* interchangeably.

Although the literature on occupations, organizations, and industries is vast, empirical studies that focus on the dynamics surrounding physical, social, and/or moral taint almost always (a) target a single occupation, organization, or industry at a time, with occupational studies far outnumbering the others, and (b) use qualitative methodologies (particularly observation and interviews). This approach has led to a rich understanding of many occupations, organizations, and industries and to much inductive theorizing. What has been largely absent, however, is more integrative research that simultaneously looks at taint dynamics across multiple types and locales of dirty work, as well as quantitative research oriented toward explicitly testing taint-focused theory. Thus, much of the discussion to follow is necessarily speculative in the sense that these arguments have not been formally tested in field settings.

Our discussion is based on the *normalization model* (Ashforth & Kreiner, 1999; Ashforth, Kreiner, Clark, & Fugate, 2007; Kreiner et al., 2006), which outlines how members of dirty work occupations deal with their taint and draw positive meaning from their work. Specifically, we focus on the use of occupational ideologies—reframing, recalibrating, and refocusing, each defined later—to derive a sense of meaningfulness. Dirty work ideologies almost always strive to bridge the gulf between the occupation's stigma as dirty or bad and societal standards of clean or good. That is, the dirt is not extolled as valuable in and of itself but as a symbol of a higher purpose and significance that society should (and perhaps does) recognize. So, when a taxidermist tells a somewhat gory story about skinning a duck, the denouement is "I'll . . . make it look like it's flying away . . . like Mother Nature intended" (Bowe et al., 2000, p. 94). Ironically, in recasting dirty or bad as clean or good, dirty work ideologies uphold and reinforce the societal standards of clean or good that problematized the work in the beginning.

The *re* in reframing, recalibrating, and refocusing indicates a cognitive shift in the positive meaning that incumbents derive from dirty work. This is most clearly seen in studies of the occupational culture of various forms of dirty work, where members have collectively recast society's view of the work in more edifying terms (e.g., Applebaum, 1981; Trice, 1993), and in studies of the subsequent socialization of neophyte stigmatized workers, where individuals are taught to understand and internalize these edifying ideologies (e.g., Chappell & Lanza-Kaduce, 2010; Gusterson, 1996). However, it needs to be recognized that, at the level of the individual, there may be no *re* if the individual

■ has been brought up to internalize the ideologies (what the socialization literature refers to as *anticipatory socialization*; Merton, 1957). For example, occupations such as fishing, funeral work, and policing often run in the family such that children are exposed to and accept the edifying ideologies from a young age (e.g., Michaelson, 2010; Miller & Van Maanen, 1982).

- is innately attracted to the stigmatized features of the work. Kidder (2006) described the passion that many bike messengers feel for their dangerous job precisely because of the thrill seeking that it allows.
- rejects the ideologies. Occupational ideologies can be viewed as a social resource that the individual may or may not actually use. Bryan (1966), for instance, found that despite an occupational ideology that edified call girls at the expense of johns (clients), call girls tended to rate occupational members (although not themselves) as inferior to johns. It should be noted, however, that even if individuals reject a particular ideology as implausible, unhelpful, or unnecessary (although they may nonetheless extol it for self-persuasion and impression management purposes), they may accept other edifying ideologies or have their own idiosyncratic ideology (e.g., Fine, 1996). As a minimum, one needs to account to oneself.

Before continuing, it is important to recognize what meaningfulness is not. Meaningfulness does not include defensive tactics that enable individuals to merely cope with the stigmatized features of the work or the stigma itself (although meaning making can serve as a defensive tactic in its own right). On the basis of interviews with managers from 18 dirty work occupations, Ashforth, Kreiner, et al. (2007) described various defensive tactics, including physically avoiding stigmatizing tasks and judgmental audiences, passing as normal, using gallows humor, accepting one's situation and personal limits, condemning condemners, blaming and/or distancing from clients, and distancing from the role.[3] Although such tactics certainly abet adjustment to the work and stigma—and may even abet the social construction of positive meaning—they do not actually instill a sense of purpose and significance in the work itself.

Reframing, Recalibrating, and Refocusing

REFRAMING

This ideological practice refers to transforming the meaning of the work by infusing the means (how one does the work) or ends (for what purpose) with positive value and by neutralizing the negative value. As an example of infusing means, Mills (2007) described the appeal to truckers of

---

[3]Ashforth, Kreiner, et al. (2007) also included social comparison, which we discuss later as a major facilitator of meaningfulness.

salutary popular images of them as working-class heroes, cowboys, white knights, and kings of the road. Such images romanticize what truckers do. Similarly, the quality of the work process can be touted to emphasize positive aspects even when the work itself is dirty, such as construction workers performing exceptional craftsmanship. As an example of infusing ends, Arluke (1994) found that animal shelter workers viewed euthanasia as preferable to the risk of animals suffering through abuse or neglect.

Regarding neutralizing, Pande (2010) studied commercial surrogacy, where women are paid to carry babies to term for other individuals who then keep them as their own. One surrogate neutralized the moral stigma as follows:

> I don't think there is anything wrong with surrogacy. We need the money and they need the child. The important thing is that I am not doing anything wrong for the money—not stealing or killing anyone. And I am not even sleeping with anyone. (Pande, 2010, p. 299)

Although neutralizing does not instill edifying meaning directly, it can do so indirectly by clearing the ground for infusing. Thus, despite the fact that the surrogacy agency emphasized the contractual nature of the relationship between the surrogate and sponsoring couple, some surrogates emphasized the special bond they enjoyed with their sponsors and fantasized about a longer term relationship with their sponsor's family. The upshot of this and the other reframing processes is that the meaning of work is changed in the mind of the worker by injecting positivity and/or negating negativity.

RECALIBRATING

Recalibrating involves "adjusting the implicit standards that are invoked to assess the magnitude (how much) and/or value (how good) of a given dirty work attribute" (Ashforth & Kreiner, 1999, p. 422). For example, although less than 10% of the emergency calls in one study of firefighters pertained to fires and most of these were minor, the firefighters nonetheless strove to define their work in the heroic light of firefighting (Tracy & Scott, 2006). In contrast, the firefighters actually devalued their far more common emergency medical services (EMSs): "We'll sit and talk about a really long, complicated EMS call for a minute, but we'll talk about a little fire, say a dumpster fire, for an hour and a half" (Tracy & Scott, 2006, p. 20). Reliving firefights at the expense of EMS events reinforced the desired identity of firefighter.

Dirty work ideologies—which of course include reframing and refocusing in addition to recalibrating—often draw on wider societal discourses about what is considered valuable (Grandy, 2008; Tracy & Scott, 2006; Wicks, 2002). Tracy and Scott (2006) argued that one reason firefighters have a much more positive reputation than correctional officers is that firefighting dovetails with a privileged discourse of masculine physical prowess and bravery, whereas correctional work dovetails with a devalued discourse of feminine caregiving. Moreover, "many of the studies that associate dirty work and strong organizational culture and identification are based on research with male dirty workers doing 'manly' jobs" (Tracy & Scott, 2006, p. 10). As an example, Tracy and Scott contrasted Ackroyd and Crowdy's (1990) study of English slaughtermen, who assigned high status to the job of killing livestock and who left work proudly wearing their bloodstained clothes, with studies of domestic workers and careworkers, who pointedly did not wear the physical dirt associated with their feminine-typed jobs as a badge of honor.

Pratt and Ashforth (2003) noted that there are likely to be a "limited number of meaning archetypes [discourses] in a given society" (p. 311). In the case of dirty work, popular discourses appear to include masculinity, performing a vital service, self-sacrifice and heroism, achievement and excellence, and attaining rewards. Yet, as the notion of subjectivity suggests, there remains some latitude in the meaningfulness that may be socially constructed and, thus, a certain arbitrariness in which discourses are invoked. For instance, door-to-door insurance selling is socially tainted by servility (e.g., flattering, not giving offense) and morally tainted by intrusive sales techniques (Leidner, 1991). It is telling that this occupation is dominated by women in Japan and is correspondingly feminine-typed—even while it is dominated by men in the United States and correspondingly cast in more masculine terms (e.g., "contests of wills"; Leidner, 1991, p. 166).

Discourses often vary greatly across contexts, including industries, national boundaries, and geographic regions. During a talk at INSEAD (Institut Européen d'Administration des Affaires) in France about dirty work, the first author mentioned the severe moral stigma that attends sex work but was quickly corrected that the stigma is far less pronounced in Europe. Discourses are also organic and can gradually change over time (Meisenbach, 2010). In the United States, for instance, recent decades have witnessed the gradual erosion of the moral taint that historically suffused gambling (Munting, 1996) and tattooing (Adams, 2009). Similarly, key events can change or punctuate discourses, such as how the pervasive images of firefighters at Ground Zero during 9/11 raised the collective consciousness about the heroic discourse associated with firefighting.

REFOCUSING

In *refocusing*, attention is deliberately shifted from the tainted aspects of the work to the nontainted aspects. Although refocusing instills positive meaning, it nonetheless leaves the stigma intact. First, attention can be refocused to nontainted *intrinsic qualities* of the work. For instance,

Chiappetta-Swanson (2005) described how some hospital nurses who performed abortions redirected their attention to the nontainted tasks of physical and emotional caregiving. Second, attention can be refocused on the *intrinsic rewards* one gains from performing the tainted tasks, such as opportunities for learning, using diverse skills, and significantly affecting others inside or outside the organization.[4] Mike Rowe, host of the TV program *Dirty Jobs,* told an interviewer,

> Nobody follows their passion into waste water treatment or window washing. You do it because you're hungry and you've found a job nobody else wants to do, and then you do it well, with a good attitude, with an entrepreneurial spirit. People are going to need to be willing to do work for work's sake and find their happiness in learning to enjoy a job that they might not have dreamed about their entire lives. (Rentilly, 2010, p. 92)

Third, attention can be refocused on the *extrinsic rewards* of work, such as pay, recognition, opportunities for promotion, and camaraderie. A paparazzo contrasted his former career as a news photographer with his current one:

> Being a news photographer, you have more of an interest in getting your pictures published than making a good living at it. And now this is the opposite, doing this paparazzi work. I don't care where the pictures go. I don't even care if anybody knows my name. Just send me the check. (Bowe et al., 2000, p. 240)

Without reframing and recalibrating, extrinsic rewards may compensate for the taint, but they do not instill intrinsic meaningfulness. This raises the question of whether intrinsic meaningfulness is actually a luxury that many individuals simply cannot afford. Ehrenreich (2001) discussed the treadmill faced by menial workers in the United States, many of whom perform low-prestige dirty work (e.g., maid, store greeter), where simply making ends meet is a major preoccupation. Indeed, many people in such jobs refer to having had few occupational choices ("What else could I do?"; e.g., Bryant & Perkins, 1982; Wicks, 2002). Although claiming that one had no choice helps to justify one's involvement in tainted work, it is a backhanded rationale because it implies one is helpless, and it fails to provide edifying meaning (it may even forestall meaning seeking, in that one can blame one's plight on external factors). For these reasons, we suspect that *no choice* does not provide a palatable justification for long-term involvement in dirty work for most individuals and that they are therefore likely to eventually find edifying compensations in the intrinsic qualities, intrinsic rewards, or extrinsic rewards of work.

---

[4]As these examples suggest, this latter form of refocusing blurs somewhat with reframing, specifically, infusing the means (how one does the work) with positive value.

Finally, it is important to note that the distinction between tainted and nontainted is often fuzzy because the taint associated with core tasks tends to color all tasks (e.g., the nurse providing emotional care-giving is nonetheless doing so in the context of an abortion) and, perhaps to a lesser extent, the intrinsic and extrinsic rewards derived from those tasks (e.g., blood money received by a private investigator). Thus, refocusing may be difficult to sustain in the absence of reframing or recalibrating the core tasks.

Major Facilitators of Reframing, Recalibrating, and Refocusing

Various factors facilitate the creation, dissemination, acceptance, and maintenance of dirty work ideologies. Here, we consider occupational prestige, social validation, and social comparison.

OCCUPATIONAL PRESTIGE

Occupational prestige reflects the "social standing of the job and job holder" (Fujishiro, Xu, & Gong, 2010, p. 2100) and is an amalgam of status, education, work quality, income, and power (Treiman, 1977). Although physical, social, and moral taint undermine an occupation's social standing, many tainted occupations nonetheless retain relatively high prestige because of the elements listed previously (Ashforth & Kreiner, 1999). Examples include dentist, social worker, funeral director, defense attorney, proctologist, and animal experimenter. Furthermore, some occupations enjoy immense popular support and thus some prestige because of their resonance with wider societal discourses about what is valued, as suggested by our earlier discussion of the valorization of masculinity (as in, e.g., the military, sports, and construction).

Prestige facilitates dirty work ideologies in two ways. First, the more prestigious the occupation, the more institutionalized and socially accepted the occupation's ideologies are likely to be (and the so-called professions and quasi professions actively promulgate their ideologies in medical schools, police academies, mortuary science programs, and so on; e.g., Cahill, 1999; Chappell & Lanza-Kaduce, 2010). Thus, few would argue with a dentist's claim to be focused on the well-being of her patients, even if people nonetheless wonder, "How can you do it?" Social acceptance of an occupation's ideology helps validate that ideology, as discussed later. In turn, an institutionalized and socially accepted dirty work ideology helps sustain the occupation's prestige.

Second, during encounters with outsiders, prestige provides what Hochschild (1983) described as a *status shield*. Hochschild coined the term to explain why male flight attendants experience more deference and less verbal abuse than do their female counterparts. The deference afforded by a status shield makes it easier for a stigmatized worker to view a given occupational ideology as valid. For example, the status shield afforded doctors enables them to ask intrusive questions and inflict pain in the course of treatment with less pushback from patients, facilitating the ideological claim to be providing important health care. Indeed, doctors define their dirty work not so much in terms of the actual medical tasks they perform but in terms of dealing with recalcitrant patients who deny the doctors their status shield (Shaw, 2004).

SOCIAL VALIDATION

A *socially validated* ideology is one that has been deemed legitimate by other individuals or groups, thereby reinforcing the ideology. As noted, if others appear to share or endorse one's beliefs, those beliefs are taken to be valid ("How could we all be wrong?"). Perhaps the most critical audience for dirty work beliefs is one's coworkers and managers because they share the occupational identity, have intimate knowledge of the work, interact regularly with one, and have a major impact on the quality of one's work experiences (Rosso et al., 2010). Indeed, those in dirty work occupations often band together as a defense against the derogatory views and voyeurism of outsiders and (as mentioned) form strong and insular subcultures. Stigmatized workers do not need to convince everyone of the meaningfulness of their work, only a sufficiently large proportion of insiders to form a social buffer against outsiders (Ackroyd & Crowdy, 1990; Ashforth, Kreiner, et al., 2007).

Nonetheless, outsiders—including other members of the organization, clients (if relevant), family and friends, the general public, and the media—remain quite important because they typically represent an ongoing challenge to the positive meaning constructed by the stigmatized workers. In regard to organizational members, Kreiner et al. (2006; see also Bergman & Chalkley, 2007) argued that the more central the dirty work occupation is to the mission of the organization (e.g., bill collectors in a collection agency vs. in a department store), the more likely that the organization itself will internalize the ideology of the occupation, thus increasing social validation. In regard to clients, because stigmatized workers are acutely aware of their stigma, they tend to be quite sensitive to signs of disrespect and thus wary in their dealings with clients. Many of the defensive tactics briefly noted earlier pertain to avoiding or handling problematic encounters with clients and the public (Ashforth, Kreiner, et al., 2007; Clair & Dufresne, 2004). Ghidina (1992) quoted a high school custodian:

> There was a guy who wouldn't pick up his towel in the locker room. All he had to do was throw it in the barrel on his way out, it was right by the door. I fixed him by putting his towels in his locker. I put three or four in there. He started picking them up after that. . . . He knew what they meant. (p. 81)

Indeed, dirty work subcultures often contain stories of heroic members, such as these, who confronted the disrespectful behavior of outsiders (e.g., Paules, 1991; Santino, 1990). These stories are told and retold because they affirm the dignity of those doing the dirty work, particularly where the erring outsider is made to the see the light. Conversely, dirty work employees appear to be appreciative of clients who express sincere gratitude for the employees' ministrations (e.g., Maynard-Moody & Musheno, 2003; Wicklund, 2007).

SOCIAL COMPARISON

When individuals and groups feel threatened, comparisons with other individuals or groups that are perceived as worse off—downward social comparisons—are often used to bolster self- and collective esteem (Wills, 1981). The stigma of dirty work constitutes an ongoing threat to the well-being of those who perform that work. Thus, Ashforth, Kreiner, et al. (2007) found that dirty work managers engaged in downward social comparisons with other occupations, other individuals or subgroups within the dirty work occupation, other organizations, and even their own past. An animal researcher stated, "There's a big difference between animal testing and animal research. . . . [Testing is] terrible. Nobody likes to deal with that. You watch animals OD [overdose]" (Ashforth, Kreiner, et al., 2007, p. 164). Ashforth, Kreiner, et al. suggested that stigmatized workers prefer comparisons with other occupations, as in the preceding example, because the differences are starker and the comparison involves collectives such that the stigmatized workers can rely on their peers' social validation. Indeed, many instances of reframing, recalibrating, and refocusing rely at least implicitly on social comparisons to underscore the favorability of work aspects rather than extolling the aspects in their own right.

Perhaps surprisingly, tainted workers may also engage in upward social comparisons. We speculate that individuals and groups are inclined to compare upward when they

- identify with or can claim affinity with their superiors (cf. assimilation effect; Martinot & Redersdorff, 2006). A nurse aide may identify with the field of health care or her hospital and thus define herself accordingly.

- are seeking cues for self-improvement (Helgeson & Mickelson, 1995). Individuals who view their dirty work as a stepping stone to something better may compare upward for aspirational purposes and not view their current inferior standing as diagnostic of their future standing.
- can claim superiority on other criteria (cf. social creativity; Tajfel & Turner, 1986). Stacey (2005) cited home care aides who felt they were better caregivers than the much higher status doctors and nurses. As one put it, "Nurses only give medications and do none of this intimate or personal thing with the patient" (Stacey, 2005, p. 848).

In sum, reframing, recalibrating, and refocusing are greatly facilitated by the occupation's prestige, by social validation from important insider and outsider audiences, and by downward and upward comparisons with various targets.

Applications to the Workplace

The challenge for individuals and groups associated with dirty work is to clearly explicate the purpose and significance of such work in the face of pervasive taint that instead tends to marginalize the work. As noted, studies of dirty work have relied almost exclusively on qualitative explorations of a single occupation, organization, or industry at a time. Thus, our recommendations for enhancing the perceived meaningfulness of dirty work for its practitioners are made on the basis of a combination of (a) what some individuals, groups, organizations, and industries are presently doing (referred to in Table 6.1 as "Tested in practice"); (b) our extrapolations from the reframing, recalibrating, and refocusing dynamics discussed earlier ("Derived from theory"); and (c) largely indirect empirical assessments of these recommendations ("Supported by research").

Because meaningfulness is subjective and socially constructed, there is considerable latitude in what sense occupational members make of their work and, consequently, the meaningfulness that management may proffer for the work. Given space limitations, we focus on reframing, recalibrating, and refocusing the views of occupational members rather than outsiders (for examples of the latter, see Drew & Hulvey, 2007; Weitzer, 1991). We assume that the tasks that gave rise to the stigma do not change, only the way in which members come to think of those tasks. This attests to the power that meaningfulness has to fundamentally remake how individuals relate to their work and organization.

JOINTLY APPLYING REFRAMING, RECALIBRATING, AND REFOCUSING

As suggested in Footnote 3, although the distinctions between reframing, recalibrating, and refocusing are clear in theory, these occupational ideologies tend to blur and overlap in practice (Meisenbach, 2010; Tracy & Scott, 2006). Moreover, in many dirty work qualitative studies, there are multiple examples of each (supplemented with defensive tactics). This raises the question of how the three ideologies might be jointly used in practice.

Because reframing transforms the meaning of the work, it has the most potential to challenge attributions of taint (Ashforth & Kreiner, 1999) and should therefore be most actively pursued by practitioners. However, precisely because reframing bucks conventional thinking, it is difficult for a lone worker and manager to accomplish and likely requires a stronger subculture than do recalibrating or refocusing. Hence, reframing works best in conjunction with the development of a strong subculture within a given workplace and/or across an occupation. In addition, within reframing, *neutralizing* can mitigate the stigma, whereas *infusing* imputes new value; thus, neutralizing and infusing should be pursued simultaneously.

Although recalibrating does not transform meaning, it does change the significance of whatever meaning preexists. Thus, recalibrating can bolster reframing and should therefore also be actively pursued. Indeed, recalibrating is likely to have its biggest impact when the subculture is not strong enough to support reframing (Ashforth & Kreiner, 1999), and recalibrating should be actively pursued under such circumstances.

Similarly, refocusing can bolster both reframing and recalibrating by shifting attention away from any residual taint and should therefore be pursued as a supplemental ideology. That said, refocusing is likely to matter most when reframing and recalibrating are absent and should therefore be aggressively pursued at such times. Within refocusing, attention to the intrinsic qualities and intrinsic rewards of work complements attention to the extrinsic rewards such that all forms of refocusing can be pursued simultaneously. However, the intrinsic qualities and rewards speak directly to the enactment of the work itself and thus tend to be more salient than extrinsic rewards on a moment-to-moment basis, and a pronounced emphasis on the extrinsic rewards may actually undermine the credence of the intrinsic qualities and rewards (Deci, Koestner, & Ryan, 1999). Furthermore, because substantial extrinsic rewards can usually be obtained through nonstigmatized jobs, extrinsic rewards may provide a less compelling justification (e.g., "There are better ways to earn good money than that").

The more a given ideology is couched in terms of valued societal discourses (e.g., masculinity, achievement, reward), the less likely that outsider audiences will balk at the ideology and the more likely that occupational members will quickly and uncritically internalize it. What is dirt in one discourse may be dear in another; ideologies should not apologize for dirt in light of societal discourses but extol the dirt by selectively using those discourses.

Finally, social comparisons are inevitable in meaning making. Practitioners should endeavor to draw flattering and motivating downward and upward comparisons but not by undermining respect for others, particularly if groups are task interdependent (e.g., doctors and nurses) or the others are clients (Ashforth, Kreiner, et al., 2007).

KEY MANAGEMENT PROCESSES

Because reframing, recalibrating, and refocusing attempt to recast the meaningfulness of dirt in the face of societal perceptions, it is when individuals are entering—or contemplating entering—an occupation that they are most curious about and receptive to occupational ideologies. However, our impression from dirty work ethnographies and our own research is that managers tend to take the question "Why does this occupation matter?" for granted and focus instead on the intricacies of how to actually do the work—just as managers in other occupations typically do. But dirty work is not like other occupations. Thus, practitioners would do well to broach the reality of taint and the aspects of the work that give rise to the taint during recruitment, socialization, and ongoing leadership.

Although organizations routinely hire for person–occupation fit, that fit is usually predicated on a person's knowledge, skills, and abilities (or capacity to learn them). In the case of dirty work, practitioners should also consider a person's comfort (or willingness to become comfortable) with the tainted aspects of the work and with the taint itself. This can be assessed through some form of realistic job preview (RJP), supported by open discussion of the dirt and how occupational members make sense of and cope with it. Examples of promising RJPs include touring facilities, viewing video depictions of the work and workers' views, shadowing workers as they perform tasks, and actually performing sample tasks (e.g., Faller et al., 2009).

Once hired, the socialization process can have a dramatic impact on occupational identification (Ashforth, Sluss, & Harrison, 2007). Newcomers are often hungry for positive meaning, and management can extol meaning that is consistent with the mission and means of the occupation and organization. Practitioners should use what Jones (1986) referred to as *institutionalized socialization,* entailing, in particular, the use of veterans to impart positive meaning and defensive tactics, preset developmental experiences to gradually shape exposure to and comfort with the tainted aspects, and opportunities for newcomers to share their experiences, learning, and concerns with one another (e.g., Cahill, 1999).

Even if newcomers and the work group or wider occupational subculture have internalized an edifying ideology, ongoing leadership is needed to sustain that ideology in the face of the countervailing views of outsiders (e.g., Arnold, Turner, Barling, Kelloway, & McKee, 2007; Sparks & Schenk, 2001). As with any ideology, leaders should capitalize on opportunities and carve out moments to illustrate and reaffirm the ideology. For example, sharing thank-yous from appreciative clients can remind individuals of the positive impact of their efforts. Furthermore, given that groups can sustain ideologies better than can individuals, a major role for dirty work managers is to encourage group cohesion (through, e.g., group-based rewards, social events, buddy systems, and connections to broader groups such as national conventions and professional organizations).

WHAT ABOUT THE FORMS OF TAINT?

How might the forms of taint affect these recommendations? Ashforth and Kreiner (1999) argued that although dirty work is seen as a necessary evil, physically and socially tainted work tends to be seen as more necessary than evil, whereas morally tainted work tends to be seen as more evil than necessary. In support, Ashforth, Kreiner, et al. (2007) found that a sample of six morally tainted occupations was seen as dirtier than six physically and six socially tainted occupations. Thus, all else being equal, it is likely more difficult for occupational members to find uplifting rationales for morally tainted work, and society is likely to be more skeptical of a given rationale. Moreover, because occupations that are morally tainted typically interact with similarly tainted outsiders (e.g., repossessors with deadbeat debtors), moral taint often implicates a certain social taint, exacerbating the difficulty of normalizing the activity.

By the same token, precisely because moral taint is typically seen as dirtier than physical or social taint, members of morally tainted occupations tend to be that much hungrier for edifying meaning, and morally tainted occupations have the potential for stronger (and more insular) subcultures. If that potential is realized, the resulting gulf between the occupation and outsiders provides managers with a greater license to reframe and recalibrate at will.[5] Johnson (1990) noted how members of a deathwatch team, who guard condemned prisoners during their final 24 to 48 hours, are regarded as an elite unit in the prison, accountable only to the warden and deserving of the extra privileges they get. Said one member, "It's an honor among ourselves [correctional officers] to be on the team" (Johnson, 1990, p. 81).

As discussed, all that is really needed to socially validate beliefs is a critical mass of affirming insiders. Ironically, then, morally tainted occupations often have the most well-developed ideologies, including elaborate social comparisons. However, it is important to underscore that morally tainted occupations seldom actually reject the values of society; rather, they reject the way those values are applied to their own work. Reframing and recalibrating enables occupational members to revise the application of those values—and/or to invoke other values—to bestow purpose and significance on their work.

WHAT ABOUT OCCUPATIONAL PRESTIGE?

Perhaps the more problematic wrinkle is the occupation's prestige. As noted, the more prestigious the dirty work occupation, the more institutionalized and socially accepted are its ideologies and the greater is its status shield for warding off external threats. In short, meaningfulness tends to be less problematic in such occupations (Ashforth & Kreiner, 1999).

Conversely, low-prestige dirty work occupations may struggle to assert edifying ideologies. However, every occupation inherently pursues a mission beyond simply making money and does so in a way that can be couched in uplifting ways, providing grist for reframing, recalibrating, and refocusing. Indeed, our earlier examples of all three forms of ideology speak to the malleability of subjective and socially constructed meaningfulness. The challenge to practitioners is to couch the means and ends of the occupation in intrinsically meaningful ways that resonate with occupational members.

An added challenge is that members of low-prestige occupations may not trust management, particularly if the occupation is not central to the mission of the organization. Just as stigmatized workers are marginalized in society, so they may be marginalized in their own organizations, and managers have been known to cynically manipulate ide-

---

[5]Refocusing is usually less likely to be challenged by outsiders because it does not speak directly to the taint.

ologies. Ehrenreich (2001), for example, described how the advertising brochure for a maid service extolled, "We clean floors the old-fashioned way—on our hands and knees" (p. 83), a degrading and physically taxing posture that is not superior to using a mop while standing. Managers who sincerely value the vital role played by those doing the dirty work should demonstrate that sincerity through consistent and persistent words and deeds. Lucas and Buzzanell (2004) added that managers may work around distrust by considering "peer-initiated and organizationally supported recognition programs" (p. 288).

Postscripts

It should be remembered that finding salutary meaning is not the entire story of adjustment to dirty work. As mentioned, various defensive tactics can be used to buffer individuals from any residual impact of stigma (e.g., Arluke, 1994; Ashforth, Kreiner, et al., 2007; Meisenbach, 2010). However, not all defensive tactics are conducive to the mission of the occupation and organization. Thus, although management should encourage such tactics as social support, stress management, professional counseling, accepting one's situation and personal limits, routinizing procedures and using professional jargon, rotating employees (so that exposure to the most onerous tasks is limited), and avoiding judgmental audiences (if possible), it should discourage such tactics as avoiding stigmatizing but necessary tasks, gratuitously blaming clients, and distancing from the role or clients to such an extent that performance is undermined (Margolis & Molinsky, 2008; Tracy & Scott, 2006).

Perhaps surprisingly, we believe that meaningfulness is actually less difficult to impute to work that is physically, socially, or morally tainted than to work that is colloquially said to be dirty because it is simple and repetitive. Ironically, the physical, social, and moral taint that underlies scholarly definitions of dirty work often provides a cognitive hook for positive sense making. It is precisely because slaughtering cows, counseling addicts, and bounty hunting are each quite unique and repugnant for most people that individuals who routinely perform these tasks can say they are special. Conversely, nontainted work that is simple and repetitive (i.e., monotonous), such as assembly-line work, provides less of a hook for positive sense making. As a result, individuals are more likely to seek meaningfulness through refocusing on extrinsic rewards (e.g., pay, camaraderie) and playful distractions (e.g., Roy, 1959–1960; cf. Isaksen, 2000).

TABLE 6.1

Focus on the Workplace: Enhancing the Perceived Meaningfulness of Dirty Work

Recommendations	Tested in practice	Derived from theory	Supported by research
Foster *reframing* (looking at work in a different way) to transform the meaning of work.[a]	✓	✓	✓
Within reframing, use *neutralizing* (to mitigate stigma) simultaneously with *infusing* (to impute new value).		✓	
Encourage *recalibrating* (a reapportionment of what is more or less important to the job) to accentuate the positive and minimize the negative.[b]	✓	✓	✓
Foster *refocusing* (shifting attention away from stigmatized part of work toward the nonstigmatized part), especially when reframing and recalibrating are absent.[b]	✓	✓	✓
Within refocusing, intrinsic qualities and intrinsic and extrinsic rewards complement each other and can be pursued simultaneously. Intrinsic qualities and rewards should be emphasized because they are germane to the work itself and therefore provide a more compelling justification.		✓	
To support a given ideology for the job, appropriate societal discourses should be drawn on that match the inherent nature of the work (e.g., masculinity discourse for physically oriented dirty work, femininity discourse for helping-oriented dirty work).[c]		✓	✓
Draw flattering and motivating downward and upward comparisons with other groups but not by undermining respect for others, especially coworkers and clients.		✓	
To facilitate desired ideologies, promote the development of group cohesion and a strong subculture within a given workplace and/or across an occupation.[d]	✓	✓	✓
During hiring, in addition to traditional person–job fit concerns, assess applicants' comfort with the type and degree of dirty work and the taint itself through realistic job previews (e.g., touring facilities, shadowing workers, video depictions of the work).[e]	✓	✓	✓
After hiring, emphasize institutionalized socialization, which uses veterans, preset developmental experiences, and opportunities for shared learning and meaning making.[f]	✓	✓	✓
To increase retention and maintain high motivation, sustain ideologies over time (e.g., reaffirming beliefs, sharing success stories, reinforcing group cohesion).	✓	✓	

Note. [a]Arnold, Turner, Barling, Kelloway, & McKee (2007). [b]Ashforth, Kreiner, Clark, & Fugate (2007). [c]Leidner (1991). [d]Salzinger (1991). [e]Faller et al. (2009). [f]Cahill (1999).

Finally, it is important to add that there are limits to how much any set of occupational ideologies can accomplish. Occupational members remain part of the wider society with its derogatory beliefs, and they interact regularly with people outside their occupation. Thus, occupational members are apt to remain somewhat ambivalent about their membership, at least when the derogatory beliefs of outsiders are made salient (Ashforth & Kreiner, 1999; Tyler, 2011). In the poignant words of an exotic dancer,

> Sometimes you will feel good as a woman, sometimes you will feel bad, sometimes you will feel degraded, sometimes you will feel like you have been put on a pedestal. I have gone through stages of hating men, loving men, understanding men . . . to feeling much better than them to feeling less [than] them. (Grandy, 2008, p. 186)

In closing, so-called dirty workers are performing the vital tasks that many outsiders find personally abhorrent and would prefer to disavow. Fortunately, because meaningfulness is subjective and socially constructed, individuals in dirty work occupations are often able to assert purpose and significance as a bulwark against society's unwarranted disdain.

References

Ackroyd, S., & Crowdy, P. A. (1990). Can culture be managed? Working with "raw" material: The case of the English slaughtermen. *Personnel Review, 19*(5), 3–13. doi:10.1108/00483489010142655

Adams, J. (2009). Marked difference: Tattooing and its association with deviance in the United States. *Deviant Behavior, 30,* 266–292. doi:10.1080/01639620802168817

Applebaum, H. A. (1981). *Royal blue: The culture of construction workers.* Fort Worth, TX: Holt, Rinehart & Winston.

Arluke, A. (1994). Managing emotions in an animal shelter. In A. Manning & J. Serpell (Eds.), *Animals and human society: Changing perspectives* (pp. 145–165). New York, NY: Routledge.

Arnold, K. A., Turner, N., Barling, J., Kelloway, E. K., & McKee, M. C. (2007). Transformational leadership and psychological well-being: The mediating role of meaningful work. *Journal of Occupational Health Psychology, 12,* 193–203. doi:10.1037/1076-8998.12.3.193

Ashforth, B. E., & Kreiner, G. E. (1999). "How can you do it?": Dirty work and the challenge of constructing a positive identity. *Academy of Management Review, 24,* 413–434.

Ashforth, B. E., Kreiner, G. E., Clark, M. A., & Fugate, M. (2007). Normalizing dirty work: Managerial tactics for countering occupational taint. *Academy of Management Journal, 50,* 149–174. doi:10.5465/AMJ.2007.24162092

Ashforth, B. E., Sluss, D. M., & Harrison, S. H. (2007). Socialization in organizational contexts. *International Review of Industrial and Organizational Psychology, 22,* 1–70.

Bergman, M. E., & Chalkley, K. M. (2007). "Ex" marks a spot: The stickiness of dirty work and other removed stigmas. *Journal of Occupational Health Psychology, 12,* 251–265. doi:10.1037/1076-8998.12.3.251

Bowe, J., Bowe, M., & Streeter, S. C. (Eds.). (2000). *Gig: Americans talk about their jobs at the turn of the millennium.* New York, NY: Crown.

Brewer, M. B. (1991). The social self: On being the same and different at the same time. *Personality and Social Psychology Bulletin, 17,* 475–482. doi:10.1177/0146167291175001

Bryan, J. H. (1966). Occupational ideologies and individual attitudes of call girls. *Social Problems, 13,* 441–450. doi:10.2307/798593

Bryant, C. D., & Perkins, K. B. (1982). Containing work disaffection: The poultry processing worker. In P. L. Stewart & M. G. Cantor (Eds.), *Varieties of work* (pp. 199–212). Beverly Hills, CA: Sage.

Cahill, S. E. (1999). Emotional capital and professional socialization: The case of mortuary science students (and me). *Social Psychology Quarterly, 62,* 101–116. doi:10.2307/2695852

Chappell, A. T., & Lanza-Kaduce, L. (2010). Police academy socialization: Understanding the lessons learned in a paramilitary-bureaucratic organization. *Journal of Contemporary Ethnography, 39,* 187–214. doi:10.1177/0891241609342230

Chiappetta-Swanson, C. (2005). Dignity and dirty work: Nurses' experiences in managing genetic termination for fetal anomaly. *Qualitative Sociology, 28,* 93–116. doi:10.1007/s11133-005-2632-0

Clair, J. A., & Dufresne, R. L. (2004). Playing the grim reaper: How employees experience carrying out a downsizing. *Human Relations, 57,* 1597–1625. doi:10.1177/0018726704049991

Deci, E. L., Koestner, R., & Ryan, R. M. (1999). A meta-analytic review of experiments examining the effects of extrinsic rewards on intrinsic motivation. *Psychological Bulletin, 125,* 627–668. doi:10.1037/0033-2909.125.6.627

Douglas, M. (1966). *Purity and danger: An analysis of concepts of pollution and taboo.* London, England: Routledge & Kegan Paul. doi:10.4324/9780203361832

Drew, S. K., & Hulvey, M. (2007). Cops, crimes, and community policing. In S. K. Drew, M. Mills, & B. M. Gassaway (Eds.), *Dirty work: The social construction of taint* (pp. 169–193). Waco, TX: Baylor University Press.

Ehrenreich, B. (2001). *Nickel and dimed: On (not) getting by in America.* New York, NY: Metropolitan Books.

Emerson, R. M., & Pollner, M. (1976). Dirty work designations: Their features and consequences in a psychiatric setting. *Social Problems, 23,* 243–254. doi:10.2307/799771

Faller, K. C., Masternak, M., Grinnell-Davis, C., Grabarek, M., Sieffert, J., & Bernatovicz, F. (2009). Realistic job previews in child welfare: State of innovation and practice. *Child Welfare, 88*(5), 23–47.

Fine, G. A. (1996). Justifying work: Occupational rhetorics as resources in restaurant kitchens. *Administrative Science Quarterly, 41,* 90–115. doi:10.2307/2393987

Fujishiro, K., Xu, J., & Gong, F. (2010). What does "occupation" represent as an indicator of socioeconomic status?: Exploring occupational prestige and health. *Social Science & Medicine, 71,* 2100–2107. doi:10.1016/j.socscimed.2010.09.026

Ghidina, M. J. (1992). Social relations and the definition of work: Identity management in a low-status occupation. *Qualitative Sociology, 15,* 73–85. doi:10.1007/BF00989714

Grandy, G. (2008). Managing spoiled identities: Dirty workers' struggles for a favourable sense of self. *Qualitative Research in Organizations and Management, 3,* 176–198. doi:10.1108/17465640810920278

Gusterson, H. (1996). *Nuclear rites: A weapons laboratory at the end of the Cold War.* Berkeley: University of California Press.

Helgeson, V. S., & Mickelson, K. D. (1995). Motives for social comparison. *Personality and Social Psychology Bulletin, 21,* 1200–1209. doi:10.1177/01461672952111008

Hochschild, A. R. (1983). *The managed heart: Commercialization of human feeling.* Berkeley: University of California Press.

Hughes, E. C. (1958). *Men and their work.* Glencoe, IL: Free Press.

Hughes, E. C. (1962). Good people and dirty work. *Social Problems, 10,* 3–11. doi:10.2307/799402

Isaksen, J. (2000). Constructing meaning despite the drudgery of repetitive work. *Journal of Humanistic Psychology, 40,* 84–107. doi:10.1177/0022167800403008

Johnson, R. (1990). *Death work: A study of the modern execution process.* Pacific Grove, CA: Brooks/Cole.

Jones, G. R. (1986). Socialization tactics, self-efficacy, and newcomers' adjustments to organizations. *Academy of Management Journal, 29,* 262–279. doi:10.2307/256188

Kidder, J. L. (2006). "It's the job that I love": Bike messengers and edgework. *Sociological Forum, 21,* 31–54. doi:10.1007/s11206-006-9002-x

Kreiner, G. E., Ashforth, B. E., & Sluss, D. M. (2006). Identity dynamics in occupational dirty work: Integrating social identity and system justification perspectives. *Organization Science, 17,* 619–636. doi:10. 1287/orsc.1060.0208

Leidner, R. (1991). Serving hamburgers and selling insurance: Gender, work, and identity in interactive service jobs. *Gender & Society, 5,* 154–177. doi:10.1177/089124391005002002

Lucas, K., & Buzzanell, P. M. (2004). Blue-collar work, career, and success: Occupational narratives of *sisu. Journal of Applied Communication Research, 32,* 273–292. doi:10.1080/0090988042000240167

Margolis, J. D., & Molinsky, A. (2008). Navigating the bind of necessary evils: Psychological engagement and the production of interpersonally sensitive behavior. *Academy of Management Journal, 51,* 847–872. doi:10.5465/AMJ.2008.34789639

Martinot, D., & Redersdorff, S. (2006). The variable impact of upward and downward social comparisons on self-esteem: When the level of analysis matters. In S. Guimond (Ed.), *Social comparison and social psychology: Understanding cognition, intergroup relations, and culture* (pp. 127–150). Cambridge, England: Cambridge University Press. doi:10.1017/CBO9780511584329.008

Maynard-Moody, S., & Musheno, M. (2003). *Cops, teachers, counselors: Stories from the front lines of public service.* Ann Arbor: University of Michigan Press.

Meisenbach, R. J. (2010). Stigma management communication: A theory and agenda for applied research on how individuals manage moments of stigmatized identity. *Journal of Applied Communication Research, 38,* 268–292. doi:10.1080/00909882.2010.490841

Merton, R. K. (1957). *Social theory and social structure* (rev. ed.). Glencoe, IL: Free Press.

Michaelson, J. (2010). *Step into our lives at the funeral home.* Amityville, NY: Baywood.

Miller, M. L., & Van Maanen, J. (1982). Getting into fishing: Observations on the social identities of New England fishermen. *Urban Life, 11,* 27–54.

Mills, M. (2007). Without trucks we'd be naked, hungry & homeless. In S. K. Drew, M. Mills, & B. M. Gassaway (Eds.), *Dirty work: The social construction of taint* (pp. 77–93). Waco, TX: Baylor University Press.

Munting, R. (1996). *An economic and social history of gambling in Britain and the USA.* Manchester, England: Manchester University Press.

Pande, A. (2010). "At least I am not sleeping with anyone": Resisting the stigma of commercial surrogacy in India. *Feminist Studies, 36,* 292–312.

Paules, G. F. (1991). *Dishing it out: Power and resistance among waitresses in a New Jersey restaurant.* Philadelphia, PA: Temple University Press.

Pratt, M. G., & Ashforth, B. E. (2003). Fostering meaningfulness in working and at work. In K. S. Cameron, J. E. Dutton, & R. E. Quinn

(Eds.), *Positive organizational scholarship: Foundations of a new discipline* (pp. 309–327). San Francisco, CA: Berrett-Koehler.

Purser, G. (2009). The dignity of job-seeking men: Boundary work among immigrant day laborers. *Journal of Contemporary Ethnography, 38*, 117–139. doi:10.1177/0891241607311867

Rentilly, J. (2010, May). Dream job. *Spirit, 92*, pp. 88–90.

Ritzer, G., & Walczak, D. (1986). *Working: Conflict and change* (3rd ed.). Englewood Cliffs, NJ: Prentice-Hall.

Rosso, B. D., Dekas, K. H., & Wrzesniewski, A. (2010). On the meaning of work: A theoretical integration and review. *Research in Organizational Behavior, 30*, 91–127. doi:10.1016/j.riob.2010.09.001

Roy, D. F. (1959–1960). "Banana time": Job satisfaction and informal interaction. *Human Organization, 18*, 158–168.

Salzinger, L. (1991). A maid by any other name: The transformation of "dirty work" by Central American immigrants. In M. Burawoy et al. (Eds.), *Ethnography unbound: Power and resistance in the modern metropolis* (pp. 139–160). Berkeley: University of California Press.

Santino, J. (1990). The outlaw emotions: Narrative expressions on the rules and roles of occupational identity. *American Behavioral Scientist, 33*, 318–329. doi:10.1177/0002764290033003006

Shaw, I. (2004). Doctors, "dirty work" patients, and "revolving doors." *Qualitative Health Research, 14*, 1032–1045. doi:10.1177/1049732304265928

Sparks, J. R., & Schenk, J. A. (2001). Explaining the effects of transformational leadership: An investigation of the effects of higher-order motives in multilevel marketing organizations. *Journal of Organizational Behavior, 22*, 849–869. doi:10.1002/job.116

Stacey, C. L. (2005). Finding dignity in dirty work: The constraints and rewards of low-wage home care labour. *Sociology of Health & Illness, 27*, 831–854. doi:10.1111/j.1467-9566.2005.00476.x

Sudnow, D. (1967). *Passing on: The social organization of dying.* Englewood Cliffs, NJ: Prentice-Hall.

Tajfel, H., & Turner, J. C. (1986). The social identity theory of intergroup behavior. In S. Worchel & W. G. Austin (Eds.), *Psychology of intergroup relations* (2nd ed., pp. 7–24). Chicago, IL: Nelson-Hall.

Tracy, S. J., & Scott, C. (2006). Sexuality, masculinity, and taint management among firefighters and correctional officers: Getting down and dirty with "America's heroes" and the "scum of law enforcement." *Management Communication Quarterly, 20*, 6–38. doi:10.1177/0893318906287898

Treiman, D. J. (1977). *Occupational prestige in comparative perspective.* New York, NY: Academic Press.

Trice, H. M. (1993). *Occupational subcultures in the workplace.* Ithaca, NY: ILR Press.

Tyler, M. (2011). Tainted love: From dirty work to abject labour in Soho's sex shops. *Human Relations, 64,* 1477–1500. doi:10.1177/0018726711418849

Weitzer, R. (1991). Prostitutes' rights in the United States: The failure of a movement. *Sociological Quarterly, 32,* 23–41. doi:10.1111/j.1533-8525.1991.tb00343.x

Wicklund, S. (2007). *This common secret: My journey as an abortion doctor.* New York, NY: Public Affairs.

Wicks, D. (2002). Institutional bases of identity construction and reproduction: The case of underground coal mining. *Gender, Work and Organization, 9,* 308–335. doi:10.1111/1468-0432.00162

Wills, T. A. (1981). Downward comparison principles in social psychology. *Psychological Bulletin, 90,* 245–271. doi:10.1037/0033-2909.90.2.245

Robert W. Lent

Promoting Meaning and Purpose at Work

A Social-Cognitive Perspective

7

W hat does it mean to have purpose and meaning in life—and in the workplace in particular? What, exactly, is meaningful work? Can anyone attain it, or is it conferred only on a lucky few? To what extent is it a matter of personal agency, traits, cognitions, environmental conditions, or other factors? Can only certain forms of work offer meaning and purpose? Or can these virtues be found in any job or career? Do they lead to other positive outcomes, such as happiness, or are they their own rewards? Assuming that meaningful work can be cultivated, how does one go about doing so? Such questions have long intrigued observers of human behavior. Recent research and theoretical developments in several areas of psychology offer promise in the effort to understand and promote meaning and purpose—and other aspects of eudaimonic well-being—in work and other life contexts.

At a general level, the concepts of *meaning* and *purpose* can be distinguished from one another. Synonyms for meaning include significance, importance, and value; those for purpose include intention, objective, and goal. Despite these

http://dx.doi.org/10.1037/14183-008
Purpose and Meaning in the Workplace, B. J. Dik, Z. S. Byrne, and M. F. Steger (Editors)

conceptual differences, measures of meaning and purpose in life in the psychological literature often treat the two constructs as one, interspersing meaning and purpose items on the same scale (e.g., Ryff, 1989; Steger, Frazier, Oishi, & Kaler, 2006). This practice is understandable, given the common wisdom that the two usually go together. Yet, by failing to distinguish between them, it is difficult, among other things, to examine the ways in which they may interrelate or serve unique functions. For example, does having overarching goals (or purpose) lead to a sense of meaning in life? Do the two uniquely predict life satisfaction or other outcomes?

Meaning and purpose have also been studied specifically in the work domain. Steger, Dik and Duffy (2012) noted that "there is little consensus on the *meaning* of meaningful work" (p. 323). They also noted an absence of measures of meaningful work that are theory based and psychometrically sound. To remedy this situation, Steger et al. developed a novel measure of meaningful work. In the course of assessing the measure's factor structure, they observed that the conceptually derived dimensions of work meaning and work purpose were not clearly distinguishable from one another empirically. They subsequently eliminated the purpose factor, though items referring to purpose remain on two of the three remaining factors (B. J. Dik, personal communication, June 15, 2011). One way to more clearly distinguish these concepts may be to assess purpose in relation to goals (e.g., having salient, specific, personally set work goals) rather than through more general statements that may be interchangeable with meaning (e.g., "My work provides me with a sense of purpose" may sound a lot like "My work adds meaning to my life").

Other recent inquiry has focused on the concepts of *calling* and *vocation,* viewing meaningful work in terms of the extent to which individuals feel "a transcendent summons to a particular career" that aims to serve the welfare of others (Dik, Duffy, & Eldridge, 2009, p. 625). The research and theoretical efforts of Steger, Dik, and their colleagues represent an important programmatic approach to the study of meaningful work. At the same time, a number of questions remain regarding their conception and measurement of meaningful work. For example, can meaning be derived from careers that do not explicitly serve society? How does meaningful work differ from a variety of seemingly related constructs, such as social service interests, intrinsic work values, career commitment, or work-role salience? Should the desire for, or the experience of, meaningful work be viewed as a trait? Such questions have thus far received limited or uneven inquiry (e.g., see Dik & Duffy, 2009).

Although it is not the purpose of this chapter to try to resolve such challenging issues, it seems important to draw some conceptual boundaries around my treatment of the topic. First, although acknowledging the value of viewing life and work meaning in global, trait-like terms (Ryff, 1989; Steger et al., 2006), I focus on more domain- and state-specific aspects of meaning and purpose—in particular, variables that may be relatively dynamic and intervention friendly. Second, I take a phenomenological view of work meaning, interpreting meaning not as an inherent quality of one's work but rather as a function of the individual's view of it. In other words, much like beauty, work meaning lies in the eye of the beholder; it is an idiographic matter. Individuals may derive meaning from any of a number of different aspects of their work (e.g., opportunities for personal growth, self-expression, service to others); alternatively, they may view their work less in existential/intrinsic than in utilitarian/extrinsic terms (e.g., as a source of pay rather than self-definition).

Third, and related to this second point, although it is tempting to bestow on certain types of work the crown of meaning—on occupations, for example, that contribute explicitly to the well-being of others (e.g., teachers, counselors), to environmental sustainability (e.g., green jobs), or to a particular spiritual ideology (e.g., religious calling)—this temptation may reflect a somewhat narrow, if well-intended, view of meaningful work. According to such a view, meaningful work equals work that seems altruistic or is ostensibly directed at a common good. But to define meaningful work narrowly or to vest meaning only in certain forms of work rather than in the person's view of his or her work is to ignore the obvious, if morally unsettling, fact that criminals and terrorists, no less than the virtuous, can derive a sense of meaning from their work. Indeed, what is altruistic (e.g., defeating poverty vs. infidels) is also a matter of perspective. Although I much prefer to emphasize the prosocial aspects of meaningful work (i.e., activities that help rather than harm others), it is important to acknowledge that there can also be an amoral side to meaning and that purpose is limited only by humans' capacity to fashion work-related goals, whether prosocial, asocial, or antisocial. Heroes and villains may have opposite objectives, but neither lack purpose.

In the following sections, I provide an overview of a social-cognitive view of work well-being that incorporates a focus on meaning, purpose, and other eudaimonic outcomes (e.g., personal growth, social connectedness). In this framework, my concept of meaningful work closely resembles what Berg, Dutton, and Wrzesniewski (Chapter 4, this volume) refer to as *meaningfulness*—a subjective belief that one's work is significant. The social-cognitive theoretical base and its nascent empirical literature are then used to derive practical ideas for promoting well-being at work. I end with a consideration of directions for future inquiry.

Social-Cognitive Career Theory of Work Well-Being

The model of work satisfaction and adjustment described in this section represents an effort to extend social-cognitive career theory (SCCT; Lent, Brown, & Hackett, 1994) to the understanding of well-being in the work domain. SCCT originally consisted of models of educational and vocational interest, choice, and performance. Each model features an overlapping set of variables (e.g., self-efficacy, outcome expectations, goals) drawn from general social-cognitive theory (Bandura, 1986, 1997). For example, SCCT's interest model maintains that people develop vocational interests in activities for which they possess favorable self-efficacy (beliefs about one's performance capabilities) and outcome expectations (beliefs about the outcomes that can be attained). The newest model assumes that work well-being is subject to personal (e.g., traits, cognitions), behavioral (e.g., task participation), and environmental (e.g., social, cultural) influences. Although the predictors and dependent variables in the model are drawn from psychological inquiry, it is important to acknowledge the extensive philosophical roots of the literature on human well-being (see, e.g., Ryan & Deci, 2001).

Hedonic and Eudaimonic Views of Well-Being

Ryan and Deci (2001) observed that the psychological study of well-being has been approached from two relatively distinct perspectives. In the *hedonic* view, well-being is defined in terms of pleasure, happiness, or the balance between positive and negative affect. From this perspective, feeling happy or satisfied (and relatively free of negative feelings) is the key criterion of well-being. In the *eudaimonic* view, by contrast, well-being involves the effort to actualize one's potential, to make meaning, and to seek purpose in one's life. Rather than emphasizing personal feelings, the eudaimonic position focuses on aspects of thought and behavior that may enable one to lead the good life. Parenthetically, the title and content of this volume may be seen as firmly grounded in the eudaimonic tradition. Its implicit concern is with the thinking and doing versus feeling aspects of well-being.

The hedonic position is associated with the study of emotional or *subjective well-being* (SWB). SWB is often defined as consisting of three distinct but related parts: life satisfaction, positive affect, and negative affect (Diener, Suh, Lucas, & Smith, 1999). Life satisfaction entails a global evaluation of one's life (e.g., "I am satisfied with my life"); positive and negative affect involve, respectively, the extent to which one generally experiences positive and negative feelings. The eudaimonic position has given rise to the study of *psychological well-being* (PWB), which Ryff (1989) defined in terms of six characteristics (e.g., personal growth, purpose in life, positive social relations).

Both the hedonic/SWB and eudaimonic/PWB approaches view well-being as a multidimensional concept, and many measures have been developed to assess its various facets. Consistent with the conceptual differences between hedonic and eudaimonic well-being, factor analyses have found support for a two-factor latent structure underlying a variety of these measures. In one factor analytic study, the two factors were labeled *happiness* and *meaning* (McGregor & Little, 1998), with SWB measures (e.g., life satisfaction, positive affect) loading on the happiness factor and PWB measures (e.g., growth, purpose) comprising the meaning factor. In another study, the two factors, labeled *SWB* and *personal growth,* were moderately interrelated (Compton, Smith, Cornish, & Qualls, 1996). Other studies have found moderate to strong relations among hedonic and eudaimonic measures of well-being (e.g., Ryff & Keyes, 1995; Steger et al., 2006, 2012).

Such findings raise interesting questions about the nature of the relations between these two forms of well-being. Lent (2004) proposed a unifying theoretical framework in which the hedonic and eudaimonic traditions each offer valuable, complementary perspectives on achieving and sustaining optimal adjustment. In particular, eudaimonic variables and processes are hypothesized to form a central route leading to hedonic well-being. For example, people help to create meaning in their lives and contribute to their own growth and sense of purpose—eudaimonic markers of the good life—in part by setting, committing to, and pursuing personal goals, engaging in valued activities, and interacting with others in their social environments. Goal progress, behavioral engagement, and social connectedness are, in turn, likely to enhance feelings of SWB (cf. Cantor & Sanderson, 1999).

Pathways to Well-Being in the Social-Cognitive Model

Lent's (2004) framework was intended to help explain well-being both generally (e.g., overall life satisfaction) and within specific life domains (e.g., school, work, leisure). To flesh out its implications for the occupational domain, Lent and Brown (2006, 2008) offered a work-specific extension of the general framework focusing on the prediction of job (or work) satisfaction. They adopted the traditional definition of job satisfaction as the extent to which people like or feel pleasantly about their work. Lent and Brown intended for their model extension to be relevant both to global job satisfaction (i.e., general feelings about the job) and to facet satisfaction (i.e., satisfaction with specific aspects of one's job, such as the rewards, working conditions, and coworkers).

As in the earlier SCCT models of vocational interest development, choice making, and performance (Lent et al., 1994), the work satisfaction model includes the core social-cognitive person variables of self-efficacy beliefs, outcome expectations, and goals; it also incorporates additional person, behavior, and contextual variables found to be predictive of satisfaction outcomes. Some of the variables in the model (e.g., affective traits) point to relatively stable and hedonic aspects of well-being, whereas others (e.g., goals, social support) reflect presumably more malleable and eudaimonic features that suggest ways to create more meaningful (eudaimonic) and satisfying (hedonic) work. Specifically, as shown in Figure 7.1, the model examines the interplay among seven sets of variables: (a) work satisfaction, (b) overall life satisfaction, (c) personality and affective traits, (d) goal-directed activity, (e) self-efficacy, (f) work conditions and outcomes, and (g) goal- and efficacy-relevant environmental supports and obstacles.

FIGURE 7.1

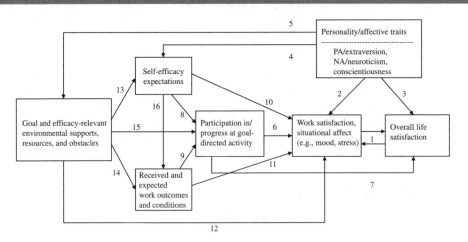

A Social-Cognitive Model of Work Satisfaction. PA = positive affect; NA = negative affect. From "Social Cognitive Career Theory and Subjective Well-Being in the Context of Work," by R. W. Lent and S. D. Brown, 2008, *Journal of Career Assessment, 16,* p. 10. doi:10.1177/1069072707305769. Copyright 2008 by SAGE Publications, Inc. Adapted with permission.

WORK AND LIFE SATISFACTION

Job satisfaction is often studied in conjunction with overall life satisfaction (one of the central components of SWB). An enduring question has been whether job satisfaction leads to life satisfaction or vice versa. Research offers support for both directional paths (e.g., Heller, Watson, & Ilies, 2004), although some evidence suggests that the path from life satisfaction to job satisfaction may be the more potent of the two (Judge & Watanabe, 1993). The social-cognitive model incorporates the view that work and life satisfaction influence one another bidirectionally, as reflected by the reciprocal paths (1) between the two variables in Figure 7.1 (the numbers in parentheses refer to the paths in Figure 7.1). It is also assumed that the strength and primary direction of the causal arrows may depend on certain moderator variables, such as the personal importance of work relative to one's other life roles (cf. Rain, Lane, & Steiner, 1991).

PERSONALITY AND AFFECTIVE TRAITS

Both job and life satisfaction have been found to relate to positive and negative affectivity (Thoresen, Kaplan, Barsky, Warren, & de Chermont, 2003) and to certain of the Big Five personality factors—in particular, neuroticism, extraversion, and conscientiousness (Heller et al., 2004). The social-cognitive model posits cognitive, affective, behavioral, and social paths by which traits may be linked to work and life satisfaction. For example, positive affect may influence work satisfaction partly indirectly by coloring workers' perceptions of their efficacy (4) and of environmental resources (5). Those who frequently experience high positive affect may be inclined to view their personal capabilities and social supports in more favorable terms than do those at low levels of positive affect or high levels of negative affect. The model also assumes a more direct path from affective traits to work (2) and life satisfaction (3) because emotional predispositions may have a pervasive effect on satisfaction across life contexts.

GOALS AND GOAL-DIRECTED BEHAVIOR

Some writers have argued that hedonic satisfaction can simply be attributed to traits (McCrae & Costa, 1991); they are thus not optimistic about the prospects for change in SWB. Others are more sanguine about the plasticity of SWB. For example, Heller et al. (2004) suggested that traits define a characteristic range of satisfaction for each individual but that "within this broad range, changes in people's environments, perceptions, feelings, and behaviors can increase or decrease their level of satisfaction" (p. 593). In keeping with this view, the social-cognitive model posits that certain influences on satisfaction are relatively modifiable. For example, it is assumed that satisfaction is partly determined by cognitive and behavioral processes, such as the setting and pursuit of personally relevant goals, over which individuals can assert some measure of personal agency.

Goal-directed behavior may be seen as forming an important eudaimonic route to well-being in that it fosters involvement in valued activities, provides opportunity to give and receive social support, and lends a sense of life purpose and meaning (Cantor & Sanderson, 1999). A variety of goal properties have been found to relate to well-being (e.g., simply having goals, having valued goals, making progress toward one's goals; Ryan & Deci, 2001). On the basis of such evidence, the social-cognitive model maintains that goals and goal-directed behavior are likely to promote both job (6) and life (7) satisfaction. This linkage is likely to be strongest when people set, are highly committed to, and perceive they are making progress at personally valued work goals, particularly goals that are proximal, intrinsic, and challenging but attainable. Goal–satisfaction relations may also be moderated by work-role salience. For instance, progress at work goals may be especially satisfying for those who view the work role as central to their identity.

SELF-EFFICACY AND WORK OUTCOMES

Self-efficacy beliefs and outcome expectations represent two additional, relatively tractable sources of work satisfaction in the social-cognitive model. Self-efficacy can be defined as beliefs about one's ability to perform the tasks required for success in one's work role (task self-efficacy) or, specifically, to perform the behaviors necessary to achieve one's work-related goals (goal self-efficacy). Outcome expectations refer to the consequences one anticipates that are contingent on performing one's work tasks or pursuing one's work goals (e.g., beliefs about receiving valued outcomes). In addition to the outcomes people anticipate from their work, the model is concerned with the conditions and outcomes that people perceive they have actually received or are currently receiving. Thus, expected and received work conditions and outcomes are classified together in Figure 7.1.

Both self-efficacy (Caprara, Barbaranelli, Borgogni, & Steca, 2003) and positive work conditions and outcomes (both those that are expected—Singer & Coffin, 1996—and those received—Dawis, 2005) have been linked reliably to job satisfaction in past research. In the social-cognitive model, self-efficacy (10) and favorable work conditions and outcomes (11) are hypothesized to affect work satisfaction directly; those who perceive themselves to be more efficacious and as having access to valued tasks and rewards are likely to be satisfied at work. Self-efficacy is seen as a partial determinant of outcome expectations (16) because those with stronger self-efficacy beliefs are likely to hold more optimistic expectations about obtaining the work outcomes they value. In addition to their direct paths to job satisfaction, self-efficacy (8) and perceived work conditions and outcomes (9) may indirectly affect satisfaction by motivating goal-directed behavior. That is, higher self-efficacy and favorable work conditions are likely to promote and sustain goal pursuit (i.e., efforts to attain one's goals), which in turn fosters work satisfaction.

GOAL- AND EFFICACY-RELEVANT ENVIRONMENTAL CONDITIONS

The category of work conditions and outcomes, described previously, incorporates a variety of variables that reflect the extent to which the individual experiences the environment as generally responsive or supportive (e.g., perceived organizational support). The social-cognitive model also includes a second type of environmental influence focusing on features of the environment that specifically support (or undermine) self-efficacy development or pursuit of one's personal goals. Prior theory and research have linked goal-relevant supports and resources (e.g., social or material support for one's central goals) to satisfaction outcomes (Cantor & Sanderson, 1999). In the social-cognitive model, goal- and efficacy-relevant supports, resources, and obstacles are expected to affect work satisfaction both directly (12) and indirectly by facilitating goal pursuit (15) and by helping to promote self-efficacy (13) and outcome expectations (14).

In sum, the foregoing may be seen as an effort to construct a process model integrating several classes of variables through which people achieve and maintain well-being at work. This model incorporates a focus on meaning and purpose but does not treat them as ultimate outcomes. It is concerned with common routes through which people derive meaning and purpose (e.g., setting and progressing toward personal goals, engaging in valued activities, receiving valued outcomes; see Figure 7.1), but its larger concern is with the ways in which eudaimonic mechanisms (including those that promote meaning and purpose) interrelate with hedonic ones in the service of optimal adjustment.

Tests of the Model

There have been several cross-sectional tests of the social-cognitive model of satisfaction in U.S. samples. Lent et al. (2005) found that the model fit the data well in predicting both the academic and social domain satisfaction of college students. Lent, Singley, Sheu, Schmidt, and Schmidt (2007) also reported good overall model–data fit in predicting college students' academic satisfaction. In each of these studies, the model explained substantial variation in domain satisfaction, though some individual paths were not supported (e.g., outcome expectations did not yield significant paths to goal progress or academic satisfaction). In testing the model with a sample of school teachers, Duffy and Lent (2009) found that the model fit the data well overall, though only three of five predictors (perceived organizational support, positive affectivity, self-efficacy) produced significant direct paths to work satisfaction.

In addition to these cross-sectional studies, there have thus far been three longitudinal tests of the satisfaction model, two with college students and one with adult workers. Singley, Lent, and Sheu (2010) collected data at two times (8 weeks apart) during an academic semester. Lent, Taveira, Sheu, and Singley (2009) assessed students at two intervals, 15 weeks apart, using the model to predict perceived college adjustment and stress as well as academic satisfaction. Self-efficacy and environmental support were significant predictors of subsequent goal progress in both studies, though the predictors of satisfaction or adjustment outcomes varied somewhat between the two studies (e.g., goal progress and support were the significant predictors in Singley et al., 2010, whereas self-efficacy and support were the significant predictors in Lent et al., 2009). Verbruggen and Sels (2010) adapted the model to the study of adult career clients, finding that the model predicted career and life satisfaction 6 months after counseling. It is noteworthy that the Lent et al. and Verbruggen and Sels studies were conducted in Portugal and Belgium, respectively, which lends a cross-cultural dimension to the study of the work well-being model.

Implications for Workplace Intervention

As noted earlier, the social-cognitive model is intended to help explain how multiple variables, both hedonic (e.g., affective traits) and eudaimonic (e.g., goal pursuit, task engagement) in nature, jointly operate to promote (or hinder) work satisfaction. Although the model incorporates a number of predictions that are consistent with prior theory and research findings, it is important to emphasize that formal tests of the model as a whole, or of substantial subsets of it, are still relatively few in number. Nevertheless, I believe the model may provide a source of practical ideas for efforts to promote work (and life) satisfaction. In this section, I offer several provisional suggestions for applying the theoretical model to practice. These are summarized in Table 7.1. I primarily direct my comments at implications for counseling, but many of the ideas could also be applied to self-directed efforts or organizational interventions (e.g., delivered through mentoring, coaching, or educational seminars).

People seek career counseling or employee assistance for a wide array of reasons (e.g., conflicts with supervisors, a wish to change careers, concerns about performance). From the perspective of the hedonic and eudaimonic conceptions of well-being, many of these reasons for help seeking can probably be classified into two larger categories: (a) dissatisfaction with one's job or with particular parts of it and (b) a desire to achieve greater growth, learning, or meaning in one's work. The first category is synonymous with hedonic notions of well-being; the second represents eudaimonic well-being. Persons in the latter category may express existential concerns and see work in terms of its potential for self-expression or self-actualization.

Of course, the two categories are not mutually exclusive. For instance, people may become unhappy with their current work precisely because they view it as lacking the meaning or growth they seek. They don't see the point of it anymore or may prefer to do something that allows them to be the sort of person they wish to be—to reveal or develop their true selves. They may have taken their current job for extrinsic reasons (e.g., pay, prestige) but are now more focused on intrinsic reasons to work (e.g., the self-satisfaction that accompanies helping others or creating art). Although the two categories may overlap, it may be useful to view them in terms of their relative alignment with remedial and developmental interventions—efforts to fix a problem and restore hedonic well-being versus to promote, in a more proactive way, the personal growth and meaning objectives that are associated with eudaimonic well-being.

Remedial Implications

People are more likely to seek work-related counseling when they are feeling dissatisfied, demoralized, or stressed with some aspect of their work lives. As I have described elsewhere (e.g., Lent, 2005), a social-cognitive approach considers various possible sources of work dissatisfaction, such as failure to attain the intrinsic or extrinsic outcomes that one expects from work (e.g., poor correspondence between work needs and reinforcers), obstacles to the fulfillment of one's self-set work goals, exposure to stressful or punitive work conditions, low self-efficacy regarding one's job capabilities, insufficient organizational supports for one's work well-being or career progress, and possession of affective traits that can adversely affect both hedonic and eudaimonic well-being.

A variety of affect-promoting interventions can be derived from the theory and its research base. Depending on the basis for one's dissatisfaction, an SCCT approach would, for example, foster strategies to enable clients, where possible, to attain valued work outcomes and progress at self-set work goals (or to identify new ones), cope with or change distressing work conditions, cultivate self-efficacy beliefs and skills regarding work tasks and coping capabilities, and access needed work supports and resources. Individuals, of course, will vary in their potential to affect their current work environments. Where environmental, self, and job change options are constrained (e.g., for economic or family reasons), an SCCT-based counselor might work to identify nonwork routes to satisfaction.

The social-cognitive literature contains a number of specific suggestions, such as self-efficacy enhancement (e.g., Brown & Lent, 1996), for accomplishing these sorts of objectives. In the work context, for example, well-matched mentors can serve as coping models who help to foster robust self-efficacy beliefs in the mentee and also convey information about successful goal attainment, environmental change, and coping strategies within the current organization. Brown and Lent (1996) provided two case examples involving counseling for job dissatisfaction. In both instances, the clients identified and eventually pursued alternative career options that were, compared with their current work, more correspondent with their personal values and interests and, thus, likely to offer opportunities for meaningful work. In both cases, it was also necessary to focus on a variety of counseling subgoals (e.g., boosting self-efficacy, building social support, managing barriers) to create the scaffolding needed to support career change.

A social-cognitive counseling approach to work satisfaction would focus on cognitive, behavioral, and social targets that are relevant to both hedonic and eudaimonic well-being. For example, as noted earlier, the literature on goals highlights the beneficial effects on well-being of having, and making progress on, personally salient goals, both at work and in other life spheres (Diener et al., 1999; Locke & Latham, 2002; Ryan & Deci, 2001). Among its eudaimonic benefits, the goal-pursuit process can foster a sense of life structure, purpose, and agency. Goal-focused interventions can be designed to help clients identify and prioritize central goals, develop plans for goal pursuit, marshal goal-relevant supports, and manage barriers to goal pursuit (Lent, 2004). Where opportunities for meaningful goal pursuit are limited in the work context—or where work is simply not as central to an individual's identity as are other life roles or settings—counseling can focus on alternative forums for developing and pursuing personally meaningful goals (e.g., through volunteer experiences or leisure pursuits). A number of conditions have been identified that may facilitate goal progress, such as setting goals that are relatively clear, specific, challenging, and broken into proximal subgoals (e.g., Bandura, 1986).

Another important focal point for eudaimonic well-being is behavioral involvement in valued life tasks (Cantor & Sanderson, 1999). Although some individuals find great meaning and enjoyment in solitary pursuits (e.g., writing, painting), many find social interactions to be of particular value for deriving both a sense of meaning and satisfaction. When people lack outlets for valued life-task participation, such as performing preferred work tasks or leisure activities, or when previously available outlets have been blocked (e.g., through job, physical health, or social changes), people are likely to experience decrements in SWB and PWB, such as a diminished sense of life structure and meaning. Existential angst and depression are not uncommon in such circumstances. Where access to valued task participation, either at work or in other central life contexts, has been impeded or may be so in the future (e.g., by retirement), counseling can profitably be directed at encouraging engagement in alternative activities that offer potential for personal growth and meaning fulfillment. A variety of tools can be adapted for this purpose, such as measures of personal strivings, personal projects, or flow activities (see Lent, 2004). Interest assessment can also be used to identify previously underdeveloped areas for vocational or avocational involvement.

Developmental Implications

People do not always seek counseling when their concerns are eudaimonic in nature, unless the mismatch between what they want from work and what their work environment provides (e.g., in terms of opportunities for growth, meaning, or purpose) has become excessive, resulting in a diminution of hedonic well-being and a sense that one is stuck in a poor-fitting, meaningless job. (Even then, economic or other factors may limit one's sense of coping options.) Many organizations attempt to ward off worker burnout or rustout and retain their most productive workers by offering an array of job-enrichment and career-renewal opportunities, such as skill training, mentoring, coaching, promotions, and career management seminars. Although all of these can be helpful, they are predicated on the assumption that the organization has work that the individual would find meaningful and that would offer the sort of opportunities for growth or goal pursuit that he or she values. Where this assumption does not hold, an individual may need to look beyond the current job or work organization in order to become the sort of person, or perform the sort of activities, that would fulfill his or her eudaimonic objectives.

Many of the counseling elements described earlier in the remedial section could be adapted for proactive, developmental purposes (e.g., goal-focused interventions). Because meaningful work lies in the eye of the beholder and can take many forms, a necessary starting point would be to help the client articulate those values or conditions that would constitute meaningful (or growth-promoting or purposeful) work for him or her. For different persons, the values may involve work, for example, that allows for self-expression, that provides a sense of belonging or mattering to a valued reference group, that serves one's concept of a higher spiritual power, or that would allow one to make a contribution to the world that exceeds one's own existence. A few, perhaps fairly intuitive, orienting questions may be useful in defining the client's concept of meaningful work. Such questions may include, What things give (or could give) your life a sense of meaning? How important is it for you to pursue these things through your work? How much opportunity is there in your current job to do these things? Are there ways to change your current job to make it more meaningful to you? If so, how? If not, what other kinds of work—or nonwork routes—have you considered to make your life feel more meaningful?

These sorts of questions could be pursued in a more or less openended way in counseling, with client and counselor working together to identify the client's intrinsic work values, value-consistent goals or dreams, and forms of work that could enable their expression. Many clients are likely to know what is missing and what would imbue their work lives with greater meaning. Others may be aware of the existential void but have little idea of how they might fill it. Questions about meaning may well be pursued along with assessment of additional person and environment attributes (e.g., interests, abilities, availability of social and financial supports for a career change). For example, a given client might derive meaning from having greater opportunity to help others, but there are many ways to help others, some of which will be more or less consistent with his or her vocational personality (e.g., directing hunger-relief efforts, teaching math in an inner-city school, restructuring loans, designing bridges, becoming a counselor).

Standard vocational assessment activities may be quite useful in helping to clarify the individual's work personality and in suggesting work environments that may allow him or her to do meaningful work or get other eudaimonic needs (e.g., self-actualization) met. For example, there are a variety of values inventories that could be used to help identify intrinsic personal or work values (e.g., see Rounds & Armstrong, 2005), the fulfillment of which could help to define meaningful work for a given individual. There are also many less-structured or informal ways to clarify values and life goals. For example, clients can be led through a future career fantasy exercise or be asked to write their own epitaphs, describing the sort of life for which they would like to be remembered— an exercise clearly designed to get to the heart of the existential matter. Ways to fulfill core values could be explored through one's current job (e.g., shifting the focus from task productivity to organizational citizenship behaviors that promote the welfare of others) or through job restructuring, change, or nonwork activities.

Future Directions for Theory, Research, and Practice

Although these applied suggestions hint at the social-cognitive model's practical utility, there is need for much additional inquiry, especially efforts to test the model with employed workers and to examine moderators of particular model relations. For example, does the strength of the relation of goal progress to work satisfaction depend, as hypothesized, on the degree to which the individual is committed to his or her goal? Is pursuit of particular types of goals (e.g., intrinsic vs. extrinsic, approach vs. avoidance, proximal vs. distal, challenging vs. routine) more likely to lead to work satisfaction? Although some of these issues have received attention and more cross-sectional tests would be useful, particularly if they extend study of the model to diverse occupational and cultural contexts, there would be particular value in testing the model using longitudinal and, especially, experimental designs. Longitudinal studies can examine whether the temporal predominance of the predictors is consistent with hypotheses, whereas experimental studies can provide compelling tests of the causal relations among the variables. Controlled intervention studies can both examine causal questions (e.g., does increased support for work goals lead to greater work satisfaction?) and establish the utility of theory-derived methods for enhancing the eudaimonic and hedonic aspects of work satisfaction.

In keeping with the larger focus of this book and the questions raised at the outset of this chapter, it would also be valuable to pursue more basic research on the concepts of work meaning and purpose. In essence, what do different people mean when they refer to meaningful and purposeful work? Both qualitative and quantitative research may be useful in this effort. For example, is meaningful work defined differently as a function of social class, educational status, occupational type, or culture? Do blue- and white-collar workers mean the same thing when they talk about meaningful work? Are they equally likely to seek meaning in their work? Does the concept of meaningful work have salience for those who perform particularly arduous, dangerous, or routine tasks? If so, how do they pursue meaning in their work? Is the desire to find meaning in work more likely to be found among those whose more basic, extrinsic work needs (e.g., adequacy of pay) have been met?

Even if meaning in work is an idiographic matter, it may be useful to create a *taxonomy of meaningful work*—a set of categories that capture the most common ways in which meaningful work can be manifested (along with the frequencies of each category among persons of different groups, e.g., in terms of socioeconomic status, culture). Such a taxonomy, and measures derived from it, could be useful for counseling, research, and theoretical purposes. For example, at a theoretical level, it could clarify whether meaningful work is distinct from, or merely synonymous with, the larger concept of intrinsic work values (i.e., values associated with performing the work itself rather than the extrinsic consequences of the work, such as pay or prestige). Moreover, as suggested at the beginning of this chapter, more basic quantitative research on the measurement and construct validity of meaning and purpose at work would be useful. For example, can purer (i.e., in terms of non-overlapping content), more psychometrically distinct measures of work meaning and purpose be developed? In what ways do these constructs relate to other indicators of eudaimonic (e.g., flow, engagement, vitality) and hedonic work well-being?

Conclusion

In this chapter, I have presented a social-cognitive model that attempts to incorporate both eudaimonic (thinking- and doing-focused) and hedonic (feeling-focused) aspects of work well-being. In addition to describing the basic model, I have briefly considered its empirical base and applied implications and cited a few directions for future inquiry, both regarding the model per se and on the broader topic of meaningful work. As noted in several places in the chapter, there are many factors that may constrain one's desire to find meaning, purpose, or growth at work. And individuals differ in the extent to which they look to work as an essential context for constructing meaning. For many, work is a way to put bread on the table or a way to spend time before one's real life begins—at home, with friends, or in other life contexts. Moreover, not everyone works for pay, either by choice (e.g., staying home to raise a family) or because of extenuating conditions (e.g., disability, difficulty finding job openings in the current economy). Given these realities, I suggest that hedonic and eudaimonic strategies for work well-being described in this chapter can be adapted to other life domains that may be more salient to a given individual or that afford him or her greater opportunities for exercising personal agency than does work.

TABLE 7.1

Focus on the Workplace: A Social-Cognitive Perspective

Recommendations	Tested in practice	Derived from theory	Supported by research
Help the client to identify or develop work goals that have personal significance, are challenging but attainable, and are broken into proximal subgoals.[a,b]	✓	✓	✓
Assist the client to mark and make progress toward these goals, including accessing environmental resources (and overcoming obstacles) to goal pursuit.[c]	✓	✓	✓
Identify work activities that are consistent with the client's intrinsic work values or provide opportunities to experience flow.[c]	✓	✓	✓
Encourage involvement in these work activities to the extent possible.[d]	✓	✓	✓
Identify and encourage participation in social activities at work, especially ones that offer the potential to give and receive social support (e.g., mentoring) and convey a sense of belonging or mattering.[d]	✓	✓	✓
Where opportunities for valued task engagement, goal pursuit, or social support are limited at work, identify other work options or life contexts (e.g., volunteer roles) that may offer such activities.[c]	✓	✓	✓
Where job and environmental change is being considered, assist the client to identify and access needed supports and resources.[e]	✓	✓	✓
Focus on enhancement of self-efficacy, skills, and outcome expectations in the service of goal pursuit, valued task involvement, and social support seeking.[a,e]	✓	✓	✓

Note. [a]Bandura (1986). [b]Locke & Latham (2002). [c]Lent (2004). [d]Cantor & Sanderson (1999). [e]Brown & Lent (1996).

References

Bandura, A. (1986). *Social foundations of thought and action: A social cognitive theory.* Englewood Cliffs, NJ: Prentice-Hall.

Bandura, A. (1997). *Self-efficacy: The exercise of control.* New York, NY: Freeman.

Brown, S. D., & Lent, R. W. (1996). A social cognitive framework for career choice counseling. *Career Development Quarterly, 44,* 354–366. doi:10.1002/j.2161-0045.1996.tb00451.x

Cantor, N., & Sanderson, C. A. (1999). Life task participation and well-being: The importance of taking part in daily life. In D. Kahneman,

E. Diener, & N. Schwarz (Eds.), *Well-being: The foundations of hedonic psychology* (pp. 230–243). New York, NY: Russell Sage Foundation.

Caprara, G. V., Barbaranelli, C., Borgogni, L., & Steca, P. (2003). Efficacy beliefs as determinants of teachers' job satisfaction. *Journal of Educational Psychology, 95,* 821–832. doi:10.1037/0022-0663.95.4.821

Compton, W. C., Smith, M. L., Cornish, K. A., & Qualls, D. L. (1996). Factor structure of mental health measures. *Journal of Personality and Social Psychology, 71,* 406–413. doi:10.1037/0022-3514.71.2.406

Dawis, R. V. (2005). The Minnesota theory of work adjustment. In S. D. Brown & R. W. Lent (Eds.), *Career development and counseling: Putting theory and research to work* (pp. 3–23). New York, NY: Wiley.

Diener, E., Suh, E. M., Lucas, R. E., & Smith, H. L. (1999). Subjective well-being: Three decades of progress. *Psychological Bulletin, 125,* 276–302. doi:10.1037/0033-2909.125.2.276

Dik, B. J., & Duffy, R. D. (2009). Calling and vocation: Definitions and prospects for research and practice. *The Counseling Psychologist, 37,* 424–450. doi:10.1177/0011000008316430

Dik, B. J., Duffy, R. D., & Eldridge, B. M. (2009). Calling and vocation in career counseling: Recommendations for promoting meaningful work. *Professional Psychology: Research and Practice, 40,* 625–632. doi:10.1037/a0015547

Duffy, R. D., & Lent, R. W. (2009). Test of a social cognitive model of work satisfaction in teachers. *Journal of Vocational Behavior, 75,* 212–223. doi:10.1016/j.jvb.2009.06.001

Heller, D., Watson, D., & Ilies, R. (2004). The role of person versus situation in life satisfaction: A critical examination. *Psychological Bulletin, 130,* 574–600. doi:10.1037/0033-2909.130.4.574

Judge, T. A., & Watanabe, S. (1993). Another look at the job satisfaction–life satisfaction relationship. *Journal of Applied Psychology, 78,* 939–948. doi:10.1037/0021-9010.78.6.939

Lent, R. W. (2004). Toward a unifying theoretical and practical perspective on well-being and psychosocial adjustment. *Journal of Counseling Psychology, 51,* 482–509. doi:10.1037/0022-0167.51.4.482

Lent, R. W. (2005). A social cognitive view of career development and counseling. In S. D. Brown & R. W. Lent (Eds.), *Career development and counseling: Putting theory and research to work* (pp. 101–127). Hoboken, NJ: Wiley.

Lent, R. W., & Brown, S. D. (2006). Integrating person and situation perspectives on work satisfaction: A social-cognitive view. *Journal of Vocational Behavior, 69,* 236–247. doi:10.1016/j.jvb.2006.02.006

Lent, R. W., & Brown, S. D. (2008). Social cognitive career theory and subjective well-being in the context of work. *Journal of Career Assessment, 16,* 6–21. doi:10.1177/1069072707305769

Lent, R. W., Brown, S. D., & Hackett, G. (1994). Toward a unifying social cognitive theory of career and academic interest, choice, and performance [Monograph]. *Journal of Vocational Behavior, 45,* 79–122. doi:10.1006/jvbe.1994.1027

Lent, R. W., Singley, D., Sheu, H., Gainor, K. A., Brenner, B. R., Treistman, D., & Ades, L. (2005). Social cognitive predictors of domain and life satisfaction: Exploring the theoretical precursors of subjective well-being. *Journal of Counseling Psychology, 52,* 429–442. doi:10.1037/0022-0167.52.3.429

Lent, R. W., Singley, D., Sheu, H., Schmidt, J. A., & Schmidt, L. C. (2007). Relation of social–cognitive factors to academic satisfaction in engineering students. *Journal of Career Assessment, 15,* 87–97. doi:10.1177/1069072706294518

Lent, R. W., Taveira, M., Sheu, H., & Singley, D. (2009). Social cognitive predictors of academic adjustment and life satisfaction in Portuguese college students: A longitudinal analysis. *Journal of Vocational Behavior, 74,* 190–198. doi:10.1016/j.jvb.2008.12.006

Locke, E. A., & Latham, G. P. (2002). Building a practically useful theory of goal setting and task motivation. *American Psychologist, 57,* 705–717. doi:10.1037/0003-066X.57.9.705

McCrae, R. R., & Costa, P. T. (1991). Adding *liebe und arbeit:* The full five-factor model and well-being. *Personality and Social Psychology Bulletin, 17,* 227–232. doi:10.1177/014616729101700217

McGregor, I., & Little, B. R. (1998). Personal projects, happiness, and meaning: On doing well and being yourself. *Journal of Personality and Social Psychology, 74,* 494–512. doi:10.1037/0022-3514.74.2.494

Rain, J. S., Lane, I. M., & Steiner, D. D. (1991). A current look at the job satisfaction/life satisfaction relationship: Review and future considerations. *Human Relations, 44,* 287–307.

Rounds, J. B., & Armstrong, P. I. (2005). Assessment of needs and values. In S. D. Brown & R. W. Lent (Eds.), *Career development and counseling: Putting theory and research to work* (pp. 305–329). New York, NY: Wiley.

Ryan, R. M., & Deci, E. L. (2001). On happiness and human potentials: A review of research on hedonic and eudaimonic well-being. *Annual Review of Psychology, 52,* 141–166. doi:10.1146/annurev.psych.52.1.141

Ryff, C. D. (1989). Happiness is everything, or is it? Explorations on the meaning of psychological well-being. *Journal of Personality and Social Psychology, 57,* 1069–1081. doi:10.1037/0022-3514.57.6.1069

Ryff, C. D., & Keyes, C. L. M. (1995). The structure of psychological well-being revisited. *Journal of Personality and Social Psychology, 69,* 719–727. doi:10.1037/0022-3514.69.4.719

Singer, M. S., & Coffin, T. K. (1996). Cognitive and volitional determinants of job attitudes in a voluntary organization. *Journal of Social Behavior & Personality, 11,* 313–328.

Singley, D., Lent, R. W., & Sheu, H. (2010). Longitudinal test of a social cognitive model of academic and life satisfaction. *Journal of Career Assessment, 18,* 133–146. doi:10.1177/1069072709354199

Steger, M. F., Dik, B. J., & Duffy, R. D. (2012). Measuring meaningful work: The Work and Meaning Inventory (WAMI). *Journal of Career Assessment, 20,* 322–337. doi:10.1177/1069072711436160

Steger, M. F., Frazier, P., Oishi, S., & Kaler, M. (2006). The Meaning in Life Questionnaire: Assessing the presence of and search for meaning in life. *Journal of Counseling Psychology, 53,* 80–93. doi:10.1037/0022-0167.53.1.80

Thoresen, C. J., Kaplan, S. A., Barsky, A. P., Warren, C. R., & de Chermont, K. (2003). The affective underpinnings of job perceptions and attitudes: A meta-analytic review and integration. *Psychological Bulletin, 129,* 914–945. doi:10.1037/0033-2909.129.6.914

Verbruggen, M., & Sels, L. (2010). Social–cognitive factors affecting clients' career and life satisfaction after counseling. *Journal of Career Assessment, 18,* 3–15. doi:10.1177/1069072709340516

LEADING A MEANINGFUL ORGANIZATION

Michael G. Pratt, Camille Pradies, and Douglas A. Lepisto

Doing Well, Doing Good, and Doing With

Organizational Practices for Effectively Cultivating Meaningful Work

8

> Work is about a search for daily meaning as well as daily
> bread, for recognition as well as cash, for astonishment
> rather than torpor, in short, for a sort of life rather than
> a Monday through Friday sort of dying.
>
> —*Studs Terkel,* Working

Work, as Studs Terkel (1995) reminds us, provides a variety of functions and opportunities in our lives including "a search for daily meaning" (p. xiii). Given the large portion of our waking lives devoted to it and its centrality in modern life, it is perhaps not surprising that we look to work as a source of meaning beyond daily bread and cash. But can the places we work for help make work meaningful—something more than a "Monday through Friday sort of dying" (Terkel, 1995, p. xiii)?

Historically, the search for meaning in and at work has tended to focus on the individual meaning-maker (Rosso, Dekas, & Wrzesniewski, 2010). This is appealing given that meaning is often in the eye of the beholder. However, we argue that meaning is not simply self-constructed; it is also socially constructed (e.g., Weick, 1995). That is, we draw upon social cues from people, culture, symbols, and the like when making sense of what is meaningful. Because work is often conducted in socially rich contexts, organizations are in a unique position to help members cultivate and enact meaningful work. Unfortunately, there is a paucity

http://dx.doi.org/10.1037/14183-009
Purpose and Meaning in the Workplace, B. J. Dik, Z. S. Byrne, and M. F. Steger (Editors)

of research that examines how organizations and organizational practices might foster work that is *meaningful* (Rosso et al., 2010)—that is, work perceived as purposeful and significant (Pratt & Ashforth, 2003). The aim of this chapter, therefore, is to explore how organizations can effectively foster meaningfulness. But to understand how to best foster meaningfulness, we must first briefly discuss how individuals find or create meaningfulness.

We take as our starting point Pratt and Ashforth's (2003) research linking organizational practices with fostering meaningfulness in and at work, given that it is one of the few comprehensive treatments of how organizations influence work meaning (Rosso et al., 2010). Like many, Pratt and Ashforth began with the assumption that individuals construct meaningfulness; that is, certain jobs or organizations are not intrinsically meaningful in themselves. In particular, individuals interpret what is meaningful through their own identities. Pratt and Ashforth further argued that to influence meaningfulness, organizations must influence how people view themselves. Research has suggested two main paths for such influence: what one does (i.e., one's roles) and with whom one surrounds oneself (i.e., one's membership in a community or culture). Organizational practices that can influence meaningfulness, therefore, are of two main types: those that alter roles and tasks, known as *meaningfulness in work* practices, and those that change the nature of an individual's social context, known as *meaningfulness at work* practices (Pratt & Ashforth, 2003).

Though considered a critical first step, Pratt and Ashforth's (2003) linkages between practices and individual meaningfulness are quite broad: Because everyone has an identity, anyone could potentially be equally influenced by meaningfulness *in* and *at* practices. However, given their assertion that individuals construct meaningfulness, it seems unlikely that different individuals will react to organizational attempts to influence meaningfulness in the same way. Because our focus is on the effectiveness of these organizational practices, we decided to explore this question of differential impact. In particular, we wondered, "If what is meaningful to one person is not necessarily meaningful to another, how might companies effectively manage meaningfulness?" To get at this question, we moved beyond the notions of how individuals viewed themselves (i.e., their identities) to a similarly fundamental issue: What makes work as a major life domain worthwhile? We argue that work orientation is a useful lens to examine the various, but finite, ways people answer such a question.

Next, we briefly review and define the concept of work orientation. We then evaluate the dominant three-orientation approach—job, career, and calling—and offer an alternative five-orientation approach that we believe provides much-needed clarity. We spend the bulk of the chapter tying specific organizational practices to these new work orientations.

Work Orientation

Although conceptualizations of *work orientations* vary, we define them as internalized evaluations about what makes work worth doing. The impetus of our conceptualization of work orientation draws from Bellah, Madsen, Sullivan, Swidler, and Tipton's (1985) original tripartite model of job, career, and calling. However, given that the focus of their book was broadly on American life, Bellah and colleagues devoted rather little attention to developing these orientations. We enrich this original conceptualization by building from their societal analysis to include recent developments regarding the role of culture on cognition (e.g., Vaisey, 2008, 2009).

Several points about our definition are notable. First, work orientations are evaluative: As enacted, they involve making judgments about what makes work good or bad; specifically, these judgments draw on standards about what makes work worth doing. In making these evaluations, individuals may not provide completely coherent justifications for why work is worthy (Haidt, 2001); that is, they may not be fully aware of the standards they have internalized. Rather, these evaluations tend to first come from the gut, as intuitions do (Dane & Pratt, 2007). As a result, individuals experience a feeling about what makes something good. Likewise, work orientations are manifested holistically—more like patterns of values and beliefs rather than discrete ones. Individuals likely internalize impressions and understandings about work from a variety of sources such as family, media, and society in general. These impressions, in turn, form the standards by which these judgments are made (Lepisto, Pradies, & Pratt, 2012).

Second, despite their sociocultural origins, work orientations are internalized—they reside in individuals as standards for evaluating the work. Thus, although sociocultural meanings of work exist beyond individuals in a variety of collective forms (e.g., symbols, myths, artifacts, institutions—known as cultural *codes;* Swidler, 2001), work orientations are their individual-level manifestation. They are dispositional in that they are fairly stable over time within individuals (Wrzesniewski, 1999). This is not to suggest that work orientations, like other dispositions, cannot be changed (Davis-Blake & Pfeffer, 1989); however, change is not likely easy. Third, work orientations refer to work conceptualized as a *life domain* (Berg, Grant, & Johnson, 2010) or broader *cultural category* (Abbott, 1989) that sits alongside other life domains such as marriage, education, or religion. Thus, work orientations are not about any specific job one might hold or the characteristics of one's tasks (e.g., skill variety, autonomy). Work orientations focus on what makes work worthy or good, just as one might assess what makes marriage or education worthy or good.

Although the number of work orientations that have been posited has varied (e.g., intrinsic vs. extrinsic; Amabile, Hill, Hennessey, & Tighe, 1994), the tripartite model of work orientation of job, career, and calling has emerged as the dominant model (e.g., Baumeister, 1991; Wrzesniewski, McCauley, Rozin, & Schwartz, 1997). We describe job, career, and calling as they have been conceptualized in the management literature, recognizing these interpretations differ somewhat from the traditional formulation (Bellah et al., 1985). Individuals with *job* orientations approach work as instrumental activity. They see work in terms of financial security and seek out jobs that provide such security. Because these individuals work to live, not live to work, work is meaningful to the degree that it can provide the resources necessary to pursue activities outside of work (e.g., family or hobbies; Wrzesniewski et al., 1997). However, as Bellah and colleagues (1985) noted, people with a job orientation also likely value hard work, discipline, and individual initiative. Those with *career* orientations derive meaning from work through "records of success, achievement, and status" (Baumeister, 1991, p. 122). Here, work is meaningful to the degree that it provides avenues for social achievement: promotion, recognition, and perceived career success. Finally, *calling* as a work orientation has been described in a variety of ways, but researchers often invoke Bellah et al., who noted the following:

> [A calling] subsumes the self into a community of disciplined practice and sound judgment whose activity has *meaning and value in itself* [emphasis added], not just in the output or profit that results from it. But the calling not only *links a person to his or her fellow workers* [emphasis added]. A calling links a person to the larger community, a whole in which *the calling of each is a contribution to the good of all* [emphasis added]. (p. 66)

We emphasize that this is the definition of calling as it relates to work orientation. Although the notion of calling has been conceptualized in many ways before and independently from the idea of work orientation (see Dik & Duffy, 2009; Wrzesniewski, Dekas, & Rosso, 2009), we focus on Bellah and his colleagues' (1985) original conceptualization that identifies three distinct elements apparent in the notion of a calling orientation. First, a calling orientation involves subordinating oneself to a practice or ideal that possesses meaning and value in itself. Second, a calling orientation involves connection and community with fellow workers. Finally, a calling orientation invokes helping others and the notion of contribution to the good of all. We see a partial overlap between how Bellah and colleagues conceptualized a calling orientation and extant conceptualizations of callings. In particular, conceptualizations of callings tend to explicitly or implicitly involve two of the three main elements: that callings are intrinsically valued (Berg et al., 2010) and involve helping others, often because of a sense of destiny or moral duty (Bunderson & Thompson, 2009; Wrzesniewski et al., 1997). We disentangle and enrich these two elements and build up the neglected third element of callings: good work as determined by the quality of bonds among colleagues.

Specifically, we argue that although these three elements may constitute a calling orientation, they need not necessarily go together and thus may represent orientations in their own right. For example, it is possible to view work as intrinsically self-fulfilling—pleasure that comes from doing a job well—but not directly helpful to others (e.g., creating elegant computer code). Therefore, we argue for a work orientation based solely on fulfillment from the work itself, which we refer to as a *craftsmanship orientation,* and another based solely on helping others, which we refer to as a *serving orientation.* Finally, though extant conceptualizations of calling do not appear to emphasize notions of community and connection with colleagues as Bellah et al. (1985) did, anecdotal and theoretical research has suggested a relational or socially based orientation that we refer to as a *kinship orientation.* In short, building on Bellah and colleagues, we no longer see callings as a primary orientation, but one that is perhaps a combination of three others: craftsmanship, serving, and kinship. We discuss each of these orientations in turn.

CRAFTSMANSHIP ORIENTATION: MEANINGFULNESS THROUGH "DOING WELL"

> It is important to watch for details, to be neat and technically efficient. I don't like to waste motion and so I try to make the operation as well planned and thought out as possible. I'm particular about how the needle is held, where the stitches are placed, the type of suture, and so on—things should look the best and seem easy. (Csikszentmihalyi, 1990, p. 156).

Although often associated with artistic and craft work, craftsmanship is relevant to a wide range of work and occupations (Sennett, 2008). The craftsman conducts his or her work with skill and expertise, developing pride in his or her work, not as a means to an end but as an end in itself. As C. Wright Mills (1956) argued,

> The hope in good work . . . is hope of product and hope of pleasure in the work itself; the supreme concern, the whole attention, is with the quality of the product and the skill of its making. . . . gratification is such that a man may live in a kind of quiet passion "for his work alone." (pp. 220–221)

Therefore, someone with a *craftsmanship orientation* evaluates work as worth doing when it is done well for its own sake.

Theoretical and empirical research has provided direct and indirect support for this orientation. First, recent scholars have joined classical theorists to argue that the ethic of craftsmanship—the unalienated devotion to one's labor for its own sake—is timeless and represents "a fully idealized model of work gratification" (Mills, 1956, p. 220). Research on communities of practice has provided indirect support for such a notion by highlighting how gaining expertise and defining oneself as a master practitioner among others with similar interests is of central importance (Lave & Wenger, 1991, p. 111). Likewise, studies of culinary work have demonstrated the importance of aesthetics, style, and quality to occupational life and occupational identity: "Craft is a part of all work life" (Fine, 1992, p. 1270).

Second, definitions of craftsmanship invoke notions of *competence*, which Rosso et al. (2010) identified as a means for experiencing meaningful work. Furthermore, a meta-analytic review of goal-directed achievement strivings (Hulleman, Schrager, Bodmann, & Harackiewicz, 2010) suggested that one facet of striving is *mastery*, where individuals are focused on mastering the requirements of a task and improving their competence. Individuals who take this approach would likely find meaningfulness from doing the work well rather than simply performing better than others or working solely for financial compensation.

SERVING ORIENTATION: MEANINGFULNESS THROUGH "DOING GOOD"

> As an environmental protection agency specialist reflected, "I've always felt a personal obligation to be doing something that is for the betterment of everyone. And the environment is like, well, what could be more important than that? So even though it's frustrating sometimes, I couldn't just stop and follow something that might be extremely interesting to me but didn't help the world. . . . I have this deep-rooted need to feel that my job is of public service." (Bowe, Bowe, & Streeter, 2000, pp. 578–579)

Whereas craftsmanship highlights meaningfulness from work as an end in itself, a serving orientation draws the focus outward to show how meaningfulness comes from the perceived effect on the beneficiaries of work. Thus, someone with a serving orientation evaluates work as worth doing when it betters the lives of others or advances a cause. Serving often refers to other people, but more broadly, it can refer to animals, plants, nature, an ideology, or a religion.

A service orientation is elucidated by research that has focused less on why one serves (e.g., a calling from God or one's true self) and more on who benefits from one's work. This research, which includes work on prosocial behavior and altruism, has provided support for distinguishing a serving orientation from callings. To illustrate, the notion of prosocial behaviors implies that workers are motivated by making a positive difference in the lives of other people by promoting the welfare of others (e.g., Grant, Dutton, & Rosso, 2008; Penner, Dovidio, Piliavin, & Schroeder, 2005). Similarly, research on employees with strong altruistic or prosocial values (Penner et al., 2005) or benevolent personalities (Huseman, Hatfield, & Miles, 1987) has argued that workers seek positions that allow them to do good and help others (Grant, 2008a). Taken as a whole, this drive to help others, exclusive of whether the work is otherwise engaging, suggests that serving is a distinct way of viewing one's work.

KINSHIP ORIENTATION: MEANINGFULNESS THROUGH "DOING WITH"

> We're here [at work] 24 hours a day every third day. This is our family. A lot of people don't understand that. You have to get along with your family. . . . Just like you, I love my family. This is my family here, this is what really intrigues me about this place. (Haski-Leventhal & McLeigh, 2009, pp. 85–86)

Like a serving orientation, a *kinship orientation* is focused on others and not on work itself. However, the focus here is on the quality of relationships one creates through his or her work—or, as Bellah et al. (1985) noted, through linking a worker "to the larger community" (p. 66). Kinship is similar to Bennett's (1974) *social* work orientation that focused on friendships at work. We adopt the more specific term *kinship* rather than the broader term *social* because of the quality of the tie. Kinship as it appears here does not refer to an actual blood or legally binding bond (e.g., marriages, civil unions); rather, we use it because those who appear to have it—such as the person in the quotation that opens this section—often refer to these bonds in familial terms. These bonds may be dyadic, such as seeing one's boss as a parent, or they may be more communal, as is the case of brotherhoods (or sisterhoods)—terms used to describe freemasonry, monastery inhabitants, police officers, and firefighters. Either way, someone with a kinship orientation evaluates work as worth doing when it creates close (familial) bonds.

Several lines of theoretical and empirical research have offered initial support for the existence of a kinship orientation. As noted, Bennett (1974) referred to this as a social orientation; however, his conceptualization has gone largely undeveloped. Drawing on disparate research on organizational culture and practices that blur work and nonwork spheres of life (e.g., family, spirituality), Pratt and Ashforth (2003) argued for the importance of creating community as a vehicle for creating meaningfulness at work. Similarly, Rosso et al. (2010) argued that *belongingness* is a mechanism through which meaningfulness is created (cf. *drive to bond;* Nohria, Groysberg, & Lee, 2008). Drawing on recent work on the importance of high-quality connections with others in organizations, Dutton and Heaphy (2003) viewed interpersonal connections as primary means for deriving purpose and significance from work. In addition to providing a route for meaningfulness, these connections may also be the primary rationale for working. To illustrate, surveys have shown that soldiers are more motivated to fight to protect their friends than they are to protect their country or some other ideal. In a recent study of what motivated soldiers fighting in Operation Iraqi Freedom, L. Wong and colleagues found that "fighting for my buddies" was the most common response: "U.S. soldiers continue to fight because of the bonds of trust between soldiers" (L. Wong, Kolditz, Millen, & Potter, 2003, p. 23).

Tying Organizational Practices to Work Orientations

Increasing the number of primary work orientations to five creates a good-news/bad-news situation for practitioners. Although having more orientations suggests that one-size-fits-all approaches will have limited appeal, the added orientations broaden the number of practices that may facilitate meaningful work and may, in turn, lead to more effective results. Because of space constraints, we cannot cover the full range of practices that are relevant to the five work orientations. To narrow it down, we focus on the three orientations we have introduced here, given that there has been considerable research on jobs and careers, such as on how to structure compensation systems (see Martocchio, 2010) and career paths (e.g., Chapter 3, this volume). We narrow it down further by providing only a sampling of practices that may be effective for fostering meaningfulness among those with craftsmanship, service, and kinship orientations.

These practices are illustrated in Figure 8.1 and Table 8.1. The figure was inspired by Pratt and Ashforth's (2003) work distinguishing between general practices (e.g., selection) and those more closely aligned with meaning in working (e.g., job design) and meaning at work (e.g., managing culture). We extend their logic by moving to even more tailored practices, which we refer to as *customized,* that are closely aligned with a single work orientation. The logic underlying these arguments, as well as many in the organizational literature, is one of fit or alignment (e.g., Chatman, 1989). That is, organizational practices that align with individuals' work orientations will increase the probability

FIGURE 8.1

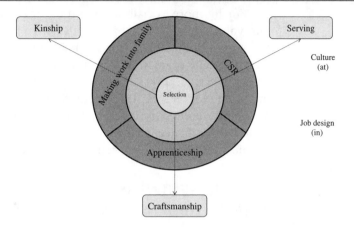

Tailoring practices for different work orientation types. Tailoring involves moving from a general (selection) to a more customized organizational practice to better foster meaningfulness for workers with specific work orientations: serving, craftsmanship, and kinship. A stronger fit between a practice and a work orientation occurs as one moves from the center of the model. CSR = corporate social responsibility.

that individuals will experience meaningfulness in or at work. Thus, as one moves out from the center of Figure 8.1, these organizational practices will provide a stronger fit with a specific work orientation and increase the likelihood for meaningful work.

For each practice, we provide theoretical evidence linking the practice to the facilitation of work meaningfulness and, where applicable, empirical evidence. Despite little empirical or theoretical work directly linking specific organizational practices to the creation of meaningfulness, we have been able to extrapolate from research linking these practices to related areas of scholarship (e.g., work motivation) as well as draw on our own research and practice in these areas.

GENERAL ORGANIZATIONAL PRACTICES FOR FOSTERING MEANINGFULNESS

Pratt and Ashforth (2003) suggested there are three main practices that can foster meaningfulness for workers: recruitment, selection, and socialization. With regard to specific work orientations, recruitment and selection are fundamental because they ensure that workers with specific orientations are attracted to and are hired by organizations. Before using work orientations as a selection criterion, however, research would have to show a clear connection between work orientation fit and job performance, thus avoiding issues of adverse impact.

Furthermore, socialization or training can be used to reinforce certain values or practices that are attractive to individuals with certain work orientations (e.g., during their initiation, emphasizing to those with a serving orientation how their organization does various public-good projects). There is also a possibility that certain practices can shape or alter a worker's existing orientation. However, as with recruitment and selection, there is no research on this topic to date. Thus, we do not review this practice in Table 8.1. That said, we discuss a specific type of socialization practice—apprenticeship practices—later in this chapter.

MEANINGFULNESS IN WORKING AND MEANINGFULNESS AT WORK PRACTICES

Although there are likely many practices that can influence those with craftsmanship, serving, and kinship orientations, our focus is on two critical areas: job design (a meaningfulness *in* practice) and managing organizational culture (a meaningfulness *at* practice). Both are broad enough that they can be tailored to fit specific work orientations.

Job Design

At its essence, job design involves how one can change the content and structure of jobs to achieve higher work motivation (Hackman & Oldham, 1980). Because this literature is broad and diverse (see Morgeson & Campion, 2003, for review), we draw primarily on two streams of research that we believe are the most relevant for meaningfulness for each work orientation: (a) the job characteristics model (JCM; Hackman & Oldham, 1980) and (b) relational job design (e.g., Grant, 2007, 2008a).

The JCM suggests there are five central job dimensions to be considered during redesign: skill variety (the degree to which a job requires various activities to be carried out), task identity (the degree to which one can complete the whole job from its beginning to its end), task significance (the degree to which the job impacts the lives of others), autonomy, and feedback (e.g., Hackman & Oldham, 1976). One of the critical psychological states stemming from work that is high on certain dimensions, such as task significance, is experienced meaningfulness (Fried, 1991; Hackman & Oldham, 1976).

We argue that jobs, designed in such a way as to align with broader conceptualizations of work will be more meaningful. To cultivate a craftsmanship orientation, at least three job characteristics should be focal points: task identity, feedback, and autonomy. Given that those with a craftsmanship orientation evaluate work as worth doing when it is done well for its own sake, having the opportunity to complete one's job as a whole rather than just doing parts of it should be especially beneficial. Because mastery is important in this orientation, feedback provides those with this orientation with information to gauge their work against standards of quality and know when they are met. This is especially critical during apprenticeships (discussed later). Finally, the hallmark of an expert craftsman is the ability to produce his or her products or services without interference from others. Thus, job autonomy is essential.

Relational job design, by contrast, is likely to appeal to an individual with a serving orientation because it taps into an individual's prosocial values to help and care for others. Relational job design broadens the focus of traditional job design to consider the *relational architecture,* "the structural properties of work that shape employees' opportunities to connect and interact with other people" (Grant, 2007, p. 396). In particular, relational job design focuses on designing jobs in such a way that workers can realize the impact their work has on other people (i.e., beneficiaries). By altering the relational architecture to increase contact with beneficiaries, workers with a serving orientation should have an increased motivation to make a prosocial difference and ultimately experience greater meaningfulness (Grant, 2007).

There is some theoretical and empirical support for the linkage between elements of relational job design and experienced meaningfulness, though not necessarily for those with a serving orientation. Work by Grant (2007, 2008a, 2008b), for example, has provided preliminary, but indirect, empirical support for this linkage. For example, lifeguards who read stories of how other lifeguards rescued drowning swimmers showed increases in job dedication and helping behavior (Grant, 2008b). Likewise, public service and telephone solicitation employees who were provided greater opportunities for impact on and contact with beneficiaries had higher levels of affective commitment to those they served and stronger prosocial motivations (Grant, 2008a). To the degree that one's attachments and motivations reflect experienced meaningfulness, the results of these studies suggest that for those with a serving orientation, conducting relational job design interventions may provide more potent opportunities for experiencing purposeful and significant work.

Those with a kinship orientation can be provided with more opportunities for meaningfulness through job design as well. Limited research has focused on how the interconnection of tasks, or *task interdependence,* increases the motivational value of jobs (e.g., C. Wong & Campion, 1991). As jobs become more interconnected, workers have greater opportunities to interact and focus their work on supporting others within the organization. In this way, those who obtain meaning through connection with others will have more opportunities for meaningfulness. To illustrate, the increasing use of team-based designs can provide additional opportunities for those with kinship orientations to feel a sense of cohesion, camarade-rie, membership, and ultimately meaningfulness (Hackman, 1987).

Managing Organizational Culture

Practices that shape an organization's culture may also enhance the mean-ingfulness that workers experience (Pratt & Ashforth, 2003). Specifically, we see opportunities for practitioners to tailor organizational cultures in different ways to align with the three orientations.

Although organizational culture has been defined in myriad ways (see Trice & Beyer, 1993, for a review), from a functional perspective, it can be defined as a relatively shared pattern of assumptions, meanings, and values about how things are done every day in the organization (Schein, 2010). By *relatively shared,* we want to emphasize that cultural meanings, values, and assumptions need not be held by all members (Martin, 1992); organizations may have multiple subcultures (Trice & Beyer, 1993). Consequently, it may be that different subcultures in a single organization can cater to those individuals with different work orientations. It is also important to note that our prescriptions are made under the assumption that organizational cultures can be managed and even changed. As Schein (1995) put it, "One could argue that the only real thing of importance that leaders do is to create and manage cul-ture" (p. 273).

For the craftsmanship orientation, we suggest that appreciation for standards and quality is important. Cultures that propagate prac-tices that emphasize these are likely to offer an environment in which an individual with a craftsmanship orientation can develop meaning-fulness. Such attempts often take the form of striving for perfection. Companies such as Intelligentsia Coffee and Lexus offer fitting exam-ples. Intelligentsia appeals to those with a craftsmanship orientation by establishing standards of excellence in their approach to coffee. Coined "The Black Cat Project," this integration of product selection and the application of high skill from baristas promotes a continuous striving for the highest standards: "the pursuit of espresso perfection in all of its manifestations" (Intelligentsia Coffee, 2011). By espousing these ideals, providing baristas with intensive training programs, utilizing special-ized equipment, and sourcing the best beans, Intelligentsia has built a culture tailored to a craftsmanship orientation.

In a similar way, Lexus cultivates craftsman-like values by adopt-ing *kaizen,* the continuous improvement of products and process. This luxury automobile manufacturer even touts "the passionate pursuit of perfection" as a central value in how work is done (Lexus, n.d.). The introduction of such practices, slogans, and guiding principles that emphasize standards of quality while keeping in mind the extant culture of the organization in order to make an adapted change should foster meaningfulness for those with a craftsmanship orientation. However, it is important to note that any cultural change is likely to involve additional fundamental changes, such as changes in leadership behavior (or in leaders), incentive structures, and the like.

Those with a serving orientation develop meaningfulness through their connection to, and impact on, the beneficiaries of their work. Therefore, organizations with rites and rituals that recognize and celebrate these various beneficiaries will be attractive to those with this type of orientation. Many nonprofit organizations offer apt examples, given that their missions often strive to promote and help those who are overlooked and underrepresented. For example, during employee appreciation dinners at Ten Thousand Villages in Champaign, Illinois, this fair-trade organization spends time discussing the stories of the artisans whose lives are positively affected by the selling of their products.

For-profit organizations can engage in similar practices. For example, the medical technology company Medtronic emphasizes the importance of connecting employees to patients. Through annual parties, employees meet patients who have seen their lives improved thanks to Medtronic's products (Grant, 2007). The CEO even promotes the expression of a "'defining moment' in which they [the employees] come face to face with a patient whose story deeply touches them" (George, 2003, p. 88). These annual rituals and the resulting connection between employees and patients reinforce an organizational culture in which caring about patients is central. For those with a serving orientation, these cultural practices provide strong opportunities to cultivate meaningfulness.

Finally, organizations can have a culture tailored to fit individuals with a kinship orientation or a drive to bond by instituting practices emphasizing teamwork, camaraderie, and community (Nohria et al., 2008, p. 279). There are various ways in which organizations can manage culture to build community. For example, Iggy's Bread of the World, a renowned Boston-based bakery, has organized intershift soccer games among employees to create a sense of camaraderie: "This common passion for soccer, despite the many cultural and linguistic differences among the workers, served to unite the employees" (Valley & Gendron, 2001, p. 6).

Practices that provide such opportunities for collaboration create stronger communities and thus greater opportunities for meaningfulness for those with a kinship orientation. Another way that companies can foster community is through practices that provide opportunities for employees to support one another. Grant et al. (2008) examined employee support programs at a large retail chain. They found that employees who gave financial contributions to assist fellow employees strengthened their affective commitment to the organization; the same effect was found for the support recipients. For those with a kinship orientation, employee support programs bring together giver and receiver, thus increasing bonds with the collective.

CUSTOMIZED ORGANIZATIONAL PRACTICES TO FOSTER MEANINGFULNESS

Having reviewed some exemplary practices that foster meaningfulness across the three orientations, we now review practices more specifically tailored to each orientation (see Figure 8.1). We identify an exemplary organizational practice for each work orientation while recognizing the possibility for many others.

Craftsmanship Practice: Apprenticeship

Historically, craftsmen served under experts as they developed from apprentices to journeymen to masters. We see potential for this to continue today through formal mentorship programs that more closely resemble this long-standing practice. Specifically, those with a craftsmanship orientation will benefit from relationships with those who embody the ideals they are attempting to approximate in their work. In the interactive process of observation, imitation, trial, and error, the master facilitates the apprentice's fine-tuned skills largely through the transmission of tacit knowledge (O'Connor, 2005). Thus, this relationship should be focused primarily on what apprentices do and how they do it rather than on how fast or efficiently work is completed (Gamble, 2001). Doctoral students learning to be academics (Kanigel, 1993) and those learning a manual trade (Crawford, 2009) offer a fitting model for how this can be achieved. Though organizations are increasingly aware of the importance of mentorship programs, viewing them as apprenticeships reframes them to focus on developing the deep skill and expertise that would resonate with a craftsmanship orientation.

Serving Practice: Corporate Citizenship

Adopting practices that promote corporate social responsibility or citizenship is uniquely suited to foster meaningfulness for those with a serving orientation. Corporate citizen practices "go beyond the traditional definition of profit-making . . . to enhance the quality of community life through active, participative, organized involvement" (Tichy, McGill, & Clair, 1997, pp. 2–3). Though corporate citizenship is a broad umbrella of practices, we see two examples as especially fitting for a serving orientation: one focused on direct employee participation and the other on promoting corporate-level initiatives.

For example, the Swiss bank UBS has created the UBS Graduate Deferral Program, which is designed to give new hires the possibility to postpone their entry by 1 year to do community service with half the base salary and a stipend for health insurance (Hewlett, Sherbin, & Sumberg, 2009). Programs such as these enable individuals with a serving orientation to directly serve others, with the support of their organizations. Merck's Mectizan Donation Program, in contrast, illustrates how corporate citizenship practices can influence even those who are not directly helping others. After being unable to find a buyer for Mectizan, a drug that treats river blindness—an affliction that devastated the poorest of countries—Merck decided not only to donate the drug for free but also to ensure its distribution for as long as it was needed. This donation had an electrifying effect on Merck members; as one noted, "It was one of the highlights of my career here" (Dutton & Pratt, 1997, p. 161). Prior research on similar practices has suggested that such initiatives allow members to see their organization in caring terms (Grant et al., 2008), thus making it especially appealing for those with a serving orientation.

Kinship Practice: Blending Work and Family

Organizations can move beyond simply creating strong community bonds to actually recreating familial dynamics, thus appealing directly to those with a kinship orientation. In their study of network marketing organizations, Pratt and Rosa (2003) identified two sets of practices that blend work and family. The first set of practices, *making work into family*, "involves the formation and management of positive family-like dynamics . . . by instituting mentor–protégé and quasi-filial relationships within the organization's structure" (Pratt & Rosa, 2003, p. 404). Here, mentors, peers, and subordinates are viewed in familial terms, such as parents, siblings, and kids, respectively. Such bonds are created as organizational members engage in practices that would normally be found in family life. For example, Quicken Loans "sends handwritten cards to employees on their anniversaries, as well as to employees' kids on their birthdays—with gift certificates enclosed" (Coombes, 2008, para. 14). Southwest Airlines emphasizes teamwork, community, and family (Godsey, 1996). This family spirit manifests itself in many ways, including voluntary contributions employees make to assist colleagues in need (O'Reilly & Pfeffer, 1995). Similarly, Pratt (2000a) described how after an Amway distributor was shot at home by a burglar, his extended family offered to donate hundreds of gallons of blood to a local hospital and cleaned and redecorated his house. Although some practices here may overlap with those we have talked about previously (e.g., building mentor–protégé relationships, supporting other employees), it should be noted that these practices are explicitly geared toward strengthening familial group cohesion.

The second set of practices, *bringing family into work,* involves incorporating family members into the workplace. Some of these practices are rather simple. To illustrate, the airline SAS provides baby seats and high chairs in their cafeterias to "encourage families to eat lunch together" (Fishman, 1998, para. 12). Others involve a greater investment of resources. The Global Family Program of the chemical company BASF is a good illustration. This program facilitates foreign exchange opportunities whereby the children of BASF employees worldwide are welcomed into the homes of BASF employees in other countries (BASF SE, 2008). Here, coworkers literally take on a parenting function for their colleagues' children.

Conclusions and Future Directions

We argue that when examining why work is worth doing and thus how to manage meaningfulness, one needs to take a step back from looking at the specific tasks that make up someone's job and the compensation structures associated with it. We feel it is critical to know how people look at work more generally (i.e., as a life domain) because these views will likely have a sizable influence on how they approach the work they do, as well as their reaction to it (e.g., job satisfaction and job engagement; Lepisto et al., 2012). Specifically, we have argued for the existence of at least five individually held, but socially derived, work orientations, and we have developed three of them: craftsmanship, serving, and kinship. These latter three orientations correspond with "doing [work] well," "doing good [work]," and "doing [work] with." We then discussed how various organizational practices, ranging from general (e.g., selection) to specific (e.g., apprenticeships), may appeal to workers with these orientations. We conclude that organizations will be the most effective in fostering meaningfulness in and at work to the degree that these work practices fit an individual's work orientation.

We make these conclusions somewhat tentatively, however, because there is more theoretical than empirical support for our claims. To obtain such empirical support, researchers could develop measures to more accurately capture work orientations. This may involve both inductive and deductive research as well as partnerships between researchers and practitioners. There is also a pressing need for research that more directly examines the effectiveness of these work practices on the experience of meaningfulness in and at work. And given our focus on effectiveness, research should not only examine these practices but also look at whether work orientations vary in the meaningfulness they provide to individuals. For example, will job and career orientations that are more self-focused ultimately lead to as much experienced meaningfulness as those that we have focused on here—ones that move beyond the self?

Even as we strive to better codify and establish empirical support for our claims, several key questions and areas for future research remain for all students of work and organizations. The first involves further exploring the notion of work orientation. For example, where do these orientations come from? Work orientation has often been conceptualized as being individually held; however, some research, including our own, has suggested that work orientations may stem from more macro sociocultural beliefs and understandings (Bellah et al., 1985; Lepisto et al., 2012). If so, more research is needed on what these sociocultural beliefs and understandings are and how they get transmitted to workers. By knowing how meaningfulness is transmitted to individuals, practitioners may in turn learn how to better cultivate meaningfulness among their workers.

Furthermore, we may need to more closely examine how work orientations are similar to and different from related concepts and terms. For example, we have argued that work orientations are likely a gestalt or pattern of values and sociocultural beliefs. They may also be different from work values in that work orientations are focused more exclusively on work as a life domain and on the worthiness of work. Thus, work orientations are about why I work rather than what I work for. A person with a service orientation and a person with a craftsmanship orientation may therefore value money for different reasons (e.g., to help others vs. to allow one to continue doing the work one loves). In this way, work orientations might share more similarities with recent research that has described different logics of worth (Boltanski & Thévenot, 2006).

Research should also attempt to determine whether we have truly captured each of the primary work orientations and in what way (if any) work orientations may be combined. For example, we have implied that what scholars today refer to as *callings* may actually involve a blending of serving, kinship, and craftsmanship orientations. Similarly, if we believe that individuals may have more than one work orientation, we should explore whether certain combinations of work orientations are more likely (e.g., a serving–kinship orientation) than other combinations (e.g., a serving–job orientation). Again, these issues have significant practical implications. If workers have more than one work orientation, what organizational practices might be attractive to them? Would they involve the creation of entirely new practices or simply the combination of practices that appeal to distinct orientations? Alternatively, might organizations need to get closer to the center of our

Figure 8.1, pursuing broader practices that may appeal to a wider range of work orientations? And might both of these approaches (broader and combined) have the potential to dilute their positive effects for workers with a strong dominant orientation compared with those with mixed orientations? Pratt and Ashforth (2003) argued that the implementation of practices based on different logics (meaningfulness at work and meaningfulness in working) might be, at best, difficult. To illustrate, some practices that enhance meaningfulness for an individual with a kinship orientation, such as encouraging members to disengage from their tasks to participate in community-building events, might conflict with practices that foster meaningfulness for an individual with a craftsmanship orientation who prefers to focus on her or his work.

Finally, future studies may also be done to better understand the development of work orientations over time and how changeable they are. Although we have acknowledged the relatively stable nature of work orientations, researchers could try to understand how malleable these orientations truly are. For example, will work orientations change in a time of personal crisis or change? And if they are embedded in sociocultural meanings, might changes and upheavals in sociocultural meanings lead to changes in varieties or predominance of certain work orientations? Certainly, there is some belief that orientations toward work that move beyond self-interest (e.g., noninstrumental and non-materialistic) have gained ascendance in recent decades (Joas, 2000). Does this mean more people will have service (or even kinship and craftsmanship) orientations? Furthermore, might work orientations naturally evolve over time? If so, are there any common trajectories for work orientation change? Do individuals move back and forth between certain orientations? Moreover, if orientations are malleable to some degree, are there ever points in individuals' lives when their orientations are not well articulated? Scholars have recently commented on the confusion and ambiguity individuals encounter when not possessing clear standards on which to draw to assess what makes life and work good (Bellah et al., 1985; Sennett, 2008). Future research may benefit from validating these arguments and offering insights for the role of organizations in this dilemma.

Whatever results this research ultimately yields, we conclude by stressing the importance of integrity and honesty in developing practices that foster meaningfulness. Indeed, some organizations might not have their members' wellness in mind. Rather, they might adopt some practices to appeal to external stakeholders (e.g., institute corporate social responsibility practices to improve reputation). Such a strategy might lead to disillusionment, which in turn can lead to higher turnover (Pratt & Ashforth, 2003). As Pratt and Ashforth (2003) justly put it, "Creating meaningfulness is not only a means of increasing performance—it is also an end in itself" (p. 326).

TABLE 8.1

Focus on the Workplace: Overview of Organizational Practices

Recommendations	Tested in practice	Derived from theory	Supported by research
Job design[a,b,c]		✓	✓
Culture[d]		✓	✓
Apprenticeship for those with a craftsmanship orientation[e]		✓	✓
Corporate citizenship program for those with a serving orientation[f,g]		✓	✓
Blending work and family for those with a kinship orientation[h,i]		✓	✓

Note. [a]Hackman & Oldham (1980). [b]Grant (2008a, 2008b). [c]C. Wong & Campion (1991). Scholars (e.g., Hackman & Oldham, 1980) have argued that skill variety, task identity, and task significance lead to meaningfulness. We suggest, on the basis of the job characteristics model, that replacing skill variety and task significance with autonomy and feedback will lead to greater meaningfulness for those with a craftsmanship orientation. Relational job design (e.g., Grant, 2008a, 2008b) suggests that individuals who are connected to beneficiaries experience greater motivation and persistence. We infer from this that those who seek to serve others will experience more meaningful work—through altering the relational architecture of jobs—because of a logic of fit. Similarly, jobs can be redesigned to create increased interdependence (e.g., C. Wong & Campion, 1991), which we believe—again using a fit logic—may be meaningful to those with a kinship orientation. [d]Schein (2010). Although the academic and practitioner literature on culture is sizable, to our knowledge, theory and interventions have not directly explored its influence on experienced work meaningfulness. However, given that cultures shape how individuals make sense (or make meaning) of their workplace, we extrapolate to argue that organizational culture may also increase the likelihood that individuals will experience meaningfulness on the basis of a logic of fit. [e]Kanigel (1993). To our knowledge, research that has empirically tested apprenticeships is limited. That limited research has, however, suggested that the process is made meaningful through the slow accumulation of skill and knowledge gained by mirroring a master. [f]Tichy, McGill, & Clair (1997). [g]Thompson & Bunderson (2003). Theoretical work has suggested that individuals develop ties with their organization on the basis of the organization's mission and ideology (Thompson & Bunderson, 2003). Specifically, these ties result from a fit between an individual's values and the organization's. Extrapolating from this research, we argue that a similar fit may result in enhanced meaningfulness for those with a serving orientation. [h]Pratt & Rosa (2003). [i]Pratt (2000a, 2000b). To our knowledge, there is no academic or practitioner literature that has suggested that these practices identified by Pratt and Rosa (2003) will result in meaningful work. However, Pratt's ethnographic work with Amway distributors suggests that such practices do facilitate the transformation of work into something meaningful for the participants. This would be particularly fitting for those with a kinship orientation (see Pratt, 2000a, 2000b).

References

Abbott, A. (1989). The new occupational structure: What are the questions? *Work and Occupations, 16,* 273–291. doi:10.1177/0730888489016003002

Amabile, T. M., Hill, K., Hennessey, B., & Tighe, E. (1994). The Work Preference Inventory: Assessing intrinsic and extrinsic motivational orientations. *Journal of Personality and Social Psychology, 66,* 950–967. doi:10.1037/0022-3514.66.5.950

BASF SE. (2008). *Combining career and family* (BASF SE Human Resources Publication 1-6). Ludwigshafen, Germany: Author. Retrieved from http://www.docstoc.com/docs/23654074/Combining-career-and-family

Baumeister, R. F. (1991). *Meanings of life.* New York, NY: Guilford Press.

Bellah, R. N., Madsen, R., Sullivan, W. M., Swidler, A., & Tipton, S. M. (1985). *Habits of the heart.* Berkeley: University of California Press.

Bennett, R. (1974). Orientation to work and some implications for management. *Journal of Management Studies, 11,* 149–162. doi:10.1111/j.1467-6486.1974.tb00881.x

Berg, J. M., Grant, A. M., & Johnson, V. (2010). When callings are calling: Crafting work and leisure in pursuit of unanswered occupational callings. *Organization Science, 21,* 973–994. doi:10.1287/orsc.1090.0497

Boltanski, L., & Thévenot, L. (2006). *On justification: Economies of worth.* Princeton, NJ: Princeton University Press.

Bowe, J., Bowe, M., & Streeter, S. (2000). *Gig: Americans talk about their jobs.* New York, NY: Three Rivers Press.

Bunderson, J. S., & Thompson, J. A. (2009). The call of the wild: Zookeepers, callings, and the double-edged sword of deeply meaningful work. *Administrative Science Quarterly, 54,* 32–57. doi:10.2189/asqu.2009.54.1.32

Chatman, J. A. (1989). Improving interactional organizational research: A model of person-organization fit. *Academy of Management Review, 14,* 333–349.

Coombes, A. (2008). Ports in a storm: Job security may play a part in Fortune's "100 best places to work" this year. *Market Watch.* Retrieved from http://www.marketwatch.com/story/job-security-camaraderie-key-factors-at-100-best-places-to-work

Crawford, M. B. (2009). *Shop class as soulcraft: An inquiry into the value of work.* New York, NY: Penguin.

Csikszentmihalyi, M. (1990). *Flow: The psychology of optimal experience.* New York, NY: Harper & Row.

Dane, E., & Pratt, M. G. (2007). Exploring intuition and its role in managerial decision making. *Academy of Management Review, 32,* 33–54. doi:10.5465/AMR.2007.23463682

Davis-Blake, A., & Pfeffer, J. (1989). Just a mirage: The search for dispositional effects in organizational research. *Academy of Management Review, 14,* 385–400.

Dik, B. J., & Duffy, R. D. (2009). Calling and vocation at work. *The Counseling Psychologist, 37,* 424–450. doi:10.1177/0011000008316430

Dutton, J., & Heaphy, E. (2003). The power of high-quality connections. In J. E. Cameron, J. E. Dutton, & R. E. Quinn (Eds.), *Positive organizational scholarship* (pp. 263–278). San Francisco, CA: Berrett-Koehler.

Dutton, J., & Pratt, M. G. (1997). Merck & Company: From core competence to global community involvement. In N. M. Tichy, A. R. McGill,

& L. St. Clair (Eds.), *Corporate global citizenship: Doing business in the public eye* (pp. 150–168). San Francisco, CA: New Lexington.

Fine, G. A. (1992). The culture of production: Aesthetic choices and constraints in culinary work. *American Journal of Sociology, 97,* 1268–1294.

Fishman, C. (1998). Sanity Inc. *Fast Company.* Retrieved from http://www.fastcompany.com/36173/sanity-inc

Fried, Y. (1991). Meta-analytic comparison of the Job Diagnostic Survey and Job Characteristics Inventory as correlates of work satisfaction and performance. *Journal of Applied Psychology, 76,* 690–697. doi:10.1037/0021-9010.76.5.690

Gamble, J. (2001). Modelling the invisible: The pedagogy of craft apprenticeship. *Studies in Continuing Education, 23,* 185–200. doi:10.1080/01580370120101957

George, B. (2003). *Authentic leadership: Rediscovering the secrets to creating lasting value.* San Francisco, CA: Jossey-Bass.

Godsey, K. (1996). Flying lessons: 10 Southwest strategies to apply to your business. *Success, 43,* 24–25.

Grant, A. M. (2007). Relational job design and the motivation to make a prosocial difference. *Academy of Management Review, 32,* 393–417. doi:10.5465/AMR.2007.24351328

Grant, A. M. (2008a). Designing jobs to do good: Dimensions and psychological consequences of prosocial job characteristics. *Journal of Positive Psychology, 3,* 19–39. doi:10.1080/17439760701751012

Grant, A. M. (2008b). The significance of task significance: Job performance effects, relational mechanisms, and boundary conditions. *Journal of Applied Psychology, 93,* 108–124. doi:10.1037/0021-9010.93.1.108

Grant, A. M., Dutton, J. E., & Rosso, B. (2008). Giving commitment: Employee support programs and the prosocial sensemaking process. *Academy of Management Journal, 51,* 898–918. doi:10.5465/AMJ.2008.34789652

Hackman, J. R. (1987). The design of work teams. In J. Lorsch (Ed.), *Handbook of organizational behavior* (pp. 315–342). Englewood Cliffs, NJ: Prentice-Hall.

Hackman, J. R., & Oldham, G. R. (1976). Motivation through the design of work: Test of a theory. *Organizational Behavior and Human Performance, 16,* 250–279. doi:10.1016/0030-5073(76)90016-7

Hackman, J. R., & Oldham, G. R. (1980). *Work redesign.* Englewood Cliffs, NJ: Prentice Hall.

Haidt, J. (2001). The emotional dog and its rational tail: A social intuitionist approach to moral judgment. *Psychological Review, 108,* 814–834. doi:10.1037/0033-295X.108.4.814

Haski-Leventhal, D., & McLeigh, J. D. (2009). Firefighters volunteering beyond their duty: An essential asset in rural communities. *Journal of Rural Community Development, 4,* 80–92.

Hewlett, S. A., Sherbin, L., & Sumberg, K. (2009, July). How Gen Y & Boomers will reshape your agenda. *Harvard Business Review, 87*(7), 71–76.

Hulleman, C. S., Schrager, S. M., Bodmann, S. M., & Harackiewicz, J. M. (2010). A meta-analytic review of achievement goal measures: Different labels for the same constructs or different constructs with similar labels? *Psychological Bulletin, 136,* 422–449. doi:10.1037/a0018947

Huseman, R. C., Hatfield, J. D., & Miles, E. W. (1987). A new perspective on equity theory: The equity sensitivity construct. *Academy of Management Review, 12,* 222–234.

Intelligentsia Coffee. (2011). *Black Cat Project.* Retrieved from http://www.intelligentsiacoffee.com/content/black-cat-project

Joas, H. (2000). *The genesis of values.* Chicago, IL: University of Chicago Press.

Kanigel, R. (1993). *Apprentice to genius: The making of a scientific dynasty.* Baltimore, MD: Johns Hopkins University Press.

Lave, J., & Wenger, E. (1991). *Situated learning: Legitimate peripheral participation.* New York, NY: Cambridge University Press.

Lepisto, D. A., Pradies, C., & Pratt, M. G. (2012). *The worth of work: Toward a reorientation of the meaning of work.* Manuscript in preparation.

Lexus. (n.d.). *The passionate pursuit of perfection: 30 years of Lexus.* Retrieved from http://www.lexus-global.com/about_lexus/index.html#30YearsLexus

Martin, J. (1992). *Cultures in organizations.* New York, NY: Oxford University Press.

Martocchio, J. (2010). *Strategic compensation* (6th ed.). Upper Saddle River, NJ: Prentice Hall.

Mills, C. W. (1956). *White collar: The American middle classes.* New York, NY: Oxford University Press.

Morgeson, F. P., & Campion, M. A. (2003). Work design. In W. Borman, D. Ilgen, & R. Klimoski (Eds.), *Handbook of psychology: Vol. 12. Industrial and organizational psychology* (pp. 423–452). Hoboken, NJ: Wiley.

Nohria, N., Groysberg, B., & Lee, L.-E. (2008, July). Employee motivation: A powerful new model. *Harvard Business Review, 86*(7), 78–84.

O'Connor, E. (2005). Embodied knowledge: The experience of meaning and the struggle towards proficiency in glassblowing. *Ethnography, 6,* 183–204. doi:10.1177/1466138105057551

O'Reilly, C., & Pfeffer, J. (1995). *Southwest Airlines: Using human resources for competitive advantage.* Boston, MA: Harvard Business School Publishing.

Penner, L. A., Dovidio, J. F., Piliavin, J. A., & Schroeder, D. A. (2005). Prosocial behavior: Multilevel perspectives. *Annual Review of Psychology, 56,* 365–392. doi:10.1146/annurev.psych.56.091103.070141

Pratt, M. G. (2000a). Building an ideological fortress: The role of spirituality, encapsulation and sensemaking. *Studies in Cultures, Organizations and Societies, 6,* 35–69.

Pratt, M. G. (2000b). The good, the bad, and the ambivalent: Managing identification among Amway distributors. *Administrative Science Quarterly, 45*, 456–493. doi:10.2307/2667106

Pratt, M. G., & Ashforth, B. E. (2003). Fostering meaningfulness in working and at work. In K. S. Cameron, J. E. Dutton, & R. E. Quinn (Eds.), *Positive organizational scholarship* (pp. 309–327). San Francisco, CA: Berrett-Koehler.

Pratt, M. G., & Rosa, J. A. (2003). Transforming work–family conflict into commitment in network marketing organizations. *Academy of Management Journal, 46*, 395–418. doi:10.2307/30040635

Rosso, B. D., Dekas, K. H., & Wrzesniewski, A. (2010). On the meaning of work: A theoretical integration and review. *Research in Organizational Behavior, 30*, 91–127. doi:10.1016/j.riob.2010.09.001

Schein, E. H. (1995). Defining organizational culture. In J. T. Wren (Ed.), *The leader's companion: Insights on leadership through the ages* (pp. 271–281). New York, NY: Free Press.

Schein, E. H. (2010). *Organizational culture and leadership* (4th ed.). San Francisco, CA: Jossey-Bass.

Sennett, R. (2008). *The craftsman.* New Haven, CT: Yale University Press.

Swidler, A. (2001). *Talk of love: How culture matters.* Chicago, IL: University of Chicago Press.

Terkel, S. (1995). *Working.* New York, NY: Ballantine Books.

Thompson, J. A., & Bunderson, J. S. (2003). Violations of principle: Ideological currency in the psychological contract. *Academy of Management Review, 28*, 571–586. doi:10.2307/30040748

Tichy, N. M., McGill, A. R., & Clair, L. S. (1997). *Corporate global citizenship: Doing business in the public eye.* San Francisco, CA: Lexington Books.

Trice, H. M., & Beyer, J. M. (Eds.). (1993). *The cultures of work organizations.* Englewood Cliffs, NJ: Prentice Hall.

Vaisey, S. (2008). Socrates, Skinner, and Aristotle: Three ways of thinking about culture in action. *Sociological Forum, 23*, 604–622. doi:10.1111/j.1573-7861.2008.00079.x

Vaisey, S. (2009). Motivation and justification: A dual-process model of culture in action. *American Journal of Sociology, 114*, 1675–1715. doi:10.1086/597179

Valley, K., & Gendron, A. (2001). *Iggy's Bread of the World* (Harvard Business School Case 9-801-282). Boston, MA: Harvard Business School.

Weick, K. E. (1995). *Sensemaking in organizations.* Thousand Oaks, CA: Sage.

Wong, C., & Campion, M. (1991). Development and test of a task level model of motivational job design. *Journal of Applied Psychology, 76*, 825–837. doi:10.1037/0021-9010.76.6.825

Wong, L., Kolditz, T. A., Millen, R. A., & Potter, T. M. (2003). *Why they fight: Combat motivation in the Iraq war.* Carlisle, PA: Strategic Studies Institute, U.S. Army War College.

Wrzesniewski, A. (1999). *Jobs, careers, and callings: Work orientation and job transitions* (Unpublished doctoral dissertation). University of Michigan, Ann Arbor, MI.

Wrzesniewski, A., Dekas, K., & Rosso, B. (2009). Calling. In S. J. Lopez & A. Beauchamp (Eds.), *The encyclopedia of positive psychology* (pp. 115–118). Malden, MA: Wiley-Blackwell.

Wrzesniewski, A., McCauley, C., Rozin, P., & Schwartz, B. (1997). Jobs, careers, and callings: People's relations to their work. *Journal of Research in Personality, 31*, 21–33. doi:10.1006/jrpe.1997.2162

Fred O. Walumbwa, Amanda L. Christensen, and Michael K. Muchiri

Transformational Leadership and Meaningful Work | 9

Over the past 3 decades, there has been considerable interest in *work meaningfulness*—that is, the degree to which an employee experiences work as inherently fulfilling and rewarding, judged in relation to her or his own ideals or standards (Hackman & Oldham, 1980). Meaningfulness can be experienced at work in several ways, including through self-transcendence—that is, by serving the greater good (Steger & Dik, 2010)—or by the cultivation of important and valued relationships at work (Pratt & Ashforth, 2003). Empirical evidence shows that to the extent that employees experience work meaningfulness, they are more likely to be engaged in their jobs, thereby enhancing their effectiveness and job performance (Arnold, Turner, Barling, Kelloway, & McKee, 2007; May, Gilson, & Harter, 2004; Sparks & Schenk, 2001). Therefore, it is important to understand what predicts or makes more meaningful work. Given the dominant role of leadership in the workplace (Avolio, Reichard, Hannah, Walumbwa, & Chan, 2009; Avolio, Walumbwa, & Weber,

http://dx.doi.org/10.1037/14183-010
Purpose and Meaning in the Workplace, B. J. Dik, Z. S. Byrne, and M. F. Steger (Editors)

2009; Yukl, 2010), one key situational factor that may have substantial impact on meaningful work is leadership.

Among leadership theories, transformational leadership (e.g., Bass, 1985) perhaps provides the most intuitive link to meaningful work. Transformational leadership has been studied extensively and intensively (Avolio, Walumbwa, & Weber, 2009) and has been linked to employee attitudes and behaviors, including meaningful work (Arnold et al., 2007; Bono & Judge, 2003; Piccolo & Colquitt, 2006) in a variety of settings across cultures (Judge & Piccolo, 2004; Kirkman, Chen, Farh, Chen, & Lowe, 2009; Lowe, Kroeck, & Sivasubramaniam, 1996; Walumbwa, Lawler, & Avolio, 2007). *Transformational leadership* refers to leader behavior that focuses on broadening follower aspirations, goals, and values and on providing followers with confidence to perform beyond the expectations specified in the implicit or explicit exchange work agreement (Bass, 1985; Dvir, Eden, Avolio, & Shamir, 2002). Transformational leadership also emphasizes each follower's sense of self-worth in order to engage the follower in true commitment and involvement in her or his work. Thus, it is an emotional and value-based aspect of leadership that often leads to exceptional performance by individuals and teams (e.g., Bono & Judge, 2003; Dvir et al., 2002; Piccolo & Colquitt, 2006; Schaubroeck, Lam, & Cha, 2007; Walumbwa, Avolio, & Zhu, 2008; Walumbwa & Hartnell, 2011). Dimensions of transformational leadership, such as inspirational motivation, have an implicit consideration of how leaders manage followers' meaning and purpose in the workplace, inspiring followers to willingly sacrifice their selfish interests for a higher cause (Yukl, 2010).

The purpose of this chapter is to provide an integrative framework that illuminates the processes underlying the relationship between transformational leadership and meaningful work. We achieve this objective by identifying important factors that mediate and moderate the transformational leadership–meaningful work relationship (see Figure 9.1). We begin by providing a brief overview of the four dimensions of transformational leadership behaviors.

Transformational Leadership Behaviors

Transformational leaders have been described as leaders who motivate their associates, colleagues, followers, and clients to move beyond their individual self-interests for the good of the group, organization, or society (Bass, 1985; Bass & Bass, 2008). They achieve this by emphasizing one or more of the following four dimensions: idealized influence (serving

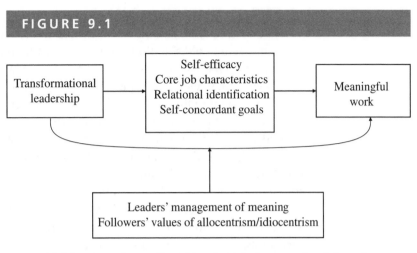

FIGURE 9.1

Linking transformational leadership to meaningful work. The underlying processes as well as the boundary conditions for the influence of transformational leadership on meaningful work.

as followers' role model such that followers seek to identify with their leaders and emulate them), inspirational motivation (energizing followers by articulating a compelling vision for the future), intellectual stimulation (challenging followers to question assumptions and status quo to reformulate problems in novel and creative ways), and individualized consideration (providing followers with support, mentoring, and coaching while also attending to their individual aspirations and needs). Each of these four dimensions can be assessed with the Multifactor Leadership Questionnaire (see Bass & Avolio, 2004).

Idealized influence leadership is described as leaders behaving in ways that make them role models for their followers. The leaders put the followers' needs above their own personal needs, sharing risks with followers, acting consistently rather than arbitrarily, being counted on to do the right thing, and demonstrating high standards of ethical and moral conduct. These leaders avoid using their power except when needed. Idealized influence also occurs when the leader does the right thing and thereby engenders the trust and respect of his or her followers.

Inspirationally motivating leaders behave in ways that motivate and inspire those around them by providing meaning and challenge to their followers' work. They do this through arousing team spirit, displaying enthusiasm and optimism, and involving followers in envisioning attractive future states. The leader clearly communicates expectations that followers want to meet and demonstrates commitment to goals and to a shared vision. Inspirationally motivating leaders hold high expectations and encourage followers to achieve more than what they thought was possible.

Intellectually stimulating leaders encourage their followers to be innovative and creative by questioning assumptions, reframing problems, and approaching old situations in new ways. When followers fall short or make mistakes, such leaders do not criticize them publicly; rather, they solicit their views to understand what caused the problem and work with them to find solutions from the followers' perspective.

Finally, *individually considerate* leaders pay special attention to each individual's need for achievement and growth by acting as coach or mentor. They do this by personalizing their interactions with followers, listening effectively, and delegating tasks as a means of helping followers to develop. These leaders also recognize individual differences in terms of needs and desires and behave in ways that demonstrate an acceptance of individual differences (e.g., some employees receive more encouragement, some more autonomy, and others more task structure).

A Model of Transformational Leadership and Meaningful Work

Transformational leaders raise followers' levels of morality and activate higher order needs in followers by infusing work with moral purpose and commitment (Arnold et al., 2007; Shamir, House, & Arthur, 1993). Therefore, we expect followers of such leaders to find a purpose in work that is greater than the extrinsic outcomes of their work, thereby enhancing work meaningfulness. Transformational leaders motivate followers through articulating a vision and mission in terms of the values they represent (Shamir et al., 1993). Such visionary and inspirational messages are instrumental in making work more meaningful because they structure attention and "shape the context of action in such a way that the members of that context are able to use the meaning thus created as a point of reference for their own action and understanding of the situation" (Smircich & Morgan, 1982, p. 261).

Transformational leadership also provides positive verbal cues to followers about the importance and purpose of their work (Bass, 1985). Such leader actions and behaviors are expected to lead to increased work meaningfulness because they signify to employees that their efforts are valued and appreciated. In support, emergent research has demonstrated a positive link between transformational leadership and employee perceptions of meaningful work (Arnold et al., 2007; Piccolo & Colquitt, 2006; van Dierendonck, Haynes, Borril, & Stride, 2004).

Specifically, Sparks and Schenk (2001) found that in multilevel marketing organizations, transformational leadership was positively associated with a higher purpose in the work, as characterized by members' beliefs that they were part of a cause that was bigger than simply making money. The authors concluded, "Transformational leadership indeed 'transforms' followers by encouraging them to see the higher purposes in their work" (Sparks & Schenk, 2001, p. 849).

Thus, both theory and empirical evidence suggest a positive association between transformational leadership and employee-experienced work meaningfulness. However, several questions remain unanswered. For example, what are the processes by which transformational leadership enhances employees' work meaningfulness? What are the conditions under which transformational leadership is more (or less) effective in enhancing work meaningfulness? Answers to these questions are likely to help organizations and their managers with guidance on enhancing work meaningfulness through effective transformational leadership practices.

The following sections examine theoretically and empirically derived concepts, such as self-efficacy, core job characteristics, relational identification with the leader, and self-concordant goals, through which transformational leadership works to enhance followers' perceptions of meaningful work. In addition, two other concepts are explored, followers' values of allocentrism and idiocentrism and leaders' management of meaning, that make the relationship between transformational leadership and meaningful work more (or less) effective. Figure 9.1 summarizes our overall model. We begin our discussion by focusing on the mediators.

Potential Mediators

SELF-EFFICACY

Self-efficacy refers to the "belief in one's capabilities to organize and execute the courses of action required to produce given attainments" (Bandura, 1997, p. 3). It is a strong motivator for individuals because it pertains to an individual's confidence that he or she possesses the internal resources to successfully perform a task (Bandura, 1997; Shamir et al., 1993). Through the broadening of followers' aspirations, goals, and values, transformational leaders provide their followers with confidence to perform beyond what is explicitly or implicitly stated in the work contract (Bass, 1985; Dvir et al., 2002) by helping followers to reach their full potential (Bass & Avolio, 1990). Shamir et al. (1993) suggested that by emphasizing positive visions, communicating high performance expectations, and expressing confidence in followers' abilities, transformational leaders can positively engage followers' self-concepts by enhancing their perceptions of self-efficacy.

Shamir et al. (1993) further suggested that by increasing followers' perceptions of self-efficacy, followers should be more deeply motivated through the maintenance and enhancement of their self-esteem and self-worth, which, in turn, not only affects followers' self-sacrificial behavior and personal commitment to the leader and mission but also positively influences followers' perceptions of task meaningfulness. Therefore, through the articulation of a vision and mission, transformational leaders present goals in terms of the values they represent, and thus, the accomplishment of goals becomes meaningful to followers as their self-concepts are evoked (Shamir et al., 1993). In addition, by understanding how followers view themselves, transformational leaders are able to improve followers' self-concepts so that they believe they can be successful at more challenging tasks (Walumbwa et al., 2008), thereby enhancing work meaningfulness.

Transformational leaders can further influence followers' self-efficacy by providing an ideal point of reference for followers to engage in vicarious learning with (Bass, 1985). Through role modeling and verbal persuasion—two major determinants of self-efficacy—leaders can increase individuals' self-efficacy (Walumbwa et al., 2008). Walumbwa et al. (2008) showed an empirical link between transformational leadership and followers' sense of self-efficacy and went further to show that self-efficacy, in turn, was positively related to individual performance. Other authors (e.g., Dvir et al., 2002; Walumbwa & Hartnell, 2011) have suggested that transformational leadership influences followers' self-efficacy through follower development and that it also influences followers' motivation, morality, identification, and empowerment.

CORE JOB CHARACTERISTICS

Hackman and Oldham (1980) proposed five core job characteristics—variety, identity, significance, autonomy, and feedback—that organizations can enhance to encourage positive work attitudes and increased work quality. *Variety* refers to the degree to which a job requires the use of different skills and talents, *identity* refers to the degree to which a job requires completion of a whole piece of work or the degree to which a job requires an individual to see a task through from beginning to end with a visible outcome, *significance* refers to the degree to which a job substantially affects others' lives, *autonomy* refers to the degree to which a job provides substantial freedom, and *feedback* refers to the degree to which a job provides clear information about individuals' performance.

Organizations and leaders can enhance these job characteristics to influence employees' attitudes and behaviors.

Piccolo and Colquitt (2006) argued that by managing the meaning of followers' work (Smircich & Morgan, 1982), transformational leaders can affect followers' perceptions of their jobs along the five core job characteristics dimensions, which, in turn, affects followers' intrinsic motivation and goal commitment, thereby influencing task performance and employees' extrarole behaviors. Transformational leaders are able to "frame and shape the context of action in such a way that the members of that context are able to use the meaning thus created as a point of reference for their own action and understanding of the situation" (Smircich & Morgan, 1982, p. 261). Thus, transformational leaders can use verbal persuasion and cues to influence followers' perceptions of core job characteristics. Furthermore, Smircich and Morgan (1982) suggested that leaders can influence followers by "mobilizing meaning, articulating and defining what has previously remained implicit or unsaid, by inventing images and meanings that provide a focus for new attention, and by consolidating, confronting, or changing prevailing wisdom" (p. 258).

Transformational leaders can influence how followers perceive their work environment by using verbal persuasion, providing ideological explanations, and communicating the value of the organization's mission (Shamir et al., 1993), leading to intrinsically motivating, engaging, and meaningful work. Bono and Judge (2003) showed that transformational leaders can help followers to see organizational goals as congruent with their own values. In further support, Piccolo and Colquitt (2006) found empirical evidence linking transformational leadership to followers' perceptions of core job characteristics. Perceptions of core job characteristics, in turn, were positively and significantly related to followers' intrinsic motivation and goal commitment.

Staw (1977) suggested that intrinsically motivated individuals derive greater satisfaction from work accomplishments and work harder to do well. Similarly, Shamir and his coauthors (1993) suggested that when individuals' self-concepts are engaged, individuals are more likely to be intrinsically motivated by their work and view their tasks as more meaningful, among other benefits. Thus, transformational leaders can influence followers' perceptions of their core job characteristics, namely, in regard to variety, identity, significance, autonomy, and feedback, to affect followers' intrinsic motivation and perceptions of work meaningfulness (Piccolo & Colquitt, 2006). They do this by raising followers to higher levels of potential, developing their skills, and expressing confidence in their followers' ability to perform beyond expectations (Bass, 1985). Consequently, followers express greater enthusiasm, intensity, and resilience toward achieving the work unit's objectives, thereby enhancing work meaningfulness.

FOLLOWER RELATIONAL IDENTIFICATION WITH THE LEADER

Sluss and Ashforth (2007) defined *relational identification* as the "extent to which one defines oneself in terms of a given role relationship" (p. 11). Relational identification reflects the interpersonal level of identification associated with one's role-related relationships, such as supervisor–direct report (Sluss & Ashforth, 2007). Thus, relational identification with the leader may serve as an important mechanism through which transformational leaders influence their followers' work meaningfulness.

Drawing on followers' self-concept and transformational leadership theories, Kark and Shamir (2002) proposed a framework for understanding the exceptional and diverse effects of transformational leaders on their followers. These authors suggested that transformational leadership may be able to elicit follower identification with the leader by priming follower relational aspects of self-concept. A basic assumption of the self-concept theory is that followers who view their leader behavior as congruent with their own goals will be more motivated and will perhaps see his or her work as more meaningful. Shamir et al. (1993) argued that the influence of transformational leaders is based on their success in connecting their followers' self-concept to the mission of their organization so that followers become self-expressive, or what Bass (1988) called "an absolute emotional and cognitive identification with the leader" (p. 50). Such leaders influence followers by activating an identity-based organizing construct in followers—a working self-concept that serves to structure cognitive, motivational, and social processes for followers by shifting followers' conceptions of their identity to be in line with the leader's goals, mission, and vision (Shamir et al., 1993). Similar arguments were also advanced by Lord and Brown (2004), who suggested that leaders exert powerful and enduring effects on follower's work behavior by influencing the way followers view themselves. Leaders influence followers by activating an identity-based organizing construct in followers—a working self-concept that serves to structure cognitive, motivational, and social processes for followers by shifting followers' conceptions of their identity (Lord & Brown, 2004) and ultimately what they believe is possible to accomplish, hence work meaningfulness.

We therefore suggest that transformational leaders increase followers' relational identification with the leader by displaying self-confidence, demonstrating high involvement in the task, engaging in self-sacrifice to show commitment to mission, demonstrating social and physical courage, and setting personal examples (Bass, 1985; Kark & Shamir, 2002; Walumbwa & Hartnell, 2011). Leader behaviors such as confidence, courage, self-sacrifice, and leading by personal example are important because they can collectively contribute to followers' positive perceptions (Hogg, 2001). These leadership behaviors also increase the emotional connection between the leader and the follower such that followers feel more obligated to do what they consider right, often forgoing self-interest for the collective interests of their organization (Bass, 1985; Kark & Shamir, 2002). Transformational leaders may also accomplish greater levels of relational identification by increasing intrinsic value of the efforts and outcomes (Walumbwa & Hartnell, 2011).

There is some preliminary evidence to support these arguments. Kark, Shamir, and Chen (2003) found that transformational leadership increased followers' identification with the leader, evidenced by followers displaying more self-confidence, involvement in their tasks, self-sacrifice to show support for the mission of the organization, and courage and setting personal examples. Dvir et al. (2002), in a field experiment involving Israeli Defense Force infantry platoon commanders, reported that developing transformational leadership in platoon commanders increased their direct followers' identification and motivation. Further supporting these claims, Walumbwa and colleagues (e.g., Walumbwa et al., 2008; Walumbwa & Hartnell, 2011) provided evidence to suggest that transformational leadership relates positively to followers' relational identification with their supervisor and their work unit identification.

A growing body of research has shown that identification is related to individual attitudes and behaviors (e.g., Lam, Schaubroeck, & Brown, 2004; Van Dick, Wagner, Stellmacher, & Christ, 2004; Van Knippenberg & Van Schie, 2000; Walumbwa, Cropanzano, & Hartnell, 2009; Walumbwa & Hartnell, 2011; Walumbwa et al., 2011). The reason for these significant findings is that identity and identification are a means of creating flexible capacities in employee attitudes and behaviors (Albert, Ashforth, & Dutton, 2000). In other words, they serve as rudders for navigating difficult waters—a core theme within the transformational leadership framework (Bass, 1985). Van Knippenberg (2000) argued that identification is associated with motivation to achieve goals because it induces individuals to take the target's perspective and to experience the target's goals and interests as their own (Dukerich, Golden, & Shortell, 2002).

Consistent with this literature, we expect relational identification with the leader to be positively related to followers' high levels of work meaningfulness. We suggest that to the extent that transformational leaders motivate followers to identify with the target and the importance of their work, as well as stress the importance and values associated with desired outcomes in ways that are more easily understood by followers, while simultaneously setting high performance standards (Bass, 1985; Shamir et al., 1993; Walumbwa et al., 2011), relational identification resulting from associating with such leaders is likely to have a positive effect on followers' perceptions of work meaningfulness. This is especially likely because employees with high relational identification with a supervisor may be intrinsically motivated to contribute on behalf of the supervisor, thereby increasing their work meaningfulness. More important, because identification conveys a sense of being a part of something, relational identification should provide an impetus to work meaningfulness, as workers take up work as a means of personal development or individual change so as to better fit themselves into the work unit (Walumbwa et al., 2008, 2009).

SELF-CONCORDANT GOALS

One of the most basic ideas regarding transformational leadership theory is that followers of transformational leaders view their work as more meaningful (Bass, 1985; Bono & Judge, 2003). To understand an underlying motivational process linking transformational leadership and meaningful work, Bono and Judge (2003) examined the relationship between transformational leadership and followers' setting of self-concordant goals at work. *Self-concordance* is the extent to which pursuits, such as job-related work or goals, are aligned or are in concordance with individuals' interests and core values (Sheldon & Elliot, 1999). When individuals view their goals and work as autonomous or when goals and activities are undertaken with willingness and choice, individuals are more likely to be internally motivated and, thus, exert sustained effort to reach those goals. "Work activities not only represent the job but the person doing the job" (Bono & Judge, 2003, p. 555). In line with this concept, self-concordant goals were significantly related to employees viewing their work as more important and self-congruent (Bono & Judge, 2003).

When transformational leaders help others to see their work in ideological terms and emphasize higher order values, followers come to see their work as concordant with their personal values and, in turn, see their work as more meaningful (Bono & Judge, 2003). Shamir and colleagues (1993) similarly suggested that when individuals internalize values, they are more likely to view their work as meaningful because the work is consistent with their self-concepts. Moreover, Sparks and Schenk (2001) theorized that transformational leaders can affect followers' beliefs in the higher purpose of their work through the activation of higher order needs and by appealing to ideological values. Thus, when transformational leaders describe work in ideological terms and emphasize higher order values, followers are more likely to internalize the goals and values as their own and to see their work as congruent with their personal values and, in turn, are more likely to view their work as meaningful.

Potential Moderators

FOLLOWERS' VALUES OF ALLOCENTRISM AND IDIOCENTRISM

Among followers' individual differences, *allocentrism* (i.e., the tendency to define the self in terms of the ingroups to which one belongs, where the goals of the ingroup have primacy over one's personal goals) and *idiocentrism* (i.e., the tendency to view the self as the most basic unit of social perception, where an individual goal has primacy over ingroup goals) have been found to significantly moderate the relationship between transformational leadership and followers' work-related attitudes and behaviors (Walumbwa et al., 2007). Because individual values specify appropriate attitudes and behaviors for responding to external influences and situations, including a leader's style and how individuals prescribe appropriate social structures and roles (Triandis, 1995; Walumbwa & Lawler, 2003), we argue that values such as allocentrism and idiocentrism play a critical role in moderating the influence of transformational leadership on work meaningfulness.

Triandis (1995) argued that values influence the domain of what constitutes normative behavior and also define acceptable roles for individuals within the social structure. *Allocentrics* are characterized by the importance they place on their ingroup and by striving for community, equality, and common goals. Because transformational leaders emphasize the commitment to a shared vision and putting the group's goals over individual goals (Walumbwa & Lawler, 2003), it is likely that allocentrics will more readily embrace transformational leadership, thereby facilitating the influence of transformational leaders on work meaningfulness, because their normative expectations and values appear to be in greater alignment with those espoused by transformational leadership.

Idiocentrics, however, tend to strive for individual goals; they value personal achievement and autonomy and see the self as independent of others (Markus & Kitayama, 1991). Thus, idiocentrics are expected to respond less positively to transformational leaders because such leaders strive to foster a team- or group-based atmosphere, thereby inhibiting work meaningfulness for those who do not necessarily value a team-based, communal atmosphere. In other words, transformational leaders create environments that are not directly aligned with idiocentric individuals' values. Thus, we expect those individuals who are more allocentric to experience greater work meaningfulness than those who are more idiocentric. In line with this argument, Walumbwa et al. (2007) found that allocentrics, as compared with idiocentrics, were more likely to respond positively to leader behaviors when they regarded their leader as exhibiting transformational behaviors.

LEADERS' MANAGEMENT OF MEANING

Smircich and Morgan (1982) argued that leadership situations often concern an obligation or a perceived right on the part of leaders to define followers' reality. Leadership involves creating a sense of organization and direction and generating a point of reference that followers can use to make sense of their situation and experiences. Indeed, an essential aspect of transformational leadership involves reframing problems and providing meaning to followers' work (Bass, 1985).

Leaders' actions "punctuate contexts in ways that provide a focus for the creation of meaning" (Smircich & Morgan, 1982, p. 261). In addition, Walumbwa and his colleagues (2008) suggested that leaders affect their followers through role modeling and verbal persuasion. Leaders' actions are interpreted by followers as common conceptions and understandings, which they then apply to subsequent experiences. Through the use of words, images, symbolic actions, and gestures, leaders can shape the meaning of followers' experiences. Thus, when transformational leaders are cognizant of the impact of their words, gestures, and actions and work to send consistent, positive messages to support the overall mission, transformational leaders can more effectively influence followers' perceptions of meaningful work.

To illustrate the point, Smircich and Morgan (1982) used the example of a person in a leadership role who loses his temper over an employee failing to complete a job on time. The leader could be expressing annoyance over a number of issues (e.g., the job was important, the employee is often late to complete jobs). The other employees witnessing the situation, however, might similarly interpret the issue (e.g., the job was important) or might ascribe entirely different reasons to the situation (e.g., the leader was having a bad day, the employee is a bad employee altogether). This example illustrates how followers interpret even seemingly small actions (in the leader's view) to apply to future situations. The point is made even stronger by recognizing that "while individuals may look to a leader to frame and concretize their reality, they may also react against, reject, or change the reality thus defined" (Smircich & Morgan, 1982, p. 259). In sum, it is essential for leaders to consistently and effectively manage meaning for followers through their words, actions, and gestures.

Applications to the Workplace and Future Directions

In this chapter, we have focused on how transformational leaders can influence individuals' perceptions of meaningful work. Transformational leaders activate followers' higher order needs by instilling followers' work with moral purpose and commitment (Arnold et al., 2007; Shamir et al., 1993). By accentuating behaviors that embody idealized influence, inspirational motivation, intellectual stimulation, and individualized consideration, transformational leaders can affect followers' self-efficacy, core job characteristics, and self-concordant goals, thereby influencing individuals' perceptions of meaningful work. The link between transformational leadership and meaningful work is strengthened (or lessened) by followers' values of allocentrism and idiocentrism and by leaders' management of meaning.

Practitioners can apply these ideas in the workplace. By understanding how followers view themselves and by providing them with confidence to reach their full potential, transformational leaders can help individuals to believe more strongly in their capabilities, thereby engaging their self-esteem and sense of self-efficacy (Shamir et al., 1993; Walumbwa et al., 2008), which, in turn, is expected to influence their perceptions of meaningful work. Next, by enhancing individuals' job characteristics, in terms of variety, identity, significance, autonomy, and feedback, research has shown that followers' intrinsic motivation and goal commitment are increased (Piccolo & Colquitt, 2006), suggesting that perceptions of work meaningfulness will also be increased.

In addition, by describing work in ideological terms and emphasizing higher order values such as high achievement, transformational leaders can help followers to see their work as congruent with personal values (Bono & Judge, 2003), thereby enhancing work meaningfulness. Transformational leaders can further influence meaningful work by managing followers' meaning of events in the workplace. Through role modeling and verbal persuasion (Walumbwa et al., 2008), transformational leaders can influence followers' interpretations and framing of issues and problems. Furthermore, through the use of consistent words, actions, and gestures (Smircich & Morgan, 1982), leaders can send clear messages to employees regarding the meaning of their work.

Finally, not all individuals respond equally to transformational leadership behaviors. Allocentrics, or those who value the goals of their group over their own, have been found to respond more positively to transformational leaders than idiocentrics, or those who value their own goals over their group's goals. By paying attention to individual differences in followers, transformational leaders can adjust their leadership style occasionally by recognizing that some individuals are motivated more by striving for personal goals than group goals. These ideas are summarized in Table 9.1.

Empirical evidence shows that when employees view their work as meaningful, their effectiveness and performance are enhanced at work (Arnold et al., 2007; May et al., 2004; Sparks & Schenk, 2001). In addition, especially in the midst of broad economic crises, an increased emphasis has been placed on leadership in the workplace and the inspiration of others to set aside selfish goals and to work toward a common interest. Thus, the link between transformational leadership and meaningful work is important and warrants further research attention. This chapter helps us to understand more about the conditions and processes underlying the relationship between transformational leadership and meaningful work, but because this direction is fairly nascent, more empirical evidence is needed in support of the arguments presented. Specifically, we suggest that researchers and practitioners would benefit from more research examining the mechanisms (i.e., self-efficacy, core job characteristics, and self-concordant goals) and boundary conditions (i.e., leader's management of meaning and followers' values) that might help to illuminate the relationship between transformational leadership and meaningful work. For example, Shamir et al. (1993) theorized that the engagement of followers' self-consistency, self-esteem, and self-expression (components related to followers' self-concept) is a key attribute through which leader behaviors are expected to influence individuals' task meaningfulness, and though these concepts have been evoked in theory, none has been empirically tested, as laid out in Shamir et al.'s theory relating leader behaviors to task meaningfulness.

In conclusion, the benefits of meaningful work are clear, and we can all benefit from a more positive outlook on our work. Although some of the recommendations discussed here have been tested in practice, derived from theory, or supported by empirical research, we recognize that not all individuals fit neatly into our theories and models. Thus, a truly transformational leader is one who recognizes that it is important to consider and appreciate individual differences. We leave you with these recommendations in the hope that your and others' lives can be improved, remembering that this comes from heedful practice and consideration.

TABLE 9.1

Focus on the Workplace: A Transformational Leadership Perspective

Recommendation	Tested in practice	Derived from theory	Supported by research
Show confidence in followers and their abilities to meet expectations and contribute to the mission and goals of the organization.[a]	✓	✓	✓
Provide meaning to individuals regarding their jobs' variety, identity, significance, autonomy, and feedback. When possible, enhance their jobs along these dimensions.[b]	✓	✓	✓
Describe work in ideological terms and emphasize higher order values such as high achievement.[c]	✓	✓	✓
Pay attention to followers' individual differences and adjust leadership style accordingly.[d]	✓	✓	✓
Be consistent in the words, actions, and gestures used. Followers interpret these and use them to make sense of situations.[e]	✓	✓	✓

Note. [a]Bono & Judge (2003). [b]Piccolo & Colquitt (2006). [c]Sparks & Schenk (2001). [d]Walumbwa, Lawler, & Avolio (2007). [e]Smircich & Morgan (1982).

References

Albert, S., Ashforth, B. E., & Dutton, J. E. (2000). Organizational identity and identification: Charting new waters and building new bridges. *Academy of Management Review, 25,* 13–17. doi:10.5465/AMR.2000.2791600

Arnold, K. A., Turner, N., Barling, J., Kelloway, E. K., & McKee, M. C. (2007). Transformational leadership and psychological well-being: The mediating role of meaningful work. *Journal of Occupational Health Psychology, 12,* 193–203. doi:10.1037/1076-8998.12.3.193

Avolio, B. J., Reichard, R. J., Hannah, S. T., Walumbwa, F. O., & Chan, A. (2009). A meta-analytic review of leadership impact research: Experimental and quasi-experimental studies. *Leadership Quarterly, 20,* 764–784. doi:10.1016/j.leaqua.2009.06.006

Avolio, B. J., Walumbwa, F. O., & Weber, T. (2009). Leadership: Current theories, research, and future directions. *Annual Review of Psychology, 60,* 421–449. doi:10.1146/annurev.psych.60.110707.163621

Bandura, A. (1997). *Self-efficacy: The exercise of control.* New York, NY: Freeman.

Bass, B. M. (1985). *Leadership and performance beyond expectations.* New York, NY: Academic Press.

Bass, B. M. (1988). Evolving perspectives on charismatic leadership. In J. A. Conger & R. N. Kanungo (Eds.), *Charismatic leadership* (pp. 41–77). San Francisco, CA: Jossey-Bass.

Bass, B. M., & Avolio, B. J. (1990). The implications of transactional and transformational leadership for individual, team, and organizational development. In R. W. Woodman & W. A. Pasmore (Eds.), *Research in organizational change and development* (Vol. 4, pp. 231–272). Greenwich, CT: JAI Press.

Bass, B. M., & Avolio, B. J. (2004). *Multifactor Leadership Questionnaire: Manual leader form, rater, and scoring key for MLQ (Form 5x-Short).* Redwood City, CA: Mind Garden.

Bass, B. M., & Bass, R. (2008). *The Bass handbook of leadership: Theory, research, and managerial applications.* New York, NY: Free Press.

Bono, J. E., & Judge, T. A. (2003). Self-concordance at work: Toward understanding the motivational effects of transformational leaders. *Academy of Management Journal, 46,* 554–571. doi:10.2307/30040649

Dukerich, J. M., Golden, B. R., & Shortell, S. M. (2002). Beauty is in the eye of the beholder: The impact of organizational identification, identity, and image on the cooperative behaviors of physicians. *Administrative Science Quarterly, 47,* 507–533. doi:10.2307/3094849

Dvir, T., Eden, D., Avolio, B. J., & Shamir, B. (2002). Impact of transformational leadership on follower development and performance: A field experiment. *Academy of Management Journal, 45,* 735–744. doi:10.2307/3069307

Hackman, J. R., & Oldham, G. R. (1980). *Work redesign.* Reading, MA: Addison-Wesley.

Hogg, M. A. (2001). A social identity theory of leadership. *Personality and Social Psychology Review, 5,* 184–200. doi:10.1207/S15327957 PSPR0503_1

Judge, T. A., & Piccolo, R. F. (2004). Transformational and transactional leadership: A meta-analytic test of their relative validity. *Journal of Applied Psychology, 89,* 755–768. doi:10.1037/0021-9010.89.5.755

Kark, R., & Shamir, B. (2002). The dual effect of transformational leadership: Priming relational and collective selves and further effects on followers. In B. J. Avolio & F. J. Yammarino (Eds.), *Transformational and charismatic leadership: The road ahead* (pp. 67–91). Oxford, England: Elsevier Science.

Kark, R., Shamir, B., & Chen, G. (2003). The two faces of transformational leadership: Empowerment and dependency. *Journal of Applied Psychology, 88,* 246–255. doi:10.1037/0021-9010.88.2.246

Kirkman, B. L., Chen, G., Farh, J. L., Chen, Z. X., & Lowe, K. B. (2009). Individual power distance orientation and follower reactions to transformational leaders: A cross-level, cross-cultural examination. *Academy of Management Journal, 52,* 744–764. doi:10.5465/AMJ.2009.43669971

Lam, S. S. K., Schaubroeck, J., & Brown, A. D. (2004). Esteem maintenance among groups: Laboratory and field studies of group performance cognitions. *Organizational Behavior and Human Decision Processes, 94,* 86–101. doi:10.1016/j.obhdp.2004.03.004

Lord, R. G., & Brown, D. J. (2004). *Leadership processes and follower self-identity.* Mahwah, NJ: Erlbaum.

Lowe, K. B., Kroeck, K. G., & Sivasubramaniam, N. (1996). Effectiveness correlates of transformational and transactional leadership: A meta-analytical review of the literature. *Leadership Quarterly, 7,* 385–425. doi:10.1016/S1048-9843(96)90027-2

Markus, H. R., & Kitayama, S. (1991). Culture and self: Implications for cognition, emotion and motivation. *Psychological Review, 98,* 224–253. doi:10.1037/0033-295X.98.2.224

May, D. R., Gilson, R. L., & Harter, L. M. (2004). The psychological conditions of meaningfulness, safety and availability and the engagement of the human spirit at work. *Journal of Occupational and Organizational Psychology, 77,* 11–37. doi:10.1348/096317904322915892

Piccolo, R. F., & Colquitt, J. A. (2006). Transformational leadership and job behaviors: The mediating role of core job characteristics. *Academy of Management Journal, 49,* 327–340. doi:10.5465/AMJ.2006.20786079

Pratt, M. G., & Ashforth, B. E. (2003). Fostering meaningfulness in working and at work. In K. Cameron, J. Dutton, & R. Quinn (Eds.), *Positive organizational scholarship* (pp. 309–327). San Francisco, CA: Berrett-Koehler.

Schaubroeck, J., Lam, S. S. K., & Cha, S. E. (2007). Embracing transformational leadership: Team values and the relationship between leader behavior and team performance. *Journal of Applied Psychology, 92,* 1020–1030. doi:10.1037/0021-9010.92.4.1020

Shamir, B., House, R. J., & Arthur, M. B. (1993). The motivational effect of charismatic leadership: A self-concept based theory. *Organization Science, 4,* 577–594. doi:10.1287/orsc.4.4.577

Sheldon, K. M., & Elliot, A. J. (1999). Goal striving, need satisfaction, and longitudinal well-being: The self-concordance model. *Journal of Personality and Social Psychology, 76,* 482–497. doi:10.1037/0022-3514.76.3.482

Sluss, D. M., & Ashforth, B. E. (2007). Relational identity and identification: Defining ourselves through work relationships. *Academy of Management Review, 32,* 9–32. doi:10.5465/AMR.2007.23463672

Smircich, L., & Morgan, G. (1982). Leadership: The management of meaning. *Journal of Applied Behavioral Science, 18,* 257–273. doi:10.1177/002188638201800303

Sparks, J. R., & Schenk, J. A. (2001). Explaining the effects of transformational leadership: An investigation of the effects of higher-order motives in multilevel marketing organizations. *Journal of Organizational Behavior, 22,* 849–869. doi:10.1002/job.116

Staw, B. (1977). Motivation in organizations: Synthesis and redirection. In B. Staw & G. Salancik (Eds.), *New directions in organizational behavior* (pp. 55–95). Chicago, IL: St. Clair.

Steger, M. F., & Dik, B. J. (2010). Work as meaning: Individual and organizational benefits of engaging in meaningful work. In P. A. Linley, S. Harrington, & N. Page (Eds.), *Handbook of positive psychology and work* (pp. 131–142). Oxford, England: Oxford University Press.

Triandis, H. C. (1995). *Individualism and collectivism.* Boulder, CO: Westview Press.

Van Dick, R., Wagner, U., Stellmacher, J., & Christ, O. (2004). The utility of a broader conceptualization of organizational identification: Which aspects really matter? *Journal of Occupational and Organizational Psychology, 77,* 171–191. doi:10.1348/096317904774202135

van Dierendonck, D., Haynes, C., Borril, C., & Stride, C. (2004). Leadership behaviour and subordinate well-being. *Journal of Occupational Health Psychology, 9,* 165–175. doi:10.1037/1076-8998.9.2.165

Van Knippenberg, D. (2000). Work motivation and performance: A social identity perspective. *Applied Psychology, 49,* 357–371. doi:10.1111/1464-0597.00020

Van Knippenberg, D., & Van Schie, E. C. M. (2000). Foci and correlates of organizational identification. *Journal of Occupational and Organizational Psychology, 73,* 137–147. doi:10.1348/096317900166949

Walumbwa, F. O., Avolio, B. J., & Zhu, W. (2008). How transformational leadership weaves its influence on individual job performance. *Personnel Psychology, 61,* 793–825. doi:10.1111/j.1744-6570.2008.00131.x

Walumbwa, F. O., Cropanzano, R., & Hartnell, C. A. (2009). Organizational justice, voluntary learning behavior, and job performance: A test of the mediating effects of identification and leader-member exchange. *Journal of Organizational Behavior, 30,* 1103–1126. doi:10.1002/job.611

Walumbwa, F. O., & Hartnell, C. A. (2011). Understanding transformational leadership–employee performance links: The role of relational identification and self-efficacy. *Journal of Occupational and Organizational Psychology, 84,* 153–172. doi:10.1348/096317910X485818

Walumbwa, F. O., & Lawler, J. J. (2003). Building effective organizations: Transformational leadership, collectivist orientation, work-related attitudes, and withdrawal behaviors in three emerging economies. *The*

International Journal of Human Resource Management, 14, 1083–1101. doi:10.1080/0958519032000114219

Walumbwa, F. O., Lawler, J. J., & Avolio, B. J. (2007). Leadership, individual differences and work attitudes: A cross-culture investigation. *Applied Psychology, 56,* 212–230. doi:10.1111/j.1464-0597. 2006.00241.x

Walumbwa, F. O., Mayer, D. M., Wang, P., Wang, H., Workman, K., & Christensen, A. L. (2011). Linking ethical leadership to employee performance: The rules of leader–member exchange, self-efficacy, and organizational identification. *Organizational Behavior and Human Decision Processes, 115,* 204–213. doi:10.1016/j.obhdp.2010.11.002

Yukl, G. A. (2010). *Leadership in organizations* (7th ed.). Upper Saddle River, NJ: Pearson Prentice Hall.

Dianne R. Stober, Stefanie Putter, and Lauren Garrison

Connecting the Dots

Coaching Leaders to Turn Values Into Meaningful Work

10

> "Would you tell me, please, which way I ought to go
> from here?"
> "That depends a good deal on where you want to get
> to," said the Cat.
> "I don't much care where," said Alice.
> "Then it doesn't matter which way you go," said the Cat.
> —Lewis Carroll, *Alice's Adventures in Wonderland*

The Cheshire Cat could have been a coach. Clarifying statements and pointing out logical conclusions are all part of the coaching toolkit. And though Alice was not talking about her values or moral compass, making meaning of her situation is not that different from what leaders have to consider in fostering meaning in and at work. Steger and Dik (2010) argued that people find meaning in and at work through experiencing a sense of purpose in their work and a fit between their abilities and interests and the needs of the larger group or organization. This take on meaningful work encompasses both the individual's sense of where she or he fits in the organization and the sense of purpose that is derived from her or his role in the organization. There is little doubt that meaningful work is a good thing or that individuals and organizations should be interested in increasing people's experiences of meaningful work. The question before us in this chapter is, How can leadership coaching be used to foster the experience of meaningful work? Our purpose in this chapter is to provide a map

http://dx.doi.org/10.1037/14183-011
Purpose and Meaning in the Workplace, B. J. Dik, Z. S. Byrne, and M. F. Steger (Editors)

for applying coaching in particular arenas that are known to influence people's experiences of meaningful work. The links between leadership coaching and meaningful work are indirect, and we point out areas for research and application that are ripe for the curious. Along the way, we illustrate how coaching can be applied to both developing leaders and assisting organizations in increasing the experience of meaningful work.

We propose that coaching can be a process for cultivating meaningful work by focusing on a number of areas in which meaningful work can be promoted through working with leaders. In focusing on coaching leaders, we use an executive and organizational coaching definition: "a development process that builds a leader's capabilities to achieve professional and organizational goals . . . and is based on mutual trust and respect" (Graduate School Alliance for Executive Coaching, 2011, para. 1). The coaching process generally involves assessment and an agreed-on focus that is then used to guide rich conversations, goal setting, and action planning. In addition, the coaching process provides a structure for self-reflection and feedback for the coaching client.

Coaching leaders is a potentially rich way to foster meaningful work because, as Walumbwa, Christensen, and Muchiri described (Chapter 9, this volume), leadership is intimately and intuitively connected to promoting meaning in the workplace. We feel that leadership and meaning in the workplace intersect most closely within the realm of values, both of the leader and of the organization. Thus, we consider values within the context of a well-established theory of leadership, namely, authentic leadership (e.g., Luthans & Avolio, 2003). For a leader to live his or her values within the context of work, it is necessary for that leader to develop awareness of his or her values, act in accordance with those values, and recognize how they fit within the broader values of the organization. We take a practical approach in illustrating how leaders can be coached to foster purpose and meaning in the workplace through helping them live within their values. See Figure 10.1 for a conceptual framework for coaching for meaningful work.

Case Illustrations: Stan and GenCo

Stan, a rising star in his organization, was given the leadership of a business unit that has struggled over the past few years to develop and retain leaders.[1] Without a strong team of leaders, the business had a

---

[1]All names in the cases have been changed to maintain confidentiality.

FIGURE 10.1

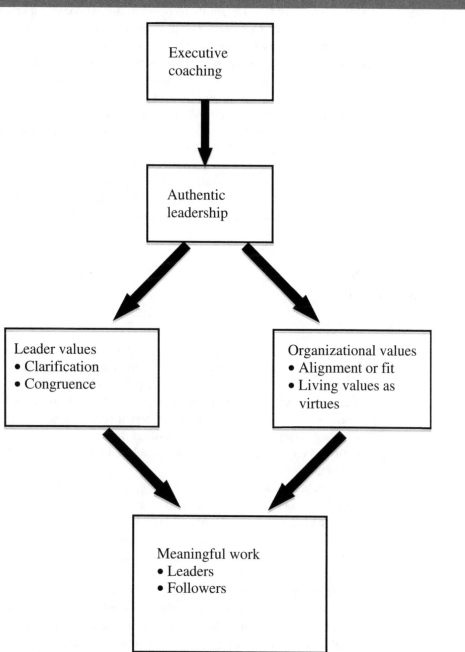

A proposed conceptual model of coaching for meaningful work. Leaders are coached to foster purpose and meaning in the workplace through helping them use authentic leadership to integrate personal and organizational values.

hard time navigating changing market conditions and delivering the level of service for which the business had historically been known. Stan was aware that his ability to develop his people was a crucial task ahead of him, so he began working with Claire, an executive coach. One area of focus for Stan and Claire was creating an atmosphere of solidarity, collaboration, and excitement for the potential of the business and enhancing his leaders' ability to see themselves as a part of something with meaning and integrity.

Likewise, GenCo (not its real name) is a global business with leaders who have recognized they would like to further develop how their corporate values guide their organization. This organization used a coach to work with the senior executive team to improve their organizational practices regarding their stated values. In both coaching illustrations, we discuss how coaches can work with leaders to connect the dots between their leadership, values, and meaningful work.

Coaching for Authentic Leadership

Today, there is renewed interest in ethical and values-based leadership (e.g., Avolio & Walumbwa, 2006; Brown, Treviño, & Harrison, 2005; George, 2003). As Avolio, Luthans, and Walumbwa (2004) proposed, "the unique stressors facing organizations throughout society today call for a new leadership approach aimed at restoring basic confidence, hope, optimism, resiliency, and meaningfulness" (p. 3). Authentic leadership development was designed to help address this need for a new approach.

Authentic leaders are those who help strengthen the organizational climate through leading with transparency, honesty, and a strong understanding of their values (Gardner, Avolio, Luthans, May, & Walumbwa, 2005). As described by Walumbwa, Avolio, Gardner, Wernsing, and Peterson (2008), *authentic leadership development theory* is founded on four components: self-awareness, relational transparency, balanced processing, and an internalized moral perspective. We focus on two of these factors for coaching leaders toward meaningful work: self-awareness and internalized moral perspective. In terms of self-awareness, a coach can guide leaders toward greater authenticity by helping them to develop insight and a deep understanding of their strengths, weaknesses, values, needs, and beliefs. Coaches help people turn insight into action (D. B. Peterson, 1996). As such, they can help leaders develop an internalized moral perspective, which means that they "walk the talk," and show consistency between their internal values and external actions (Walumbwa et al., 2008). Leaders who express authenticity are likely to promote meaning and purpose in the workplace, as we discuss next.

SELF-AWARENESS: VALUES CLARIFICATION

Leader self-awareness of core beliefs and values is a critical element of authentic leadership development theory (Avolio & Gardner, 2005; Ilies, Morgeson, & Nahrgang, 2005; Shamir & Eilam, 2005). In accordance with self-determination theory (Deci & Ryan, 2000), individuals become more authentic when they are driven by internal processes such as values and beliefs rather than external processes such as social expectations and rewards. Thus, once an individual's values become intrinsically driven versus extrinsically driven, these values become ingrained into who one is and ultimately become part of one's authentic self (Gardner et al., 2005).

High levels of self-awareness regarding personal beliefs and ideals can have a huge influence on the thoughts that leaders hold, the attitudes they form, and, ultimately, the behaviors and actions they demonstrate in the workplace (e.g., Chatman, 1991). Values are learned and strengthened over time through experiences and social-modeling processes; a coach can help a leader make meaning out of those experiences through guided self-reflection (D. B. Peterson, 1996). When leaders are coached to increase their self-awareness of their beliefs and ideals, they are more likely to be driven by values of doing what is right and fair for both themselves and their employees (Luthans & Avolio, 2003). *Values assessment* is a process often used by coaches to assist clients in clarifying which values motivate and drive their thinking and behavior. Such assessment processes lie at the heart of authentic leadership development theory and also play a critical role in several other leadership theories, such as those involving charismatic, transformational, servant, and spiritual leadership (Avolio & Gardner, 2005), highlighting the importance of values assessment in coaching leaders toward authenticity.

INTERNALIZED MORAL PERSPECTIVE: VALUES CONGRUENCE AND ALIGNMENT

In addition to values awareness and clarification, another core element of authentic leadership development is values congruence or alignment. *Congruence* has been defined as the degree of alignment and consistency between two components (Nadler & Tushman, 1980). One way that authentic leaders demonstrate values congruence is through walking the talk, or demonstrating consistency between words and actions.

Such congruence or alignment often emerges through a process of self-regulation. A coach can help leaders foster value congruence by guiding them through the following three key steps: (a) assessing one's internal standards, (b) evaluating gaps between internal standards and desired outcomes, and (c) identifying actions to help minimize the gap needed to reach intended outcomes (Stajkovic & Luthans, 1998). This approach is highly consistent with common coaching practices and can help leaders to create alignment between their internal values and their organizational behaviors (for coaching practice resources, see Hernez-Broome & Boyce, 2011; Stober & Grant, 2006). As one example, May, Chan, Hodges, and Avolio (2003) discussed how authentic leaders can address ethical issues at work through behaving in ways that align with their moral beliefs. The authors proposed a model of how to develop the moral aspects of authentic leadership (see May et al., 2003, p. 250) and highlighted how developing moral capacity, moral courage, and moral resiliency facilitates leader engagement in authentic moral actions. Thus, authentic leaders are those who are able to create alignment between their moral values and actions. Although there is still a need for further integration between the authentic leadership and values congruence literatures (Jung & Avolio, 2000; Meglino, Ravlin, & Adkins, 1991; Schwartz, 1999), initial evidence suggests that leaders who walk the talk through consistency between words and actions are likely to gain credibility, trust, and respect (Avolio, Gardner, Walumbwa, Luthans, & May, 2004).

Why Coach Authentic Leadership for Meaningful Work?

There is growing evidence that authentic leadership is a mechanism through which one can achieve positive organizational outcomes (George, 2003; George, Sims, McLean, & Mayer, 2007), such as attracting high-level talent and achieving superior bottom-line results. In addition, the leaders benefit through enhanced self-esteem, psychological well-being, and performance on the job (Grandey, Fiske, Mattila, Jansen, & Sideman, 2005; Kernis, 2003), which would likely increase their sense of meaning and fit for their work. For clients being coached with an authentic leadership focus, benefits are likely to be seen at both the individual and organizational levels.

Furthermore, if coaches focus on authentic leadership development with leaders, there are also benefits for their people. Employees of authentic leaders exhibit engagement in work, heightened well-being, and improved performance (Gardner et al., 2005), as well as congruence in their own values and actions (Walumbwa et al., 2008). Avolio, Gardner, et al. (2004) proposed that likely outcomes of authentic leadership for employees include enhanced commitment, satisfaction, meaningfulness, and engagement on the job. One reason why authentic leadership leads to enhanced meaning of work for employees may be due in part to alignment of values. We would expect that aligning one's values with those of the job might be one approach to enhance fit. People, in general, desire to engage in meaningful work that aligns with their identities, or true selves (Steger & Dik, 2010). Hence, we can expect that employees who have high alignment between personal values and values that are necessary for doing the job well would experience enhanced person–job fit and, ultimately, greater meaning in the workplace. Overall, there is an opportunity to better understand the relationship between authentic leadership, meaning at work, and how coaching leaders to develop authentic leadership can increase meaning at work for both leaders and their people. In the next section, we explore how taking a values-based approach to coaching leaders can provide an avenue to facilitate authentic leadership development and meaning in the workplace.

Coaching Application: Values Focus to Enhance Authentic Leadership and Meaningful Work

So how do we use coaching to foster meaningful work for leaders and those working with them? Many organizations and coaches use coaching as a tool or process to enhance a leader's effectiveness with a goal of benefiting the organization as a whole. Developing and enhancing authentic leadership by increasing self-awareness, especially in terms of values clarification, and assessing congruence between a leader's internal values and actions can be a direct focus of an executive coaching relationship.

To return to our illustration: Stan is a rising star executive working with Claire, an executive coach. Stan and Claire have been focusing on Stan's leadership capabilities and his ability to influence others' engagement in his organization. In focusing on key qualities of authentic leaders, Claire asked Stan to identify (a) what he values in his role and in his work and (b) what specific behaviors his values demand.

COACHING FOR WHAT IS VALUED

Stan was able to identify several aspects of his role and work that he particularly values: getting to paint the big picture for others, matching people and tasks for success, and finding new ways to meet goals for the business. Although Claire and Stan both recognized that this list was not all encompassing of Stan's values, identifying the aspects of his role that were especially important and satisfying to Stan would allow him to develop a greater self-awareness of how he leads. As a coach, Claire used a values-identification process to deepen Stan's self-reflection and understanding of himself as a leader. This could increase Stan's experience of meaningfulness in his work and his satisfaction in his role.

COACHING FOR VALUE–BEHAVIOR CONGRUENCE

Claire used the coaching process to help Stan link his self-awareness to particular actions. That is, by asking Stan to use his awareness of what he valued in his role and determine what kinds of behaviors were required to live those values, Claire helped Stan consciously move toward congruence between his values and his actions, which we know can increase authentic leadership capabilities. Focusing coaching conversations in this way can enhance *meaningfulness in work,* or a sense of meaning and purpose in one's work actions (Pratt & Ashforth, 2003; Steger & Dik, 2010). For example, the behaviors Stan identified include regularly taking time to prepare his messages of vision and mission for various work projects and to find effective forums for those communications—team meeting discussions, larger presentations, one-on-one conversations, and written communications. By linking these actions with his awareness of valuing his leadership in painting the big picture, Stan could increase his sense of meaningfulness in his leadership role and have positive effects on his team and their engagement.

In addition, the coaching process could also increase Stan's sense of *meaningfulness at work* by fostering conversations that considered the relational aspects of how he fit into the larger whole (Pratt & Ashforth, 2003; Steger & Dik, 2010). In our example, Stan recognized that he valued identifying who was the best fit for leading an initiative, project, or task and how getting the right match encouraged individuals to work to their strengths. Stan saw how this value was also connected to developing his people's capacities. By understanding his own high value for leveraging people's strengths, Stan began taking more time to work with his direct reports on identifying their skills, interests, and expertise and matching those with specific aims and tasks of his group. This awareness of values and of behaviors that align with the values could increase Stan's sense of how his leadership builds stronger relationships with his direct reports and also serves the higher needs and goals of the organizational mission. Thus, the coaching process provided the forum and focus for Stan to further develop his authentic leadership.

Another way to use coaching to increase meaningful work for leaders is through using assessments such as the Values in Action Inventory of Strengths (C. Peterson & Seligman, 2004). Coaches can use the profile to help clients identify their strengths of character and values in action and use those findings to design behavioral actions that align with their character strengths. Making sense of one's character and how that applies to one's leadership behaviors and work can facilitate a sense of meaningful work, which is then transferred to employees through authentic leadership.

Coaching can have a positive effect on meaningful work for leaders by providing a context for specific explorations of leaders' values and the congruence between those values and leadership actions. Helping leaders delineate what they value in their particular roles and how they align their behaviors with those values can increase the ways leaders make sense of the meaningfulness of their work and the meaningfulness of their role within the larger aims of the organization.

Individual–Organizational Values Alignment and Fit

Another aspect of creating meaning and purpose lies in the degree of belonging or fit individuals feel with respect to their organization. *Fit* involves congruence between aspects of two entities, such as a person and an organization. For instance, congruence can occur between organizational and personal values, personal needs and organizational resources, or job demands and job skills (Chatman, 1989). Although a number of types of fit have been explored, such as person–job fit, person–supervisor fit, person–group fit, and person–organization fit (Kristof-Brown, Zimmerman, & Johnson, 2005), person–organization (P–O) fit is of particular interest for a discussion of values and meaningful work. Specifically, Cable and Judge (1997) described congruence in terms of P–O fit or alignment between the values of individual personnel and the overall organization. With evidence that congruence between different organizational components can lead to improved outcomes (e.g., Nadler & Tushman, 1988), we propose that values congruence in the workplace can help foster meaningful work.

Posner, Kouzes, and Schmidt (1985) found that values congruence between managers and their organizations was predictive of several individual-level results including personal success, intentions to stay with the organization, and an understanding of organizational values.

Similarly, Cable and Judge (1996) found that P–O fit concerning values positively influenced employee work attitudes on the job. *Individual–organizational values alignment* (i.e., P–O fit) begins with opportunities for individual members to understand and proactively support the purpose and values of the organization (Branson, 2005, 2008).

Every structural and operational choice a leader makes sends a message to organizational members about what is valued and how to support that value (Argandoña, 2003). Leaders have a specific contribution to make in providing a meaningful forum for individual members to actively discuss their values and engage them with those of the organization. Coaching can be a vehicle for helping leaders to plan or implement such opportunities. For example, if an organization values strengthening community relationships, a coach may work with leaders to provide opportunities for individuals to network with local business owners, volunteer in their communities, or support local charities. Discussing the leaders' desires to engage the organization in planning and implementing such initiatives is one way coaches can influence leaders to build organizational structures, policies, and procedures that strengthen the virtues and purpose of the organization (Argandoña, 2003; Ostroff, Kinicki, & Tamkins, 2003). By providing such opportunities for individual members to align their personal values with organizational values, leaders are likely to experience greater meaning in their own work as well as help others experience more meaningful work.

Living Organizational Values and Virtues

In an organization, meaning can come from being or doing (Pratt & Ashforth, 2003). When people are attracted to an organization's image or culture, just being there and being a member create meaning for them. By becoming an employee, some people are self-aligning with certain values that the organization has made transparent through its image and culture (Adkins, Russell, & Werbel, 1994; Schneider, Smith, & Goldstein, 2000). Organizational values help answer the question "What is the reason for our actions?" (Argandoña, 2003), and the true test of whether an organization's values are authentic is whether individuals can see how their actions are living proof of the broader values. This goes beyond fitting the person to the organization, rather demonstrating that the organization lives within the person.

When organizational values are given dynamic form by members accepting and acting in line with those values, we speak of *organizational virtue* (Argandoña, 2003). Organizational virtues, or the doing aspect of meaning mentioned by Pratt and Ashforth (2003), are the moral characteristics of the organization as a whole rather than the composites of characteristics of individual members. Moral characteristics stem from moral goals of the organization that go beyond the traditional bottom line. For example, an organization might employ people who value sustainability, but if the organization does not have procedures in place for those employees to practice or influence sustainability, there is no organizational-level virtue or moral characteristic regarding sustainability. Organizational moral characteristics contribute to the fulfillment of organizational members and can serve as a source of identity and pride (Pratt & Ashforth, 2003). For example, if Jen's company is known for valuing creativity and innovation and Jen has the ability to demonstrate these virtues in her daily work, Jen will likely see herself as a face of innovation at her company. Thus, when a critical mass of people shares a common understanding of values and is able to live out the valued behaviors of the organization, individual contributions create a collective sense of meaning and virtue (Ostroff et al., 2003). We now turn to how this might look when coaching leaders.

Coaching Application: Using Organizational Values to Increase Meaningful Work

We have discussed how coaches can support individual leaders' authentic leadership development, which can in turn increases a sense of meaningfulness for both the leaders and their employees. We have also discussed how organizational values and virtues are linked to people's experiences of meaningful work. Coaching is a process that can be used with leaders to unite their own values with organizational values. This unification can lead to a sense of meaning and purpose for leaders to engage the broader organization in conversations regarding how organizational values support and underlie the organization's goals. As discussed previously, leaders can provide opportunities for individuals to live out organizational values as virtues in their daily work life, and coaching can help leaders put such intentions into practice. The following is an example of how this has been done.

GenCo recently benefitted from having coaches design strategies for bringing organizational values to life in support of meaningful work. Senior executives at GenCo had developed a strong model of organizational values that outlined specific areas the corporation held as guiding virtues. These organizational values included statements about leadership, innovation, integrity, superiority, effective performance and communication, and a focus on people, among others. Although the leaders of the organization had adopted a habit of regularly discussing organizational values, senior executives realized that speaking about the values did not uniformly result in people internalizing those values. In the context of ongoing conversations, the coach worked with several senior executives to design a process that would tie espoused organizational values to leader behaviors. Specifically, the coach asked the senior executives to be more explicit in their objectives for their values model. The senior executives stated that their vision for the use of their values model would lead to the values being the guideposts for all decisions, from internal hiring and promotion to how customers were engaged to how jobs were conducted. In identifying where the executive team felt the gaps existed between espoused values and behaviors in action, the team noted that they felt that lip service to the values was present at times. There was recognition that (a) the values were somewhat abstract and (b) there were opportunities to expand people's understanding of what those values in action would look like.

Through coaching the executive team, the leaders designed a new *values touch point* that could be used regularly to increase the operationalization of the organizational values for individuals in their own roles and positions. The values touch point consisted of using the regular values discussion times to engage individuals in identifying what actions they were undertaking that day to support one or more values. For example, Rick, a business development manager, might be meeting with a customer that day. Rick could link his task of fully understanding the customer's need for his company's services, and the particular project, to the organizational value of effective communications. In addition, part of Rick's role as a business development manager was building a productive relationship with the customer through (a) demonstrating openness to the customer's perspective and (b) being curious about the customer's needs. These types of behaviors linked directly to the values of consideration of people and superior service.

The executive team was able to use coaching conversations to design a program that could support leaders in explicitly and regularly linking their behaviors, tasks, and roles directly to the organizational values model. This helped living, breathing people bring the organizational values off the statement on the wall and into their daily actions. By linking these values to actions, people's experiences of meaningful work can be strengthened as their own behaviors are explicitly embedded into the larger story of the organization as a whole.

Future Directions

As Table 10.1 illustrates, the opportunities are ripe for researchers and practitioners to further explore the relationships between coaching as a development process, leadership, values, and fostering meaningful work. The recommendations listed, to the best of our knowledge, have not been empirically tested as interventions for enhancing meaningful work. Although using coaching as a vehicle for enhancing values-based leadership and meaningful work is derived from theory and in some cases indirectly supported by research, research on its effectiveness is still needed. The scarcity of research on using coaching to enhance meaningful work is consistent with the relative newness of the empirical study of coaching. Although there has been growing interest in research on coaching (see Stober & Grant, 2006, for an annotated bibliography), much remains to be done. Currently, there are a number of obstacles to conducting this type of research: privacy and confidentiality issues, access to adequate sample sizes, challenges in experimental design in applied settings (such as using control groups or random assignment), and the amount of time often involved to see outcomes, particularly at the organizational level. The popularity of coaching and the potential benefits in contributing to theory and practice make this an area ripe for exploration.

Summary

Though there is little direct research on the relationship between coaching and meaningful work, there are a number of ways in which coaching can be used to enhance leaders' and their employees' experiences of meaningful work. Values discussions have often been a part of coaching engagements (Berger, 2006; Hernez-Broome & Boyce, 2011; D. B. Peterson, 1996) and can support leaders "walking the talk." We have illustrated how clarifying internal values regarding a leader's work can help leaders engage in behaviors consistent with their values. Coaching also can be used as an intervention to enhance meaningful work through focusing on how organizational values align with individual values and work behaviors. Coaching is a promising area for practitioners and researchers alike for helping leaders and organizations connect the dots between values and meaningful work.

TABLE 10.1

Focus on the Workplace: An Executive Coaching Perspective

Recommendations	Tested in practice	Derived from theory	Supported by research
Coach leaders on identifying values, self-awareness, and clarification by using self-reflection questions and assigning an exercise that will help uncover values or value priorities.[a, b, c, d]	✓	✓	
Coach leaders on values congruency and walking the talk by talking about what values look like in action and comparing espoused value priorities to current behaviors.[e, f, g]	✓	✓	
Coach leaders on individual–organizational values alignment by talking about barriers to and resources for acting in line with values and identifying opportunities for acting in line with values.[h, i, j, k, l, m]	✓	✓	
Coach leaders to provide specific opportunities for individuals to actively demonstrate organizational values by helping to create a common situational language about values, having clients practice talking to others about values and opportunities for demonstrating values, and having clients set up a system of recognitions for demonstrating values.[n]	✓	✓	

Note. These recommendations have been tested by the authors in practice with good results. Empirical research is still needed to support the coaching–meaningful work relationship.
[a]Avolio & Gardner (2005). [b]Gardner, Avolio, Luthans, May, & Walumbwa (2005). [c]Shamir & Eilam (2005). [d]D. B. Peterson (1996). [e]Avolio, Gardner, Walumbwa, Luthans, & May (2004). [f]May, Chan, Hodges, & Avolio (2003). [g]Stajkovic & Luthans (1998). [h]Argandoña (2003). [i]Branson (2005). [j]Branson (2008). [k]Cable & Judge (1996). [l]Kristof-Brown, Zimmerman, & Johnson (2005). [m]Enz (1988). [n]Pratt & Ashforth (2003).

References

Adkins, C. L., Russell, C. J., & Werbel, J. D. (1994). Judgments of fit in the selection process: The role of work value congruence. *Personnel Psychology, 47,* 605–623. doi:10.1111/j.1744-6570.1994.tb01740.x

Argandoña, A. (2003). Fostering values in organizations. *Journal of Business Ethics, 45,* 15–28. doi:10.1023/A:1024164210743

Avolio, B., Luthans, F., & Walumbwa, F. O. (2004). *Authentic leadership: Theory-building for veritable sustained performance* [Working paper]. Lincoln: University of Nebraska, Gallup Leadership Institute.

Avolio, B. J., & Gardner, W. L. (2005). Authentic leadership development: Getting to the root of positive forms of leadership. *Leadership Quarterly, 16,* 315–338. doi:10.1016/j.leaqua.2005.03.001

Avolio, B. J., Gardner, W. L., Walumbwa, F. O., Luthans, F., & May, D. R. (2004). Unlocking the mask: A look at the process by which authentic leaders impact follower attitudes and behaviors. *Leadership Quarterly, 15,* 801–823. doi:10.1016/j.leaqua.2004.09.003

Avolio, B. J., & Walumbwa, F. O. (2006). Authentic leadership: Moving HR leaders to a higher level. In J. J. Martocchio (Ed.), *Research in personnel and human resources management* (pp. 273–304). Oxford, England: Elsevier/JAI Press. doi:10.1016/S0742-7301(06)25007-2

Berger, J. G. (2006). Adult development theory and executive coaching practice. In D. R. Stober & A. M. Grant (Eds.), *Evidence-based coaching handbook: Putting best practices to work for your clients* (pp. 77–102). New York, NY: Wiley.

Branson, C. M. (2005, October). *Personal values and principalship behaviour: Illustrating the relationship.* Paper presented at the 10th annual Values and Leadership Conference, Penn State University, University Park, PA.

Branson, C. M. (2008). Achieving organizational change through values alignment. *Journal of Educational Administration, 46,* 376–395. doi:10.1108/09578230810869293

Brown, M. E., Treviño, L. K., & Harrison, D. A. (2005). Ethical leadership: A social learning perspective for construct development and testing. *Organizational Behavior and Human Decision Processes, 97,* 117–134. doi:10.1016/j.obhdp.2005.03.002

Cable, D. M., & Judge, T. A. (1996). Person–organization fit, job choice decisions, and organizational entry. *Organizational Behavior and Human Decision Processes, 67,* 294–311. doi:10.1006/obhd.1996.0081

Cable, D. M., & Judge, T. A. (1997). Interviewers' perceptions of person–organization fit and organizational selection decisions. *Journal of Applied Psychology, 82,* 546–561. doi:10.1037/0021-9010.82.4.546

Chatman, J. A. (1989). Improving interactional organizational research: A model of person–organization fit. *Academy of Management Review, 14,* 333–349.

Chatman, J. A. (1991). Matching people and organizations: Selection and socialization in public accounting firms. *Administrative Science Quarterly, 36,* 459–484. doi:10.2307/2393204

Deci, E. L., & Ryan, R. M. (2000). "What" and "why" of goal pursuits: Human needs and the self-determination of behavior. *Psychological Inquiry, 11,* 227–268. doi:10.1207/S15327965PLI1104_01

Enz, C. A. (1988). The role of value congruity in intraorganizational power. *Administrative Science Quarterly, 33,* 284–304. doi:10.2307/2393060

Gardner, W. L., Avolio, B. J., Luthans, F., May, D. R., & Walumbwa, F. (2005). "Can you see the real me?" A self-based model of authentic leader and follower development. *Leadership Quarterly, 16,* 343–372. doi:10.1016/j.leaqua.2005.03.003

George, B. (2003). *Authentic leadership: Rediscovering the secrets to creating lasting value.* San Francisco, CA: Jossey-Bass.

George, B., Sims, P., McLean, A. N., & Mayer, D. (2007, February). Discovering your authentic leadership. *Harvard Business Review, 85*(2), 129–130.

Graduate School Alliance for Executive Coaching. (2011). *What is executive coaching?* Retrieved from http://www.gsaec.org

Grandey, A. A., Fiske, G. M., Mattila, A. S., Jansen, K. J., & Sideman, L. A. (2005). Is "service with a smile" enough? Authenticity of positive displays during service encounters. *Organizational Behavior and Human Decision Processes, 96,* 38–55. doi:10.1016/j.obhdp.2004.08.002

Hernez-Broome, G., & Boyce, L. A. (Eds.). (2011). *Advancing executive coaching: Setting the course for successful leadership coaching.* San Francisco, CA: Jossey-Bass.

Ilies, R., Morgeson, F. P., & Nahrgang, J. D. (2005). Authentic leadership and eudaemonic well-being: Understanding leader–follower outcomes. *Leadership Quarterly, 16,* 373–394. doi:10.1016/j.leaqua.2005.03.002

Jung, D. I., & Avolio, B. J. (2000). Opening the black box: An experimental investigation of the mediating effects of trust and value congruence on transformational and transactional leadership. *Journal of Organizational Behavior, 21,* 949–964. doi:10.1002/1099-1379 (200012)21:8<949::AID-JOB64>3.0.CO;2-F

Kernis, M. H. (2003). Toward a conceptualization of optimal self-esteem. *Psychological Inquiry, 14,* 1–26. doi:10.1207/S15327965PLI1401_01

Kristof-Brown, A. L., Zimmerman, R. D., & Johnson, E. C. (2005). Consequences of individuals' fit at work: A meta-analysis of person–job, person–organization, person–group, and person–supervisor fit. *Personnel Psychology, 58,* 281–342. doi:10.1111/j.1744-6570.2005.00672.x

Luthans, F., & Avolio, B. J. (2003). Authentic leadership development. In K. S. Cameron, J. E. Dutton, & R. E. Quinn (Eds.), *Positive organizational scholarship* (pp. 241–258). San Francisco, CA: Berrett-Koehler.

May, D. R., Chan, A., Hodges, T., & Avolio, B. J. (2003). Developing the moral component of authentic leadership. *Organizational Dynamics, 32,* 247–260. doi:10.1016/S0090-2616(03)00032-9

Meglino, B. M., Ravlin, E. C., & Adkins, C. L. (1991). Value congruence and satisfaction with a leader: An examination of the role of interaction. *Human Relations, 44,* 481–495. doi:10.1177/001872679104400504

Nadler, D. A., & Tushman, M. L. (1980). A model for diagnosing organizational behavior. *Organizational Dynamics, 9,* 35–51. doi:10.1016/0090-2616(80)90039-X

Nadler, D. A., & Tushman, M. L. (1988). *Strategic organization design: Concepts, tools, & processes.* Glenview, IL: Scott, Foresman.

Ostroff, C., Kinicki, A. J., & Tamkins, M. M. (2003). Organizational culture and climate. In W. C. Borman, D. R. Ilgen, & R. J. Klimoski (Eds.), *Handbook of psychology* (Vol. 12, pp. 565–593). Hoboken, NJ: Wiley. doi:10.1002/0471264385.wei1222

Peterson, C., & Seligman, M. E. P. (2004). *Character strengths and virtues: A handbook and classification.* Washington, DC: American Psychological Association.

Peterson, D. B. (1996). Executive coaching at work: The art of one-on-one change. *Consulting Psychology Journal: Practice and Research, 48,* 78–86. doi:10.1037/1061-4087.48.2.78

Posner, B. Z., Kouzes, J. M., & Schmidt, W. H. (1985). Shared values make a difference: An empirical test of corporate culture. *Human Resource Management, 24,* 293–309. doi:10.1002/hrm.3930240305

Pratt, M. G., & Ashforth, B. E. (2003). Fostering meaningfulness in working and at work. In K. S. Cameron, J. E. Dutton, & R. E. Quinn (Eds.), *Positive organizational scholarship: Foundations for a new discipline* (pp. 309–327). San Francisco, CA: Berrett-Koehler.

Schneider, B., Smith, D. B., & Goldstein, H. W. (2000). Attraction–selection–attrition: Toward a person–environment psychology of organizations. In W. B. Walsh, K. H. Craik, & R. H. Price (Eds.), *Person–environment psychology: New directions and perspectives* (2nd ed., pp. 61–85). Mahwah, NJ: Erlbaum.

Schwartz, S. H. (1999). A theory of cultural values and some implications for work. *Applied Psychology, 48,* 23–47. doi:10.1111/j.1464-0597.1999.tb00047.x

Shamir, B., & Eilam, G. (2005). "What's your story?" A life-stories approach to authentic leadership development. *Leadership Quarterly, 16,* 395–417. doi:10.1016/j.leaqua.2005.03.005

Stajkovic, A. D., & Luthans, F. (1998). Social cognitive theory and self-efficacy: Going beyond traditional motivational and behavioral approaches. *Organizational Dynamics, 26,* 62–74. doi:10.1016/S0090-2616(98)90006-7

Steger, M. F., & Dik, B. J. (2010). Work as meaning. In P. A. Linley, S. Harrington, & N. Page (Eds.), *Oxford handbook of positive psychology and work* (pp. 131–142). Oxford, England: Oxford University Press.

Stober, D. R., & Grant, A. M. (Eds.). (2006). *Evidence based coaching handbook: Putting best practices to work for your clients.* New York, NY: Wiley.

Walumbwa, F. O., Avolio, B. J., Gardner, W. L., Wernsing, T. S., & Peterson, S. J. (2008). Authentic leadership: Development and validation of a theory-based measure. *Journal of Management, 34,* 89–126. doi:10.1177/0149206307308913

Index

About the Editors

Bryan J. Dik, PhD, is an associate professor of psychology at Colorado State University and cofounder and chief science officer of Career Analytics Network/jobZology. Dr. Dik received a BA in psychology from Calvin College and a PhD in counseling psychology from the University of Minnesota. His research is primarily in the area of career development, especially perceptions of work as a calling; meaning, purpose, religion, and spirituality in career decision making and planning; measurement of vocational interests; and career development interventions. He serves on the editorial boards of six research journals, including the *Journal of Counseling Psychology,* the *Journal of Vocational Behavior,* and the *Journal of Career Assessment.* He was co-editor of *Psychology of Religion and Workplace Spirituality* and coauthor of *Make Your Job a Calling: How the Psychology of Vocation Can Change Your Life at Work.* Dr. Dik is recipient of the 2010 Early Career Professional Award from the Society for Vocational Psychology.

Zinta S. Byrne, PhD, is an industrial and organizational (I/O) psychologist with interests in employee engagement and retention, organizational (in)justice and politics, stress within the workplace, computer-mediated communication, and other related topics associated with the employee–organization relationship. Her research interests originally developed out of her 10 years of work experience as a research and development computer software design and development engineer and research and development project manager for Hewlett-Packard Company, prior to retraining as an I/O psychologist. Her experience working for Personnel Decisions International as the western regional manager for the Global Products Division shortly after completing her PhD in psychology also influenced her research interests. She is currently an associate professor of psychology at Colorado State University and owner and president of Atniz Consulting, LLC (a consulting business focused on employee–organization relations, productivity, and leadership coaching). She has published articles and chapters in psychology and management journals and books, has presented at psychology and management conferences, reviews for and serves on a number of editorial boards, and has the forthcoming books *Organizational Psychology and Behavior: An Integrated Approach to Understanding the Workplace* and *Understanding What Employee Engagement Is and Is Not: Implications for Theory, Research, and Practice.*

Michael F. Steger, PhD, is an associate professor of counseling psychology and applied social psychology at Colorado State University. Dr. Steger received his BA from Macalester College; his MS from University of Oregon; and his PhD, with a dual specialization in counseling and personality psychology, from the University of Minnesota. His research interests concern better understanding the factors that promote human flourishing and that ameliorate psychological suffering. In particular, he has focused on researching how people generate the sense that their lives are meaningful, as well as on investigating the benefits of living a meaningful life. He is intensely interested in how the concept of meaning can be applied to create healthier, happier, and more productive workplaces. His current research examines meaning in work and in life, health, and health-risking and health-promoting behaviors. He is an associate editor for the *Journal of Personality* and serves on the editorial boards of numerous journals. His previous book was *Designing Positive Psychology: Taking Stock and Moving Forward.*